The English Language

The English Language
Yesterday and Today

Charles B. Martin
Curt M. Rulon
North Texas State University

Allyn and Bacon, Inc.   Boston

To Darlyn and Susan

Contents

Preface

This book is a selected distillation of linguistic scholarship which describes from both a historical (diachronic) and a contemporary (synchronic) viewpoint that conglomerate set of dialects and idiolects called English. The emphasis, of course, is on contemporary American English. However, in an attempt to demonstrate the universality of some of the linguistic descriptions, many foreign language examples have been given, particularly in the exercises, to show some features which many modern languages have in common.

The scholarship presented in this book, besides introducing the reader to certain basic principles of language study, is designed to give him a quick overview of the history of our language and a short résumé of the history of grammar study. This includes a brief description of the more important schools of grammar, followed by a more lengthy treatment of the one which we feel has the most to offer the modern student, namely transformational-generative grammar as developed by Noam Chomsky, his colleagues, and his students. The terminology in this grammar should not prove too forbidding to the novice because it translates easily into that of such traditional scholarly grammarians as Otto Jespersen and George O. Curme, to name only two.

Since many schools today have adopted new textbooks with a transformational-generative approach, we feel that this book will offer those who teach English or those who plan to teach the necessary background for such books as the Oregon Curriculum Series (Holt, Rinehart, and Winston), the Jacobs and Rosenbaum series (Ginn and Company), and the Nebraska Curriculum series, as well as many others. The Implications chapter will be of interest especially to those who teach.

We also devote a chapter to the history of attitudes toward language use and the development of the dictionary. Our coverage of dialectal differences in American English is deliberately limited because we feel at this time that adequate research into many varieties of English (including what is called Black English Dialect) is still lacking. Though numerous surface differences are apparently manifest among the several variations from what is perhaps arbitrarily called "standard," they are exactly that—surface variations which come from the same deep structure source. We also feel that most features of any given dialect are represented as well as can be expected by conventional spelling.

We should like to express our gratitude to our many colleagues who have contributed much expertise in one way or another, among whom are Marsue Burns, Anthony Damico, Silas Griggs, Kjell Johansen, Tom Life, and Carroll Rich. They, of course, are not responsible for our errors and misconceptions.

C. B. M.
C. M. R.

Ye knowe eek, that in forme of speche is chaunge
With-inne a thousand yeer, and wordes tho
That hadden prys, now wonder nyce and straunge
Us thinketh hem; and yet they spake hem so . . . .

Chaucer, Troilus and Criseyde, II, 22–28.

And certaynly our langage now used varyeth ferre from
that whiche was used and spoken whan I was borne; for
we Englysshe men ben under the domynacyon of the mone,
whiche is never stedfaste, but ever waverynge, wexynge
one season, and waneth and dyscreaseth another season . . . .

Caxton, Preface to Eneydos, 1490

Grammatici certant et adhūc sub iudice līs est.

(Scholars dispute and yet the case is still before the courts.)

Horace, Ars Poetica

I

The Nature of Language

Of all the developments in the history of man, surely the most remarkable was language, for with it he was able to pass on his cultural heritage to succeeding generations who then did not have to rediscover how to make a fire, where to hunt, or how to build another wheel. So powerful a tool was language that some ancient tribes even attributed magical significance to the spoken word. While civilized man today does not believe that he is subject to the evil spells or magic incantations of an enemy, he is often made the victim of language of another sort: the fiery language of the demagogue, the subtle insinuations of Madison Avenue, the daily barrage of political opinion, and other forms of persuasive speech. One simply cannot escape the influence of the spoken or written word in today's world.

The precise origin of language, though still an intriguing topic, has ceased to interest the student of language as a problem in itself. No one today allies himself with such conjectural "theories" on the subject as the "bow wow theory," the "ding dong theory," or the "yo-he-ho theory." Attention is turned instead to another facet of the same problem, whether language is an acquired behavioral skill, as the psychologists once claimed, or whether it is somehow inherent so that some kind of universal grammar is hidden away in everybody's psyche. Until very recently, it was generally assumed that the human animal acquired language as a secondary activity, that there was no such thing as a natural predilection for language. The so-called "organs of speech," or so goes the argument, existed for other purposes; in time they came to serve a secondary purpose, that of talking. Such a theory, called the empiricist theory, is based on the idea that the mind is a blank slate at birth with no innate ideas or capacities.

Recent critics of such a theory ask why a normal, or even subnormal, child can learn a language when he cannot learn simple motor skills, simple arithmetic, or elementary reading. The same child will learn two languages, thus becoming bilingual, if exposed regularly to both of them at an early age. The child will also learn a language strictly through exposure to it and not through any formal schooling in it or formalized presentations of it—he somehow is able to sort out a grammatical system from this chaos of sounds and sentences which he hears. As an infant he has the ability to make innumerable sounds but within a very few months begins a sorting-out process in which he keeps only those which are used in his linguistic environment. Furthermore, no animal has as yet been taught to talk except for parroting a few words or expressions on which it has been repeatedly drilled. It utters those and those alone, never any novel sentences. Hence the rationalist theory suggests that man must have some innate capacity for language awaiting only exposure to the spoken word.

How, then, can we define that exclusively human phenomenon called language? LANGUAGE has often been defined as a system of arbitrary but conventionalized vocal symbols used for human communication. The key word in this definition is system, and each of the three thousand or more languages in the world today has its own peculiar system in which sounds are combined in certain ways to form words, and words can be arranged in certain ways to form sentences, the basic unit of all languages.

These sentences, moreover, are more than mere strings of words. We cannot punch a card for every word in an unabridged dictionary, put the cards in a computer, press a button, and expect the first ten cards to produce a sentence. Even if we reshuffle the same ten cards, we could probably not come up with the right combination for a grammatical English sentence. The secret, needless to say, is to program the computer so that more information is punched on each card and the words will assume certain combinations; that is, some words must appear with *a* or *the* in the singular ("A boy is there," "The boy is there," but not "*Boy is there") and may take *the* in the plural but not *a* ("The boys are there" but not "*A boys are there"). Other words might be used in final position, while still others of the same general category must be followed by some kind of object ("They disappeared," "They abandoned the car," but not "*They antagonized"). The following sentences, written by Spanish students learning English, illustrate very well how the students are using their own native system to form English sentences:

How long will be his daughter in the hospital? (*¿Por cuánto tiempo estará su hija en el hospital?*)

When studied he? (*¿Cuándo estudió él?*)

How much coffee bought the woman? (*¿Cuánto café compró la mujer?*)

These littles birds are pretties. (*Estos pájaros pequeños son bonitos.*)

This book will like him when he will read it. (*Le gustará este libro cuándo lo lea.*)

When did work the man there? (*¿Cuándo trabajó el hombre allí?*)

Do you have enough years for to see this movie? (*¿Tiene bastante años para ver esta película?*)

A professor at the Grand Academy of Lagado in Book III of *Gulliver's Travels* invented a writing machine with which he hoped to come up with "books in philosophy, poetry, politics, law, mathematics, and theology, without the least assistance from genius or study." The irony of Swift's satire is that, although the wooden frame has an elaborate mechanism whereby forty helpers can, with the single turn of a crank, reposition the wooden blocks on which different words are pasted, no grammatical sentences ever appear because words are pasted to the blocks "in their several moods, tenses, and declensions, but *without any order.*" (Italics added.) Every language must of necessity have some kind of system.

Another "projector" at the same Academy devised a plan for "abolishing all words whatsoever," the reason being that, "since words are only names for things, it would be more convenient for all men to carry about them such *things* as were necessary to express the particular business they are to discourse on." In Swift's day many suggestions had been made for the formation of a universal language, among them John Wilkins's *Essay Towards a Real Character and a Philosophical Language,* published by the Royal Society in 1668, which suggested that the name of a thing should disclose the nature of that thing itself, an idea from Plato, who believed in some correspondence between an idea, ultimate reality, and the word for that idea. (As Mark Twain said, Eve named the dodo, because it looked so much like a dodo.) Swift's projector would have each person carry a bundle of things and whenever he met a friend or acquaintance, set down his bundle and begin to converse by holding up certain objects. Needless to say, vocal symbols are certainly more convenient.

The fact that language is made up of vocal symbols should indicate the primacy of speech over writing. Too many people assume that language is writing and attach too much importance to the written word. This does not mean to imply that writing is not important—certainly civilized man has best been able to preserve his culture through the written symbol. Rather it means that language study must focus first on speech, the vocal symbol. When we consider that writing has existed for about six thousand years and that even today only a third of the existing languages have writing systems, then we can see the importance of the vocal aspect of language.

Linguists today would agree that the vocal symbols in a given language are purely arbitrary and that they have become conventionalized through use by a group of people speaking the same language. Quite often people ask, "What is the real meaning of____?" as if each word had one true meaning. They will also argue in favor of an older meaning, presumably because it has some unknown sanction. *Disinterested* means *not interested* if people use it that way, oblivious to its earlier meaning, *impartial*. Likewise *ghetto*, once the Jewish quarter of a city, has been extended to mean *slum*.

The last part of the definition of language suggests that language is for human communication. Just as *vocal* was added to limit the symbolic portion of language and exclude other symbols which communicate (gestures, nods, facial expressions, etc.), *human* is added in order to exclude animal cries. Surely mother hens are conveying some kind of message to their chicks, when after certain frantic clucking the chicks leave their pickings and run after the mother. Porpoises are thought to have some rudimentary signaling system, and whales presumably can sing. Bees have ritual dances and can convey messages revealing the exact location of nectar. Yet these animal systems are limited in that they are closed systems with only a few discrete signals. Animals cannot come up with novel utterances—dogs do not bark about barking and bees do not discuss last year's food supply.

Purists like to argue that one language is more logical than another. Each language must be judged on its own merits and is successful as a language if it serves well the people who use it. If it doesn't, they will change it or adopt someone else's language. To say that Russian is deficient in comparison to English because it has no definite articles is to say that there is some intrinsic merit in definite articles. We somehow do without them in newspaper headlines with only occasional humor or ambiguity. To say that German is more logical than French or Spanish because it has three genders, whereas the latter have only two, is to place undue faith in gender. Thus no one language is inherently better than another.

If no one language is better than the next, then each one must be adequate for its users. Thus there can be no such thing as a primitive language because languages are always adequate to express the ideas, thoughts, and verbal exchanges of the people using them. If not, they add to the language whatever is necessary to describe any new facet of that particular culture. Oftentimes when people talk about primitive languages, they are actually thinking that the culture of a given people is primitive.

The same person might also suggest that one language is more beautiful than another. One doctoral candidate intimated that he preferred French to German because French was more beautiful and German was such a "fractured language," though he declined to define "fractured." Numerous other students have commented on the "guttural" qualities of German, which, to them, makes it an unattractive language. However, to the Germans it is a beautiful language and much great poetry and drama and many songs have been written in it. Actually one's own cultural bias influences his tastes in language as well as in other aesthetic judgments. Beauty is relative in every society.

Contrary to popular belief, neither climate nor bodily features affect language. How many times have we been told that certain Americans have a "Southern drawl" because it is so hot in the South? If climate affects the rapidity of our speech, would we not talk faster on cold days than on warm ones? Is speech faster north of the Arctic circle? Speech patterns of blacks are frequently attributed to the physical features of the black, who, according to the linguistically unsophisticated, cannot produce certain sounds because he has thick lips. Actually every member of society, assuming he has no physical defect like a cleft palate, can learn to reproduce the speech sounds of those in his environment.

Finally, languages change. Indo-European, the parent language of so many languages of Western civilization, broke up into several branches, each one eventually giving birth to still other languages. Such change must not be considered decay. French, Spanish, Portuguese, and Italian are not debased forms of Latin. Modern English is not a decadent form of Old English, which in turn is not a degeneration from Primitive Germanic. The purist, who is skeptical of change and is hesitant to accept any innovation in language, usually looks back to an era just preceding his when language existed in a purer state. If the older form is the purer one, then he should go back as far as written records will take him and use that form of the language. The purist, though, who often appeals to logic, is not willing in this instance to be logical.

When language change becomes so great that two people who once spoke the same language can no longer understand each other, then they are speaking two different languages—a division within the language has taken place. If, however, their conversation is mutually intelligible though with some apparent difficulties at first, then they are speaking different DIALECTS of the same language. If through geographical separation from each other and through natural change which languages undergo because they are learned through imitation—and imitation is never perfect—the speakers can no longer understand each other, their divergent dialects will have become different languages.

From the rationalist point of view, however, these different languages vary only in their surface details (combinations of sounds into words, combinations of roots and affixes, arrangement of words into sentences, intonation patterns, etc.) but in their substructure have many common structural features called LANGUAGE UNIVERSALS. That is, all languages have certain sound segments in common, and all have structural possibilities for forming questions, commands, and negative statements.

Within a given society several regional dialects may develop. Often one will gain more prestige than the others, but this is not to say that it is better than the others. Usually it gains its prestige because of the political or economic importance of the group using it. Thus different Old English dialects occupied a prestigious position as the centers of power and learning shifted from Kent to Northumbria to Mercia to Wessex and finally to London.

Quite often, people from one region move to another for economic reasons. If the dialect they bring with them represents a region or a group of people with low social status, then that dialect may have no status in the area to which the people have moved. If their social and economic mobility is decreased because of their dialect, then they will try to adopt the dialect patterns of the new area. As suggested earlier, this is not to say that their dialect is inferior—it is adequate for communication in the area in which it was formerly used. Unfortunately, those speaking the prestigious dialect are so intolerant of the person deviating from their norm that they penalize the "intruder" for his speech. At one time in this country the foreigner arriving on our shores tried very hard to become assimilated into our culture. Usually he had great difficulty with the new language, English, and died never having completely mastered it. His children and grandchildren tried eagerly to eradicate whatever traces of a foreign "accent" they had, plus whatever other cultural traits which might stigmatize them and keep them from becoming a part of the great "melting pot."

Today large groups of people are being heard from who have not become acculturated to certain "norms" of American society even when several generations had lived in this country, namely the black, the poor Appalachian white, the Mexican-American, the American Indian, and other minority groups. While some barriers of discrimination are falling, others—like those related to language—are not. Many speakers of "non-standard" dialects are being discriminated against, presumably because of their dialect.[1] Thus we must move in one direction

---

[1]Some would argue that the matter is still a racial or cultural one and that employers, using language as an excuse, will not hire a prospect because he has a black or brown face or red neck or whatever. Cf. James Sledd, "Bi-Dialectalism: The Linguistics of White Supremacy," *English Journal*, 58 (1969), 1307–15; and Bernard Spolsky, "The Limits of Language Education," *The Linguistic Reporter*, 13 (Summer, 1971), 1–5.

or the other: either by helping the divergent speaker to master standard English or by changing society's attitude toward divergent dialects. The speaker whose native tongue is not English is faced with a different set of problems. Both groups will be dealt with in a later chapter.

While on the surface it might appear that the public's attitude toward language and its refusal to accept deviations from some supposed norm might be a problem for the sociologist or the psychologist, it is still within the province of LINGUISTICS, which may be defined as the scientific study of language. The LINGUIST engages in observing language as objectively as possible without passing judgments on it. He merely records the fact that r is not pronounced after vowels in New England and that r is inserted as a bridge between vowels in expressions like "lawr and order." Such a study of regional varieties within a language is within the province of DIALECT GEOGRAPHY, the linguist being called a dialect geographer or DIALECTOLOGIST. The social status of particular dialects of English falls within the study of SOCIOLINGUISTICS.

There are still other branches of linguistic study. COMPARATIVE LINGUISTICS is the study of two or more related languages. HISTORICAL LINGUISTICS traces the development of a given language from some earlier time to the present, while DESCRIPTIVE LINGUISTICS describes a language at a particular moment in time. In APPLIED LINGUISTICS the linguist applies certain scientific methods or theories to the study of language. PSYCHOLINGUISTICS is related to the mental processes involved in language acquisition.

In his formal analysis of a language the linguist constructs a GRAMMAR, which is a formal and explicit description of that language. Again, he is concerned with an objective study of what is or has been used by speakers of that language and not with what a group of purists may think about it. Unfortunately, to most people grammar means linguistic etiquette, observing certain prescribed rules of usage. How many times have we heard someone say, "He doesn't have very good grammar" or "I'm sorry I never learned my grammar"? Such responses limit language study to observing certain niceties of speech and tend to obscure the vast possibilities for studying man's greatest accomplishment, human language.

Exercises

1. Many animals obviously have a system of communication made up of distinct signals whereby they can warn their offspring of impending danger, relay messages to each other concerning the location of food, etc. Make a comparative description of how these signalling systems differ from human language as it is defined in this chapter. Are these

animal systems closed or open as compared with human systems? Do some animals have a more complex system than others?

For information on animal communication you may wish to consult John Lilly, *Man and Dolphin* (New York: Doubleday, 1961); Karl von Frisch, *Bees: Their Vision, Chemical Senses, and Language* (Ithaca, N.Y.: Cornell University Press, 1950); and Claire and W. M. S. Russell, "Language and Animal Signals," in *Language: Introductory Readings*, edited by Virginia P. Clark, Paul A. Eschholz, and Alfred F. Rosa (New York: St. Martin's Press, 1972), pp. 27–55.

2. KINESICS is the study of communication through body movements (facial expressions, gestures, etc.). Cite other examples of such non-verbal behavior. How much do we rely on these non-verbal patterns to convey meaning in our everyday conversation? Do these styles of behavior vary from one cultural group to another? Consider such matters as shaking hands with a member of the opposite sex, kissing or hugging a member of the same sex, winking, waving hello or goodbye, "bottom pinching," hand kissing, bowing, etc.

Some introductory studies of kinesics include the following: Ray L. Birdwhistell, *Introduction to Kinesics* (Louisville, Kentucky: University of Louisville Press, 1952); Edward T. Hall, *The Silent Language* (New York: Doubleday, 1959); Julius Fast, *Body Language* (New York: M. Evans, 1970); Francis Hayes, "Gestures: A Working Bibliography," *Southern Folklore Quarterly*, 21 (December, 1957), 218–317; and the volume of readings cited above in question one.

3. PROXEMICS is related to our use of the space around us, the invisible wall we build around ourselves to keep all except our most intimate associates at a distance. How does the relative distance vary between members of the same sex, the opposite sex, the president of a company and the custodian, the president and his personal secretary, and people of different social status within a community? Does the distance also vary according to the length of time they have known each other? What is the normal distance we stand from a stranger when talking to him? Is this distance different in other cultures?

Crowded elevators bring strangers closer together than they would normally like to be. Does this closeness promote more eye to eye contact? What eye movements are typical of people in a crowded elevator?

For information on proxemics see the works cited in question two and Edward T. Hall, "Proxemics," *Current Anthropology*, 9 (April–June, 1968), 83–104.

4. The kinesic behavior of blacks often differs from that of whites, particularly in large urban areas. How would you describe the "rapping stance" which black males assume when talking to a female whom they

hope to impress? What message might be conveyed by "rolling the eyes"? What are some equivalent kinesic behaviors for other groups?

Some interesting studies of black culture include the following: Ulf Hannerz, *Soulside: Inquiries into Ghetto Culture and Community* (New York: Columbia University Press, 1969); Roger D. Abrahams, *Positively Black* (Englewood Cliffs, N.J.: Prentice-Hall, 1970); Claudia Mitchell Kernan, *Language Behavior in a Black Urban Community* (University of California Language-Behavior Research Laboratory Monograph No. 2, February, 1971); and *The Florida Foreign Language Reporter*, 9, Nos. 1 and 2 (Spring/Fall, 1971), a double issue devoted to Black Language and Culture.

5. Urban blacks also have their own verbal styles. What is "marking"? What is "signifying," sometimes called "sounding"? What is "playing the dozens"? What do these clever verbal games tell us about the authenticity of statements in educational research that black children are unsuccessful in school because they come from limited verbal environments?

These and other patterns of black verbal behavior are discussed in the Kernan and Abrahams studies cited in question four and in another Abrahams work, *Deep Down in the Jungle* (Halboro, Pa.: Folklore Associates, 1964).

References

Chomsky, Noam. *Cartesian Linguistics*. New York: Harper and Row, 1968.
Langacker, Ronald W. *Language and Its Structure*. New York: Harcourt, Brace, and World, 1967.

II

The English Language: Yesterday

In the past it was assumed that only the philologist would be interested in a specialized study of the history of the English language. Since classroom teachers, both elementary and secondary, are continually involved with matters pertaining to language, it is becoming increasingly more important for them to have some grasp of the past history of their language so that they may deal more competently with the many problems related to grammar, spelling, semantics, dialects, reading, and countless other matters. This chapter is designed to be a short sketch of English from its Germanic beginnings to the present with emphasis on the major periods of development and the salient phonological, morphological, and syntactic features of each period.

Indo-European

Comparative philology, the study of correspondences between languages from a common ancestor, received its greatest impetus in the nineteenth century in the findings of certain linguists whose work led eventually to the reconstruction of a parent language for several modern European and Asiatic languages, a language named Indo-European.

The basis for these studies was laid in the previous century when Sir William Jones, an English jurist and student of both classical and oriental languages, read a paper before the Bengal Asiatic Society in 1786. He noted that the ancient language of India, Sanskrit, bore a "stronger affinity" to Latin and Greek "than could have been produced by accident" and suggested that they may have "sprung from some common source."

Franz Bopp is credited with being the first comparative grammarian who got Indo-European grammar on its feet in 1816, with a work entitled *Concerning the conjugation system of the Sanskrit language in comparison with those of Greek, Latin, Persian, and German languages.* In 1818 Rasmus Rask, a Danish scholar, published an essay on the relation of the Old Norse, Germanic, Hellenic, Italic, and Baltic groups of languages, a relationship he had suggested in 1814 to the Danish Academy of Science. Jacob Grimm (more familiar to the average reader for his fairy tales) published an essay in 1822 showing how the Germanic branch of Indo-European underwent a sound change, later called Grimm's Law, which makes certain cognate words more apparent than they had been heretofore. Later, in 1875, Karl Verner was able to discover a second sound change which accounts for certain differences between High and Low German.

Since no written records survive, these and other philologists had to work backwards, after a close comparison of similarities within certain modern languages, in order to arrive at their probable original language. (Reconstructed hypothetical forms will henceforth be marked with an asterisk.)

It must not be assumed that Indo-European was the only language family of any significance. Indeed it is only one of several which might be mentioned here—American Indian, Malay-Polynesian, Japanese, Indo-Chinese, Hamito-Semitic, Dravidian, Aleut-Eskimo, Ural-Altaic, and Basque, to name a few. Indo-European has received greater study and analysis simply because it is the parent language of languages used by countries which exemplify Western civilization.

It is generally assumed by most philologists that the Indo-Europeans lived somewhere in north central Europe in what is now modern Poland. Their homeland had to be inland in a temperate climate, since there are cognate words in surviving languages for the seasons *(spring, winter)*, for both domesticated and wild animals *(dog, cow, sheep, bear—*but not *camel)*, and for certain plants *(oak, willow, pine—*but not *palm)*, but no common word for *ocean.*

The Indo-Europeans also had some type of family organization (there are cognate words for *mother, father, brother*, etc.), a farming culture with plows and domesticated animals, and a counting system. The following table (Whitney: 196) illustrates the cognate forms for the words *seven* and *mother:*

English:	seven	mother
Dutch:	zeven	moeder
German:	sieben	Mutter
Gothic:	sibun	[*mōdar]
Lithuanian:	septyni	moter
Celtic:	secht	mathair
Latin:	septem	mater
Greek:	hepta	meter
Persian:	hapta	matar
Sanskrit:	sapta	matar

Besides having a common word stock, the Indo-European languages are highly inflected to show grammatical distinctions in number, gender, case, tense, person, and so forth.

Chart 1 shows the main branches of Indo-European with their modern descendants. (Living languages are italicized.) Armenian and Albanian might also be included, but because of so many borrowings from neighboring languages are difficult to classify. Hittite (once spoken in Asia Minor) and Tocharian (in Chinese Turkestan) also pose problems in classification, especially since the former has a word stock based primarily on some non-Indo-European language. Since the Hittite documents date from 1400 B.C. and since its grammatical structure is similar to Indo-European, some philologists may prefer to call the parent language Indo-Hittite, making Hittite a sister language to Indo-European.

Of the Hellenic dialects spoken in the Aegean Sea area, the Attic became the most important by the fifth century B.C., chiefly because of the political, commercial, and cultural supremacy of Athens. It was the dialect of Aeschylus, Sophocles, Euripides, Aristophanes, Herodotus, Thucydides, Plato, and Aristotle. Eventually this dialect became the common one, the *koinē*, and through the conquests of Alexander the Great became the established language at the eastern end of the Mediterranean. The New Testament is undoubtedly the best-known document written in this dialect.

The Italic group of languages included the Oscan and Umbrian dialects, in which some pre-Christian inscriptions were written, and Latin, the language of Latium, which emerged as the dominant one because of the political influence of the city of Rome. Spoken Latin, also called Vulgar Latin (from *vulgus*, "common people"), spread throughout the Roman empire and survives in the modern languages called Romance languages (because of their Roman origin and not because they are related to love or lovemaking)—Italian, Spanish, French, Portuguese, and Roumanian. Other languages still spoken in

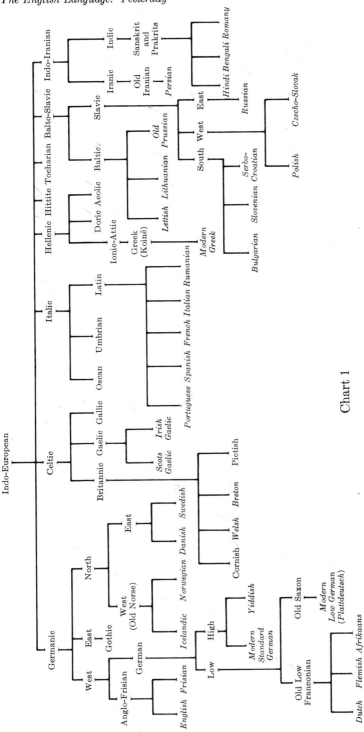

Chart 1

MAJOR INDO-EUROPEAN LANGUAGES, ANCIENT AND MODERN (living languages italicized)

Adapted from Thomas Pyles, *The Origins and Development of the English Language* Second edition, Harcourt, Brace, Jovanovich, 1971.

a few areas of France, Italy, and Spain might be added here. Provençal is slowly dying out but still is used by aged peasants in Provence, a southern province of France. Italians in the Genoa area speak Ligurian, and those in Sardinia speak Sardinian. Spaniards in Galicia, the north-west portion of Spain, speak both standard Spanish and the regional language, *gallego*. Likewise the inhabitants of northeast Spain, the region called Cataluña, speak both Spanish and Catalán.

As intimated earlier, one dialect will often emerge as the prestige dialect, as Castilian Spanish has done in Spain and as the dialects of Paris and the Ile-de-France superseded the Norman, Picard, and Bur-gundian dialects of France and the Walloon dialect of southern Bel-gium. It is commonly thought that Chaucer was gently satirizing the speech of the Prioress in the *Canterbury Tales* because she speaks Norman French ("for Frenssh of Parys was to hire unknowe"), which by his day had considerably less status than the central French of Paris.

The Celts at one time lived throughout most of Europe and even in Asia Minor in a region called Galatia. They were the original inhabitants of the island of Britain, who with the coming of the Angles, Saxons, and Jutes in the fifth century A.D. were pushed back into Wales and Cornwall, up into Scotland, and across the seas to Brittany on the mainland and the islands off the west coast of Britain. Thus Gallic was the Celtic language in Gaul (now France); Scots-Gaelic is still spoken in Scotland as well as on the Hebrides Islands and the Isle of Man; and Irish-Gaelic, rapidly waning, was recently revived in Eire, the Gaelic name for the Irish Free State. The latest attempt to prevent the demise of Irish-Gaelic was a series of government-sponsored tele-vision lessons in which two pretty girls taught a basic course in Gaelic.

In the Britannic group, Cornish (once spoken in Cornwall) and Pictish (the language of the tribes from Scotland who once harassed their Celtic neighbors to the South after the Roman troops were with-drawn) no longer exist. Breton is still spoken in Brittany (the north-eastern coastal region of France, once called Armorica), and Welsh, of course, is still spoken in Wales. The enthusiastic reception given Prince Charles in 1969 at his investiture in Caernarvon can be partially attributed to his six weeks' crash course in Welsh and his several ad-dresses in fluent Welsh to the Welsh people previous to the investiture.

Balto-Slavic and Indo-Iranian, the last two branches to be considered here, are often labeled *satem* languages to distinguish them from the others, which are called *centum* languages. Both *satem* (Old Persian) and *centum* (Latin) mean "hundred" and are mere devices for differ-entiating those languages which developed a sibilant /s/ or /š/ as in (*s*o and *sh*ow) from those which retained their palatal /k/ as in k*i*d).

The Baltic languages include Lettish (spoken in Latvia), Lithuanian, and Old Prussian (once the language of Prussia, in northern Germany).

Several modern languages of the Slavic group survive today—Bulgarian, Slovenian (in northwest Yugoslavia), Serbo-Croatian (spoken also in Yugoslavia by the once independent Serbs and Croats), Polish, Czechoslovakian, and Russian. The last one can be divided into three major dialects—White Russian (spoken in western Russia near the Polish border), Great Russian (the official and literary language of the country), and Ukranian (also called Little Russian, spoken in the south).

The oldest preserved texts in any Indo-European language are the Vedas, the sacred books of ancient India, dating from about 1500 B.C., and written in Sanskrit. Eventually other works, nonreligious in nature, were written in Sanskrit, and, under the influence of certain grammarians like Pāṇini (see Chapter III), came to have a certain fixed literary form which enabled Sanskrit to survive long after it ceased to be spoken, much as Latin has survived as a written language. Other dialects, known as Prakrits, developed alongside Sanskrit and survive in such modern languages as Hindi (in northern India); Bengali (in eastern India, now Bangla Desh); and Romany (from Gypsy *rom*, "man"), spoken by wandering tribes from northwestern India later called Gypsies because it was thought that they were from Egypt.

The Iranian languages of the Indo-Iranian family are best represented by Avestan (the language of the *Avesta*, the sacred writings of Zoroaster) and Old Persian, preserved in some cuneiform inscriptions which record the deeds of Darius (522-486 B.C.) and Xerxes (486-466 B.C.).

The Germanic Branch

The Germanic branch (also called Teutonic) is of greater interest to the student of English, however, and merits a lengthier treatment. East Germanic, best represented by Gothic, was spoken by the Goths in eastern Europe, and, thanks to a Greek missionary named Ulfilas (311-383 A.D.), was recorded for history in a translation of the Gospels and a few other New Testament passages. North Germanic is adequately represented today by Norwegian, Icelandic, Danish, and Swedish. A substantial body of heroic literature, written in Old Icelandic (also called Old Norse), survives today in the form of poetry (the early *Eddas*) and prose epics (*sagas*). In the West Germanic group, German may be subdivided into Standard German (High German); Plattdeutsch (Low German), the former spoken in the mountainous regions of southern Germany and the latter in the lowlands near the North Sea; Dutch (spoken in Holland); and Flemish (spoken in Flanders, a region in western Belgium). The Anglo-Frisian group includes English and Frisian, the latter spoken on the islands off the coast of Holland. Some textbooks, it should be noted, list Old Saxon, Old Low Franconian, Old Frisian, and Old English as branches of Low German. Divisions will vary according to the criteria selected for classifying languages.

The Germanic branch of Indo-European underwent changes which differentiate it from the other divisions. First, it lost the elaborate verbal endings which expressed various shades of meaning like imperfect or incompleted action (*was singing*) or perfect or completed action (*had sung*), etc. Only endings for two tenses survived—present and past (also called preterit, and meaning a definitely completed action). A Modern English verb like *talk*, for instance, has endings which indicate only these two tenses: *talk, talks, talking, talked* (the last two endings indicate "present perfect," or "progressive," and "past perfect," or simple past). Other shades of meaning (phase and aspect) must be given through the use of auxiliary form of *have* or *be*.

Secondly, the Germanic verbs were of two classes, those which indicated past tense through an internal change (also called an ABLAUT SERIES), as in *ring, rang, rung*, and those which indicated the past by use of a dental suffix, a /d/ or a /t/. The former are often called "strong," or "irregular," verbs though their ablaut series is often quite regular as in *ring, rang, rung; sing, sang, sung; drink, drank, drunk*, etc. The latter are called "weak" or "regular" verbs, like *talk*, and today comprise the largest number of verbs in English. Traditionally, verbs like *bring, teach, think* are also weak verbs, though some textbooks label every verb "irregular" which has a variant spelling in the preterit.

A third distinguishing feature of the Germanic languages was a twofold classification of adjectives—strong and weak. Strong adjectives were used before a noun with no other modifiers and as predicate adjectives. Weak adjectives were preceded by a modifying element (a definite article or a demonstrative or possessive pronoun). Thus Old English *god mann* ("good man") corresponds to Modern German *gut Mann* and Old English *se goda mann* ("the good man") to German *der gute Mann*. This twofold declension was lost before Middle English times.

A fourth characteristic of the Germanic branch was a fixed-stress accent; i.e., the stress on a given syllable tended to remain on that syllable no matter what affixes were added, as in *géntle, géntleman, géntlemanly, ungéntlemanly*. In non-Germanic languages the stress is not necessarily fixed; thus in Spanish we have *háblo, hábla, hablámos, habláis*, etc., and in Latin *ámō, amámus, amámini, amátur*, etc.

Finally the Germanic languages underwent a sound shift called the First Germanic Consonant Shift, or Grimm's Law, characterized by a regular shifting of stopped consonants. In the first stage the Indo-European voiceless stops /p,t,k/ became voiceless spirants /f,þ,h/[1] in

---

[1]See list of Special Symbols for the pronunciation of þ, ð, and ʒ.

Germanic. Thus Latin, an Italic language, has words like p*isc*is, p*at*er, *tu, tres, cor* (gen. c*ordis*), and c*entum*, which in English, a Germanic language, have become f*ish*, f*ather*, th*ou*, th*ree*, h*eart*, and h*undred*. In the second stage the Indo-European voiced stops /b,d,g/ become voiceless /p,t,k/ in Germanic. Thus Latin *turba* ("crowd"), d*ecem*, and *ager* become English *thor*p ("town"), *ten*, and *acre* (Old English *æcer*, "field").

In the third stage the Indo-European aspirated stops /bh,dh,gh/ became voiced spirants /ƀ,ð,ȝ/ in Germanic and later in English /b,d,g/. For example, Indo-European *bh*ratar* , Sanskrit *rudh*ir*as* , Indo-European *gh*ostis* become English b*rother*, red, and g*uest*.

The exceptions to Grimm's Law were noted by Karl Verner and later named "Verner's Law." Since the Germanic languages were characterized by a fixed stress accent, usually on the root syllable, certain Indo-European words which had stress elsewhere underwent a change when the stress was shifted in the Germanic languages. For example, /f,þ,h,s/ remained /f,þ,h,s/ initially or immediately after a stressed syllable. Everywhere else they became /b,ð,ȝ,z/ respectively. In Old English they eventually became /v,d,g,r/. These third person preterit forms from Primitive Germanic will illustrate the change:

*wurþún	→	*wúrðun	→	*wurdon* ("became" Cf.
				German *werden*)
*fluhún	→	*flúȝun	→	*flugon* ("flew")
*wæsún	→	*wǽzun	→	*wǣron* ("were")

The last change (from /s/ to /z/ to /r/) is particularly interesting, since it explains how Primitive Germanic *wæs gives us Modern English *was* and *wǣsún eventually becomes Old English *wǣren* and finally Modern English *were*. Also it explains other related forms such as Old English verbs like c*ēosan*, f*rēosan*, and l*ēosan*, which had past participle forms in *r*: *coren, froren*, and *loren*. Besides *were, lorn* has managed to survive as an archaic form and in compounds like *forlorn* and *lovelorn*. Finally Verner's Law explains how Primitive Germanic /ð/ becomes West Germanic /d/ in words like Latin *pater* (with its Indo-European /t/), which later becomes Old English *fæder*, only to change in later centuries to /ð/ again. *Sodden*, the past participle of *seethe*, also illustrates the West Germanic shift from /ð/ to /d/.

The British Celts

The first known inhabitants on the island of Britain were the Celts. Their first intruders were Romans who first invaded the island under

Julius Caesar in 55 B.C. A century later the Emperor Claudius successfully annexed Britain to the Roman empire in 43 A.D. For the next four centuries the Romanized Celts lived peacefully on the island, having been exposed both to the Roman civilization and to Christianity (through Irish missionaries), until the Roman troops were withdrawn to defend Rome from other invaders.

Although most of the troops were gone by 410, it was not long before other invaders appeared, the Picts and Scots (also Celtic in origin) from the north and west. According to Bede's *Ecclesiastical History* (ca. 730) the helpless Britons, after an unsuccessful plea for help from Rome, called on their Germanic neighbors from across the sea, the Jutes. From 449 (Bede's date) on, several shiploads of Germanic warriors arrived—Angles, Saxons, and Jutes, who not only helped defeat the Picts and Scots but also remained on the fertile island, adopting it as their new homeland. The Angles settled in Mercia and Northumbria, the Saxons in Wessex, and the Jutes in Kent. From these four regions came the four main dialects of Old English—Mercian, Northumbrian, West Saxon, and Kentish.

These pagan tribesmen brought with them an alphabet of angular letters, called RUNES, which were used to chisel religious or mystical messages in soft wood. The alphabet is sometimes called *futhorc*, after the first six letters:

ᚠᚢᚦᚨᚱᚲ

It was not long before these tribesmen adopted the Roman alphabet, retaining only two runic symbols:

the thorn þ (þ) and the wynn ƿ

and adapting some Roman symbols to fit their own needs like the ligatured æ and œ and the crossed ð. Presumably the thorn represented a voiced interdental fricative /ð/ as in (th*e*n) and the crossed *d* a voiceless one /θ/ (as in th*i*n), though in manuscripts they are used interchangeably.

Anglo-Saxon or Old English

In approaching Old English grammar it may be well to remember that the Angles, Saxons, and Jutes, who spoke mutually intelligible dialects, settled in different parts of the island of Britain and that seven kingdoms (the Anglo-Saxon Heptarchy) eventually emerged—Kent, Essex, Sussex,

OLD ENGLISH DIALECTS

Wessex, East Anglia, Mercia, and Northumbria—each one achieving some greater degree of political prominence usually associated with a powerful king. Thus Kent under Æðelberht was the most important in the sixth century, Northumbria in the seventh, Mercia in the eighth, and Wessex under Alfred the Great in the ninth.

In 597 Christianity was brought to Kent from Ireland by the missionary Augustine, who became the first Archbishop of Canterbury. By the eighth century most of the island was Christianized. In the eighth and ninth centuries the Scandinavians raided the northeast coast, and their pillage and plunder of monasteries in that area has resulted in a dearth of manuscripts today in the Northumbrian and Mercian dialects. After pushing their way inward toward the center of the island, they were finally stopped in Wessex by Alfred, and were forced to sign a treaty in 878, the Treaty of Wedmore, under which they would agree to remain within a given territory, the Danelagh, whose boundary ran diagonally across Mercia. Thus the Scandinavian languages influenced Old English grammar and vocabulary, particularly in the northeast.

Alfred's reign in Wessex was long and productive, resulting in innumerable translations from Latin into Old English of works like Boethius' *Consolation of Philosophy* and portions of the Bible. Since so many manuscripts from this area survive in the West Saxon dialect, they became the works from which later grammars of Old English are written; thus we can say that students today who study Old English are usually studying West Saxon. In fact, the greatest heroic poem of Anglo-Saxon civilization, *Beowulf*, was written in West Saxon.

Old English, in contrast to Modern English, was a highly inflected language, in which case endings, rather than word order, signaled meaning. For example, *Glædne giefend lufað God* (Cheerful-giver-loveth-God) means "God loveth a cheerful giver," the clue to subject and object being in the case endings for *God* and *cheerful giver*. Like modern German, Old English nouns, pronouns, verbs, adjectives, and adverbs were all inflected.

Old English Nouns

Nouns had five cases: the nominative (for subjects and predicate nouns), the genitive (usually to indicate possession), the accusative (for direct objects), the dative (for indirect objects), and the instrumental (used in special constructions and with prepositions to show agency). The instrumental occurs rather infrequently and almost always declines like the dative.

Since Modern German has kept its numerous noun inflections, it might be helpful to compare it with English for four different cases in the singular and the plural:

	SINGULAR	PLURAL
NOM.	Der Mann *ist zu Hause.* The man is at home.	Die Männer *sind zu Hause.* The men are at home.
ACC.	*Sie liebt* den Mann. She loves the man.	*Sie liebt* die Männer. She loves the men.
GEN.	*Das Buch* des Mannes . . . The book of the man . . .	*Die Buchen* der Männer . . . The books of the men . . .
DAT.	*Er gibt* dem Manne *das Buch.* He gives the man the book.	*Er gibt* den Männern *die Bücher.* *He gives the men the books.*

In both Old English and Modern German certain prepositions take the dative, while others take the accusative. As can be seen above, the nouns used as direct objects are in the accusative case, while those used as indirect objects are in the dative. In Modern English we have noun endings only for the plural and for one case, the genitive (possessive).

Thus it is redundant to talk about three cases (nominative, genitive, and objective) when we have case endings for only two. We might as well say Modern English has a dative case and then we would have four (or even five if we care to include the vocative, as in Latin *O patria*, "O, fatherland"). Personal pronouns, however, do have forms for three cases (*I, me, my; we, us, our; he, him, his*).

Old English nouns have been grouped according to case endings into three general categories—masculine, feminine, and neuter. As in German the Old English nouns have grammatical gender rather than natural gender; thus *wif* ("wife") is neuter and *hund* ("dog") is masculine. The masculine nouns, which make up almost half of the lexicon of nouns in Old English, may be further divided into strong nouns (also called masculine *a* stems because the stem to which inflectional endings were affixed in Germanic ended in *a*) and weak nouns (or *n* stems). The following paradigm of a typical masculine strong noun will suffice to give the beginning student some notion of Old English inflections. (Note that the words preceding each noun all mean *the* today and correspond to the various German forms mentioned above, *der, die, das,* etc.).

	SINGULAR	PLURAL
NOM.	*se cyning*, "the king"	*þā cyningas*, "the kings"
ACC.	*þone cyning*, "the king"	*þā cyningas*, "the kings"
GEN.	*þæs cyninges*, "of the king"	*þāra cyninga*, "of the kings"
DAT.	*þæm cyninge*, "to the king"	*þæm cyningum*, "to the kings"

The only endings to survive today are the genitive singular (*king's*) with an apostrophe, a printer's symbol added later, and the plural (*kings, kings'*).

Several masculine nouns (plus a few feminine and neuter) typify the weak declension (*n* stems), among them *oxa* (m. "ox"), *bēo* (f. "bee"), *tā* (f. "toe"), *ēage* (n. "eye"), and *ēare* (n. "ear").

	SINGULAR	PLURAL
NOM.	*se oxa*, "the ox"	*þā oxan*, "the oxen"
ACC.	*þone oxan*, "the ox"	*þā oxan*, "the oxen"
GEN.	*þæs oxan*, "of the ox"	*þāra oxena*, "of the oxen"
DAT.	*þæm oxan*, "to the ox"	*þæm oxum*, "to the oxen"

Obviously *oxen* has survived as the only pure form of this declension. The other words from this declension survive in Chaucer, and even then they are competing with analogical forms with -(*e*)*s*. Those who admire the magic horse of brass in the Squire's Tale murmur "as dooth a swarm of been." "Lyk asure were his legges and his toon," says the Nun's Priest of Chaunticleer. Palamon, in the Knight's Tale, cannot hide

himself from Arcita because "feeld hath eyen and the wode hath eres."
Evidently Chaucer could choose between both forms and thus chose
eres instead of *eren* to rhyme with *yeres* ("years") in the previous line.

Some neuter nouns had no ending in the plural (*dēor*, "deer"; *folc*,
"people"; *scēap*, "sheep"; *swīn*, "pig"), and others ended in *-u* or *-ru*
(*childru*, "children"). The unchanged plurals above remain the same
today with the exception of *folc*, which has become regularized to the
somewhat colloquial *folks*, though we speak of the literature and culture
of the *folk*. Chaucer kept the unchanged plural form in the General
Prologue to the *Canterbury Tales:* "Thanne longen folk to goon on
pilgrimages." To Old English *cildru* was added a weak ending; hence
children is actually a double plural. (If the nonstandard form *childrens*
ever becomes standard, then we will have a triple plural.) Other double
plurals are *brethren* (*brēðer* + *-en*), *kine* (*cȳ* + *-en*), and *breeches* (*brēc* +
-es).

A small number of nouns had a mutated vowel in the plural and still
have their irregular plural today because of their frequency of occurrence:
*foot, feet; tooth, teeth; brother, brethern; goose, geese; man, men; mouse,
mice; louse, lice; cow, kine.* In Primitive Germanic these words had the
same root vowel in both the singular and the plural, but the plural
forms had an *i* in the last syllable (**fōti, *tōði, *gōsiz, *manni*) which
was eventually lost before Old English times. Thus we had *tōþ, tēþ; gōs,
gēs; mann, menn; mūs, mȳs; lūs, lȳs; brōðer, brēðer* (+ *-en*); *cū, cȳ* (+ *-en*);
and *brōc, brēc* (+ *-es*).

Since the masculine and neuter nouns usually had *-a* in the genitive
plural, it might be of interest to note that *sēox fōta, seofon geara*, and
þrēo mila are forms which translate *six feet, seven years*, and *three miles*
in Modern English; but in Old English the second word in each expression was in the genitive case and might be loosely translated "seven
of years," etc. These forms parallel nonstandard English today, in
sentences like "I live three mile down the road" and "I worked there
seven year."

Old English Adjectives

Adjectives in Old English could be either strong or weak depending on
their use in the sentence. Strong adjectives had an indefinite use when
used alone before nouns or following indefinite articles. Weak adjectives
were used after definite articles, demonstratives, or possessive pronouns.
Thus "good" in "good kings" would be strong (*gōd cyningas*) but in the
"the good kings" or "their good kings" would be weak (*þā gōdan cyningas, heora gōdan cyningas*). The same is true today in Modern German:
gute Könige, die guten Könige, ihre guten Könige.

Adjectives were compared in Old English, usually with *-ra* and *-ost*: *glæd, glædra, gladost; lang, lengra, lengest; strang, strengra, strengest,* etc.

Some adjectives had comparative and superlative forms derived from a different root from the positive: *god, betra, betst; lȳtel, lǽssa, lǽst; micel* ("great"), *māra, mǽst; yfel* ("evil"), *wyrsa, wyrst,* etc.

An older superlative form was *-(u)ma* to which was later added the typical *-ost,* resulting in double superlatives like *foremost (fore =* "before"), *innemest* ("inmost"), *utemest* ("utmost"), *midmest* ("midmost"). Later *-most* becomes an assumed suffix in words like *uppermost* and *furthermost.*

Old English Verbs

Inflectional endings for Old English verbs were the same for both weak and strong verbs in the present indicative:

	SINGULAR	PLURAL
1.	*ic bringe*	*wē bringaþ*
2.	*þū bringest*	*gē bringaþ*
3.	*hē, hēo, hit bringeþ*	*hīe bringaþ*

Infinitives usually ended in *-an* or *-ian,* present participles in *-ende,* past participles of strong verbs in *-en,* subjunctives in *-e* (singular) and *-en* (plural), imperatives in *-e, -a,* or Ø in the singular and *-(a)ð* in the plural; and quite often past participles were prefixed with *ge-,* which is still a feature of Modern German (*haben, hatte, gehabt*).

As noted earlier, one of the characteristics of the Germanic branch of Indo-European was a twofold classification of verbs—strong and weak. The strong verbs formed their past tense (preterit) through a vowel change (called GRADATION, or ABLAUT). It is somewhat of a misnomer to call them irregular, since they are quite regular in their internal change. Philologists have been able to subclassify the Old English strong verbs according to seven different internal patterns of change. The verbs below illustrate the seven classes:

	PRESENT	PRET. SING.	PRET. PLUR.	PAST PART.
I	*drīfan,* "drive"	*drāf*	*drifon*	*drifen*
	wrītan, "write"	*wrāt*	*writon*	*writen*
II	*cēosan,* "choose"	*cēas*	*curon*	*coren*[2]
	clēofan, "cleave"	*clēaf*	*clufon*	*clofen*
	sēoðan, "seethe"	*sēað*	*sudon*	*soden*[2]

[2]Result of Verner's Law, also called *grammatical change.*

	PRESENT	PRET. SING.	PRET. PLUR.	PAST PART.
III	*bindan,* "bind"	*band*	*bundon*	*bunden*
	helpan, "help"	*healp*	*hulpon*	*holpen*
	weorþan, "become"	*wearþ*	*wurdon*	*worden*[3]
IV	*brecan,* "break"	*bræc*	*bræcon*	*brocen*
	stelan, "steal"	*stæl*	*stælon*	*stolen*
V	*licgan,* "lie"	*læg*	*lægon*	*legen*
	sittan, "sit"	*sæt*	*sæton*	*seten*
	wesan, "be"	*wæs*	*wæron*	*wæren*[4]
VI	*scacan,* "shake"	*scōc*	*scōcon*	*scocen*
	swerian, "swear"	*swōr*	*swōron*	*sworen*
VII	*blāwan,* "blow"	*blēow*	*blēowon*	*blāwen*
	bēatan, "beat"	*bēot*	*bēoton*	*bēaten*

Old English weak verbs have as their major distinction a dental suffix in the preterit, i.e., a /d/ or /t/:

PRESENT	PRETERIT	PAST PARTICIPLE
cyssan, "kiss"	*cyste*	*cyste*
lecgan, "lay"	*legde*	*legd*
lufian, "love"	*lufode*	*lufod*
secgan, "say"	*sægde*	*sægd*
tæcan, "teach"	*tæhte*	*tæht*

The paradigm which follows exemplifies a typical conjugation for both weak and strong verbs in the preterit:

PRETERIT INDICATIVE

		FOR WEAK VERBS:		FOR STRONG VERBS:
SING.	1.	*ic lufode*	1.	*ic sang*
	2.	*þū lufodest*	2.	*þū sunge*
	3.	*hē lufode*	3.	*hē sang*
PLUR.	1.	*wē lufodon*	1.	*wē sungon*
	2.	*gē lufodon*	2.	*gē sungon*
	3.	*hīe lufodon*	3.	*hīe sungon*

It should be noted also that endings existed for both the subjective and imperative moods in Old English. As in Modern English the imperative expressed a command: *Gā gē!* ("Go ye"); the subjunctive expressed a wish, a doubt, a hypothetical condition, etc.: *swelce hē tām wære* ("as if he were tame"). The passive voice could be formed with

---

[3]Cf. German *werden, wurde, geworden.*
[4]Present tense forms *eom, eart, is, sind (on), bēo, bist, biδ, bēoδ,* come from another verb *bēon. Wæron* with /r/ instead of /z/ is another example of Verner's Law.

wesan or *weorþan: Hit wæs ofer stān getimbrod* ("It [the house] was built over stone").

Unlike Latin and Greek, Old English had no endings to indicate future time; hence the present indicative was often used for the future as well: *Ic ārīse and ic fare tō mīnum fæder* ("I [will] arise and go to my father") or *and on þǣm rīptīman ic secge þǣm rīperum*, ("And at the harvest-time I will say to the reapers"). Usually clues to the time element were apparent in the context of the sentence. The preterit endings could also express pluperfect time, often with the help of an adverb of time: *Ne mētte hē ǣr nān gebrīn land* ("He [had] not found before any inhabited land").

Perfective aspect could also be expressed with *habban* ("have") and *wesan* ("be"): *habban* plus the past participle of a transitive verb (as in *hīe hæfdon hiera cyning āworpenne*, "They had deposed their king" and *nu ic hæbbe gestrīened ōþru twā*, "now I have gained another two"); and *wesan* plus the past participle of an intransitive verb (as in *hit wæs ofer stān getimbrod* above and *se hālga fæder wæs inn āgān*, "the holy father had gone in"). By the end of the Old English period, *habban* is winning out as the preferred auxiliary.

Other compound tenses in embryo in Old English were those with *sculan, scolde* ("shall," "should") and *willan, wolde* ("will," "would"), each used with an infinitive. The former with an infinitive usually, like the subjective, implied volition, as in *ic wille wyrcean mīn setl*, ("I shall make my throne"), while the latter with an infinitive implied obligation, as in *forðǣm gē sculon wēpan* ("because you will [must] weep"). Both *shall* and *will* overlap in usage. However, some prescriptive grammarians in the seventeenth century tried to settle the overlap once and for all with an elaborate set of rules which still prove a burden in many conservative classrooms.

Old English Adverbs.

Adverbs were formed from adjectives by the addition of *-e* (*wrað*, "angry"; *wraðe* "angrily") and were compared with *-or* and *-ost:*

oft, "often"	*oftor*	*oftost*
luflīce, "lovingly"	*luflīcor*	*luflīcost*

Some had a different root in the comparative and superlative forms:

lȳt, "little"	*lǣs*	*lǣst*
micle, "much"	*mā*	*mǣst*
wel, "well"	*bet, sēl*	*bētst, sēlest*
yfle, "ill"	*wyrs*	*wyrst*

The *-ly* suffix, often called an adverbial suffix in Modern English, originated in *lic*, "body." Next it was compounded with words like *mann* to form an adjective *mannlic* ("man-like," literally, "having the body of a man"), *folclic* ("folk-like," or "popular"), *heofonlic* ("heavenly"), and to these adjectives the adverbial suffix *-e* was added; hence the adverbs *bliþe-lice*, "gladly," etc. Some words like *deep* (*dēop, dēope*) and *loud* (*hlūd, hlūde*) were distinguishable in Old English because of the adverbial *-e*, but in Modern English speakers feel a need to add *-ly* as in "He drove slowly" and "He spoke loudly." And some speakers, unsure of themselves, add *-ly* to adjectives which follow verbs of the senses: "I want to sit by the door in case I get to feeling badly." Although the *-ly* suffix is frequently mislabeled the adverb suffix, one must not forget that certain adjectives also end in *-ly* (*daily, hourly, monthly, yearly, friendly,* etc.)

Old English Pronouns

Personal pronouns have changed least from Old English times to the present. The dual pronouns *wit* ("we two") and *git* ("you two") had almost completely disappeared before Middle English, a loss which need not be regretted, though these forms could be helpful in distinguishing between "you two" and "all of you" ("you-all," or even "y'all" in some parts of the country). Note the similarity between the feminine singular and the plural forms.

SINGULAR		PLURAL	
NOM. 1.	*ic*	1.	*wē*
ACC.	*mē*		*ūs*
GEN.	*mīn*		*ūre*
DAT.	*mē*		*ūs*
NOM. 2.	*þū*	DUAL:	*wit*, "we two"
ACC.	*þē*		*unc*, "us two"
GEN.	*þīn*		*uncer*, "our two"
DAT.	*þē*		*unc*, "us two"
NOM. 3.	*hē*	2.	*gē*
ACC.	*hine*		*ēow*
GEN.	*his*		*ēower*
DAT.	*him*		*ēow*
NOM.	*hēo*	DUAL:	*git*, "you two"
ACC.	*hēo, hie*		*inc*, "you two"

	SINGULAR		PLURAL
GEN.	*hire*		*incer,* "your two"
DAT.	*hire*		*inc,* "you two"
NOM.	*hit*	3.	*hīe*
ACC.	*hit*		*hīe*
GEN.	*his*		*hiera, heora*
DAT.	*him*		*him, hēom*

A Sample of Old English

Before turning to Middle English, it might be well to examine a short passage of Old English and note some of the grammatical features stated above. The passage which follows is taken from a West Saxon translation of the Gospels (Matthew 7:26-27):

> And ǣlc þara þe gehīerþ þās mīn word, and þā ne wyrcþ, sē biþ gelīc þǣm dysigan menn, þe getimbrode his hūs ofer sand-ceosal. þā rīnde hit, and þǣr cōmon flōd, and blēowan windas, and āhruron on þæt hūs, and þæt hūs fēoll; and his hryre wæs micel.

A literal translation is this:

> And each of those that heareth these my words, and them not doeth, that [one] beeth like the foolish man that built his house over [on] sand-gravel. Then rained it, and there came floods, and blew winds, and beat on the house, and the house fell; and its fall was great.

The most common relative pronoun in Old English was the particle *þe*, which may be translated *that, who,* and *which.* Thus *ǣlc þāra þe* would be translated "each of those who" (*þāra* is genitive plural). *Word* is a neuter noun which, like *dēor* and *scēap,* had no ending for the nominative and accusative plural, and thus translates "words" in Modern English, *þās* being the accusative plural form of the neuter demonstrative, *þis word. Mīn* survives as "mine" in Modern English when it follows the verb. In Middle English it alternates with *my,* which was used before consonants, and with *mine* before vowels as late as the eighteenth century (and even in a nineteenth-century hymn, "Mine eyes have seen the glory of the coming of the Lord.").
þā could mean "then" or "when" as well as "the." In the first line of the above passage it is the accusative plural *þā,* object of the third-person singular verb, *wyrcþ,* which, like *gehīerþ,* has the typical *-eþ* ending in the indicative in a contracted or syncopated form without the *-e-.* As noted earlier, *wyrcþ* may be translated "doeth" or "maketh";

and its past participle form, *wroht*, survives in archaic expressions like
"What hath God wrought?" or modern compounds like "wrought-iron."

The word *se* can be either a definite article or a demonstrative; here it
is the latter, meaning "that man." *Biþ* was often used in alternation
with *is* and often seems to denote future time. *Gelic* still survives as
"like" without the prefix. It was followed by the dative construction,
þæm dysigan menn, which shows a perfect example of a noun (*menn* is a
dative singular form of *mann*) modified by a weak adjective, *dysigan*,
rather than the strong form (*dysig*, "foolish") because it follows a
definite article.

The second particle *þe* translates "who" again and is the subject of the
verb *getimbrode*, a weak verb because of its /d/ in the preterit. In the
passage in Matthew preceding this one, the wise man's house does not fall
because *hit wæs ofer stān getimbrod*. Here *getimbrod* is a past participle
(*wesan* + past participle) rather than a preterit form. *Hūs*, like *word*, is
neuter with no ending in the accusative.

In the second sentence *þā* means "then." *Hit*, the neuter pronoun
which survives in some nonstandard dialects, is the subject of the weak
verbe *rīnde*, a preterit form (the present would be *rīneþ*). Since *cōmon*
and *blēowan* are plural, *flōd* and *windas* must also be plural. *Windas*
poses no problem since it has the typical *-s* plural from the masculine
conjugation, which survives in Modern English. *Flōd*, however, is neuter;
thus it has no ending in the nominative plural. *Cōmon*, *blēowan*, *āhruron*,
and *fēoll* (from *cūman*, *blāwan*, *ahrēosan*, and *feallan*) must be strong
verbs as evidenced by their preterit forms which have a vowel change
rather than a /d/ or a /t/.

Prepositions usually were followed by a noun in either the accusative
or the dative case; some might take either case: *on þæt hūs* and *ofer sand-
ceosal* are both accusative constructions; *þæt* was the neuter form for
both the definite article "the" and the demonstrative "that." Thus "on
the house" or "on that house" would be equally valid translations.

His, the neuter form, survives in Early Modern English, but was
quickly losing ground to its analogical counterpart, *its*. The translators
of the King James version of the Bible, reluctant to use the colloquial
its, chose a different construction, "great was the fall of it," thus avoid-
ing the archaic *his* as well as the innovative *its*. *Micel* survives today as
much rather than *great*.

Old English Syntax

Because of the large number of case endings in Old English, word order
was not quite as important in showing grammatical relationships as it is
in Modern English. However, in general, Old English word order has

many similarities to Modern English. The subject + intransitive verb, the subject + transitive verb + object, the subject + verb + complement patterns are common enough in Old English:

> *þæt hūs fēoll.* "The house fell."
> *Sum man hæfde twegen suna.* "A certain man had two sons."
> *Ic secge þæm rīperum.* "I [will] say to the reapers."
> *Ic ārīse and ic fare tō mīnum fæder.*
> "I [will] arise and I [will] go to my father."
> *And hē ārās þā and cōm tō his fæder.*
> "And he arose then and came to his father."
> *Ic wille wyrcean mīn setl.* "I shall make my throne."
> *þīn fæder of-slōh ān fæt celf.* "Thy father slew a fat calf."

The Middle English Period

By the end of the Old English period a number of inflectional endings were either lost or had fallen together, making for a much simplified system in which word order played an even greater part. The Norman invasion in 1066, with the subsequent defeat of Harold by William the Conqueror, no doubt had some influence on English, though some are of the opinion that the changes in sounds and inflections would have taken place anyway had there been no Norman invasion (Wyld: 81–82). Certainly there can be no doubt about French influence on vocabulary since, according to one estimate, over ten thousand words were borrowed from French into English during the Middle English period (Baugh: 215). The dates for this period are 1100 to 1500, though some may prefer to move them forward a few years so that the period ends as early as 1400 with the death of Chaucer. Certainly Old English is greatly changed by the time of the invasion of William of Normandy in 1066; thus 1050 would serve equally well to mark that "middle" period between Old and Modern English.

As Norman French became the language of society and government, most learned documents were written in French, thus breaking a long English scribal tradition which had begun as early as King Ethelbert's reign (860–866). Even before English was reestablished as the official language of the government and the law courts in 1363, scribes began writing again in English but with new combinations of graphs to represent both English sounds as well as newly borrowed sounds from French. Hence phonemic-graphemic correspondence is much less in Middle English than it was in Old English. To complicate matters further, the tense vowels underwent a change, called the Great Vowel Shift by later philologists, following the Middle English Period; but printing meanwhile had been introduced, thus establishing certain conventional spellings which we have with us today.

Middle English Dialects

The Northumbrian dialect of Old English (see the map below) becomes the Northern dialect of Middle English. The Mercian dialect becomes Midland, which in turn can be subdivided into East Midland (represented by London) and West Midland. The line designated by King Alfred in the Treaty of Wedmore in 878 is almost identical to the dialect boundary between the two Midland groups. West Saxon becomes the Southwestern dialect of Middle English, and Kentish remains Kentish, also called Southeastern. Chaucer's English, by the way, is late Middle English of the East Midland (London) variety, which emerged as the standard dialect because of the importance of London as a commercial center and seat of the English government.

It is not within the province of this book to treat the major differences

MIDDLE ENGLISH DIALECTS

among the various Middle English dialects except to point out those significant features which survive today, like the *-es* verbal ending for the third person singular, a Northern dialect form that eventually supplanted the *-eth* ending of Mercian, West Saxon, and Kentish. Unless otherwise indicated, the forms given to represent Middle English will be East Midland forms, generally represented in the language of Chaucer.

Middle English Nouns and Adjectives

Nouns in Middle English no longer have grammatical gender and follow in the main the inflectional pattern of the Old English masculine strong nouns, as the following paradigm illustrates:

SINGULAR

NOM.	the kyng	oxe	sheep	man	child	foot
ACC.	the kyng	oxe	sheep	man	child	foot
GEN.	the kynges	oxes	sheepes	mannes	childes	fotes
DAT.	the kynge	oxe	sheep	man	child	foot

PLURAL

NOM.	the kynges	oxen	sheep	men	children	feet
ACC.	the kynges	oxen	sheep	men	children	feet
GEN.	the kynges	—	—	mennes	—	feet
DAT.	the kynges	oxen	sheep	men	children	feet

Obviously two inflectional endings survive—the genitive *-(e)s* and the plural *-(e)s*. Even most nouns from the Old English weak declension have lost their *-n* endings (with a few exceptions like "oxen"), for example *names, bees, eyes, ears, toes*, etc. Those neuter nouns with no ending in the plural have in some instances remained unchanged (*deer, sheep, swine*), while some have followed the usual pattern of the masculine strong nouns and have added an *-s* (*folks*).

Those nouns with mutated plurals (a result of *i-umlaut*) have kept their unusual plural forms, probably because of their frequent use: *feet, geese, teeth, mice, lice, men*. The plural for *bōc* ("book") was *bēc*, which had been regularized to *books* by the end of the Middle English period. The mutated form of *cū* ("cow") was *cy*, which survives in Renaissance English as *kine*, though it has been replaced by *cows* in Modern English. *Brethren*, a double plural consisting of a mutated form (*brēþer*) plus a weak ending (*-an*), survives today along with an analogical form *sistern* used in some fundamentalist circles.

The old genitive plural forms *mila* and *fota* survive in Modern English in expressions like "a two-mile hike," "a six-foot fence," and "I went on foot." Otherwise they have a standard plural ending in -*s*.

By the end of the Old English period most of the endings for weak and strong adjectives had disappeared or had settled on one form, -*e*. Thus in Chaucer we find *the yonge sonne, his halve cours, Epicurus owne sone*. The comparative and superlative endings survive as -*er* and -*est*, as in Modern English. Chaucer says of his Lawyer, "he semed *bisier* than he was," and of his Franklin, "a *bettre* envyned man was nowher noon." The goodly Parson will not neglect "the *ferreste* in his parrisshe."

Middle English Verbs

Verb endings in Middle English are almost the same except for the present plural in which Old English -*aþ* gives way to Middle English -*e(n)*, perhaps through the influence of the preterit plural and past participle forms. Note the similarities between these Middle English forms and their Old English originals listed earlier:

SINGULAR	PLURAL
PRESENT INDICATIVE	
I bringe	*we bringe(n)*
thou bringest	*ye bringe(n)*
he, she, (h)it bringeth	*they bringe(n)*
PRETERIT FOR WEAK VERBS	
I lovede	*we lovede(n)*
thou lovedest	*ye lovede(n)*
he, she, (h)it lovede	*they lovede(n)*
PRETERIT FOR STRONG VERBS	
I song, sang	*we songe(n)*
thou song(e)	*ye songe(n)*
he, she, (h)it song(e)	*they songe(n)*

Infinitives in Middle English still end in -*n*, as they did in Old English, but like the plural, -*n* was slowly being dropped. Chaucer uses both, depending on the rhyme or meter needed at the moment. In the spring people (*folk*, pl.) "longen . . . to goon on pilgrimages / and palmeres for to seken straunge strondes." Here both infinitives and plural verbs end in -*n*, but a few lines later the *n*'s are dropped for the sake of rhyme:

> And specially from every shires ende
> Of Engelond to Caunterbury they wende,
> The hooly blisful martir for to seeke,
> That hem hath holpen whan that they were seke.

The Old English present participle ending, *-nde*, survives in Middle English (*slepinde, slepande, slepende*) but is eventually replaced by the Southern *-ing(e)*, which itself was formed from the Old English verbal noun ending *-ung*, as in *leornung*. The past participle prefix *ge-* was weakened to unstressed /i/, spelled with a *y-*: *yclept, ywrought, yfalle, ytaught*, etc. These forms also appear in Middle English poetry without the initial *y-*, especially when it is not needed in the metrical pattern.

During the Middle English period several strong verbs became weak by analogy with the larger number of weak verbs in the language: *glide, reap, cleave, flee, shove, seethe, sprout, delve, help, shear, heave, hew, leap, mow, row, sleep, weep*. Of these *cleave* has a weak form surviving in *cleft palate* and a strong form surviving in *cloven hoof*. The old preterit of *help, holp*, survives in nonstandard English.

Middle English Pronouns

Words which have a high frequency of use are less likely to disappear from a language which is changing or which is being influenced greatly by another language. Thus it is with the personal pronouns, which have remained essentially the same since Old English times. The following are typical of late Middle English:

		SINGULAR	PLURAL
1.	NOM.	*I, ik*	*we*
	ACC.	*me*	*us*
	GEN.	*min*	*our(e)*
	DAT.	*me*	*us*
2.	NOM.	*thou*	*ye*
	ACC.	*thee*	*you*
	GEN.	*thine, thy*	*your(e)*
	DAT.	*thee*	*you*
3.	NOM.	*he*	*they*
	ACC.	*him*	*hem*
	GEN.	*his*	*her*
	DAT.	*him*	*hem*
	NOM.	*she*	
	ACC.	*her(e), hir(e)*	
	GEN.	*her(e), hir(e)*	
	DAT.	*her(e), hir(e)*	

	SINGULAR	PLURAL
NOM.	*(h)it*	
ACC.	*(h)it*	
GEN.	*his*	
DAT.	*him*	

By late Old English times most of the dual pronouns had disappeared except in the south, where they are found in Southwestern Middle English in works like *The Owl and the Nightingale*. Since the Southwestern dialect is the most conservative Middle English dialect, older forms persist there the longest.

An obvious new addition to the table of Middle English pronouns above is *she*, whose precise origin has not been fully explained to everyone's satisfaction. Since it first appears in the north, it might possibly have been a Scandinavian borrowing. The neuter pronoun *hit* eventually loses its initial sound (only to regain it again in some modern nonstandard dialects). The accusative form *hine* is replaced by *hit*.

Another new pronoun in Middle English is *they*, which can with more certainty be traced to Scandinavian origin in Old Norse. The native forms from Old English *hīe* survive longer in the south but are eventually replaced by the northern *þai* (spelled variously *þay, thai,* etc.). The genitive and objective forms *þeir* and *þeim*, also of Scandinavian origin, do not appear in the Midlands and South before the fifteenth century. Thus Chaucer uses *they, hem,* and *her* or *hir* for the plural:

> So priketh hem [them] nature in hir [their] corages . . .
> So hadde I spoken with hem [them] everichon
> That I was of hir [their] felaweshipe anon . . .

Concerning the definite article, the tendency in all Middle English dialects was toward simplification; thus the masculine *se* and the feminine *seo* of Old English are eventually replaced by a new form *þe*, which is declined in the south for a while but later becomes indeclinable in all dialects of Middle English.

Early Modern English

Morphologically Early Modern English (1500-1750) differs little from late Middle English. That is, noun inflections are still found with genitive singular and with plural forms. Adjectives continue to be compared with *-er* and *-est*. Strong and weak verbs are very much in evidence, though many strong verbs like *creep* and *help* become weak through the process of analogy.

Pronoun forms remain the same in Early Modern English except for the plural forms *their* and *them*, which have completely supplanted the Middle English *her* (*hir*) and *hem*. The objective *you* was also being used alongside the nominative *ye* and gradually replaced it. The King James Bible (1611), perhaps the best representation of conservative Early Modern English, observes faithfully the older usage: "I in *you* and *ye* in me," "A new commandment I give unto *you* that *ye* love one another." The translators of the King James version were equally conservative (and consistent) in their use of *thou, thee, thy,* and *thine:* "I in *thee* and *thou* in me."

Not only does the plural objective *you* replace the plural nominative *ye* but it also comes to be used in the singular alongside *thou* as a polite form. For a time speakers used both pronouns interchangeably, depending on the person they were addressing. *Thou, thee, thy,* and *thine* were used in intimate conversations between equals and by adults or nobility when addressing children or inferiors. In addressing nobility or people above them socially, speakers of Early Modern English often used the polite *you,* and if they used *thou,* it could be a sign of contempt or disdain. In his intimate conversations with his wife, Lady Percy, Hotspur uses *thou* and its allied forms, but when he wants to be off to the war he switches to the colder and more aloof *you.* (*1 Henry IV*, II, ii). Needless to say, the wide range of nuances became too complex for the average speaker, and the *thou* forms were dropped completely except in poetry and liturgy. Even in the church ritual they are losing out and are being replaced by *you* and *your.* The newest translation of the Bible, *The New English Bible*, retains *thou* and its variant forms only in the Lord's Prayer. It should be noted, however, that many modern languages like German, French, and Spanish still have familiar forms in both singular and plural.

The four Old English masculine pronouns (*hē, hine, his, him*) were reduced to three in Middle English (*hine ⟩ him*). In Early Modern English a new analogical neuter form, *its,* begins to replace the neuter *his,* except in the King James Bible, whose translators must have felt it was too innovative. Thus they used the older *his* ("if the salt have lost his savour") or recast the sentence to avoid *its* entirely ("The earth is the Lord's and the fullness thereof."). Shakespeare vacillated among three genitive forms (*it, his,* and *its*). In *Hamlet* Horatio says of the Ghost, "Yet once methought it lifted up it head and did address itself to motion, like as it would speak." Lear's Fool says, "The hedge sparrow fed the cuckoo so long that it had it head bit off by it young." In most cases, however, Shakespeare uses *its.*

Verbal auxiliaries have become an important part of the verb phrase unit by Renaissance times. As we noted earlier, *have, shall,* and *will* were functioning as auxiliaries in late Old English and had become an increasingly more important part of the verb phrase in Middle English. In Early Modern English *be* was used with certain verbs to form perfect constructions as in the angel's statement in the Easter story: "He is not here; he is risen"; and in Falstaff's question to Bardolph: "Am I not fallen away vilely since this last action?" *Do* in older English had a causative meaning and in Renaissance English begins to take on some of its modern meanings. It was often used with a verb to express simple past action ("The serpent that did sting thy father's life now wears his crown.") as well as emphasis ("Perdition catch my soul but I do love thee.").

Negative statements in Middle English were made with *ne* (or *na*) placed before the verb and often reinforced with *not* (*noght*) after the verb. By the end of the Middle English period *not* becomes the conventionalized form, as it is today. In Early Modern English it was placed after the verb ("Weep not, sweet queen"; "He cometh not"), whereas in Modern English *not* may follow only the verb *be* ("he is not proud") or an auxiliary ("he has not arrived"). Otherwise *do* must be used. "Do not weep, sweet queen"; "They did not (didn't) arrive early."

In Early Modern English questions the subject and verb could be inverted ("Walks he forth tonight?"), whereas in Modern English *do* is obligatory ("Does he leave tonight?") unless the main verb is *be* ("He is here." → "Is he here?") or has an auxiliary ("He is leaving today." → "Is he leaving today?" "He has already gone." → "Has he already gone?").

The greatest difference between Middle English and Modern English (besides the quaint spelling which makes our students think Chaucer wrote in Old English) lies in pronunciation. Sometime between 1400 and 1450 the tense vowels underwent a change in pronunciation, called the Great Vowel Shift. Briefly its most salient changes might be summarized in the following diagram.[5]

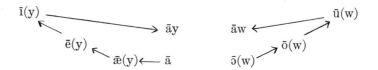

Thus Middle English *name* [nāmə] becomes Modern English *name* [nēym]; ME *swete* [swēytə] becomes MnE *sweet* [swīyt;] and ME *ride* [rīydə] diphthongizes to become MnE *ride* [rāyd]. In late Old English, the southern dialects in particular, [ā] in words like *stan* had become [ō]. In the Early Modern English period this [ō] diphthongizes and raises

[5]Key to symbols used: āy as in *ride*, īy in *we*, ēy in *say*, æy in *ash*, ā in *balm*, ōw in *law*, ōw in *go*, ūw in *who*, āw in *cow*.

to [ōw] so that Middle English *stoon* [stɔ̄n] is pronounced [stōwn].
Middle English *mona* [mōnə] becomes MnE [mūwn], and ME *hous*
[hūs] diphthongizes to MnE [hāws].

Conclusion

Thus we have seen that the language we now speak has undergone innumerable changes since its Germanic forefathers brought it to the
island of Britain in the middle of the fifth century A.D. The syntactic
structure is essentially the same, although with the loss of most inflectional endings a greater burden has been placed on word order and
function words (like prepositions) which are necessary to show grammatical relationships within the sentence.

Pronunciation, too, has undergone a number of changes. A few sounds
are no longer with us; others were added during a period of French
influence. Still others have undergone modification, like that which
affected the tense vowels. Since printing was established before many
of these changes were completed, the orthographic system of the language
gives an amazing amount of information about the phonemic history
of the underlying forms, as we shall see in Chapter V.

Furthermore, our language has been exposed to the vocabularies of
other languages and has borrowed quite freely from those languages,
giving English a cosmopolitan character. Besides wholesale borrowing
from other languages, native methods of word formation (through
compounding and through affixing of prefixes and suffixes) have taken
place to such an extent that Old English seems like a completely foreign
language to the Modern English speaker. Once he understands something of the history of the language and what actually lies beneath the
surface, he will see that those changes have not been chaotic or arbitrary but quite methodical and systematic.

Exercise

1. The following passages are translations (slightly edited) of Matthew
7:26–27, the same found in the "sample of Old English" section above.
Compare these to the Old English passage and note what major changes
have taken place in the last thousand years of English language history.
(These different selections are fairly representative of Old English,
Middle English, Early Modern English, and Modern English respectively.) What generalizations can you make about changes in English

word order, noun inflections, verb inflections, the use of auxiliary (helping) verbs, and even spelling and printing?

> Wycliffe (1389):
> And euery man þat heriþ þese my wordis, and doþ hem nat, is liche to a man fool, þat haþ bildid his hous on grauel. And rayn came doun, and floodis camen, and wyndis blewen, and þei hurliden in to þat hous; and it felle doun, and the fallying doun þereof was grete.
>
> *The Geneva Bible* (1560):
> But whosoeuer heareth these my wordes, and doeth them not, shalbe lickened vnto a foolish man, which hathe buylded his house vpon the sand: And the raine fell, and the floods came, and the windes blewe, and beat vpon that house, and it fell, and the fall thereof was great.
>
> *The New English Bible* (*NT*, 1961; 1970):
> But what of the man who hears these words of mine and does not act upon them? He is like a man who was foolish enough to build his house on sand. The rain came down, the floods rose, the wind blew, and beat upon that house; down it fell with a great crash.

2.   You may also wish to compare the passage from *The Geneva Bible* to the King James version of 1611 and note similarities and differences. How do you account for the popularity of the King James translation?

   The New English Bible passage seems much more informal or conversational than the King James. Check the Preface of each one to see how the translators conceived their task. What problems arise when translating from one language to another?

   Compare the style of *The New English Bible* to that of other contemporary translations like *Good News for Modern Man* and *The Living Bible*. How are their levels of style determined by the audience to which they are directed?

3.   Select a passage from any Shakespearean play and note in particular the use of pronouns. Try to determine when the familiar forms (*thou, thee, thine, thy*) were appropriate. If speakers shift from *you* to *thou*, is there some significance in the shift?

4.   Study the diagram of the Great Vowel Shift on p. 36. Can you determine from it how the following words would have been pronounced in Wycliffe's day, before the shift took place?

   these, do, fool, hous, rain, doun, came, to.

5.   Select a passage of one hundred or more words from any current book or periodical in English. Draw a chart with three columns labeled Anglo-Saxon (i.e. "native"), Greco-Latin, and Other. Then with the aid of a desk dictionary look up the origin of every word in the passage and note it in the proper column. If you count all words including repeats, approximately what percent of the total number is of native

origin? of foreign origin? What do these figures tell us about the cosmopolitan nature of our present English word stock?

For some more statistics on the extent of word borrowing see Stuart Robertson, *The Development of Modern English*, second ed., pp. 173–174.

References

Baugh, Albert C. *A History of the English Language*, Second Edition. New York: Appleton-Century-Crofts, 1957.

Pyles, Thomas. *The Origins and Development of the English Language*, Second Edition. New York: Harcourt Brace Jovanovich, 1971.

Robertson, Stuart. *The Development of Modern English*, Second edition, rev. by Frederic G. Cassidy. Englewood Cliffs, N. J.: Prentice-Hall, 1954.

Whitney, William Dwight. *Language and the Study of Language*, Fifth Edition. New York: Charles Scribner's Sons, 1888.

Wyld, Henry C. *A Short History of English*, Third Edition. London: John Murray, 1927.

III

Grammar Study: Then and Now

The most amazing thing about something as complex as language is that children learn it so effortlessly by the time they are three or four years old. In fact, by the time they enter school, they have mastered most of the sound patterns and most of the grammatical patterns of their system of communication. They have become native speakers who within a very short time can tell what "sounds right" in their language. Children of English-speaking parents, for example, know that *scrate* might very possibly be an English word, though they have never heard it before, because words do begin with these three consonant sounds in English. Spanish-speaking children would prefix the vowel *e-* to the word because Spanish does not permit such an initial grouping of consonants. English speakers will accept "Often he leaves early" or "He often leaves early" but not "*Early leaves often he," which sounds peculiar or foreign to the native speaker's ear.

This inherent knowledge which a native speaker possesses is called his language COMPETENCE (and what he actually utters is his PERFORMANCE). If he wants to describe the grammatical system of that language, he writes a GRAMMAR. Thus the term GRAMMAR, as we have already seen in Chapter I, has become a multi-faceted term. To the linguist it is 1) the linguistic system itself, 2) a description of that system, or 3) a theory about how that system should be described. To the purist it is a description of the language as it ought to be spoken or written.

Man has long been fascinated with the unique phenomenon of language and for various reasons (literary, social, functional) has attempted to describe his speech. These descriptions, called grammars, reflect both his attitude toward what language is or ought to be and his reasons for putting his system down in writing. In turn these descriptions have greatly influenced the study of language in the schools and subsequently the attitudes of the general public toward language.

According to the second definition above, the oldest extant grammar book of any Indo-European language would certainly be Pāṇini's grammar of Sanskrit, written about 400 B.C. to preserve a great body of liturgical literature like the Vedic hymns since Sanskrit was slowly dying as a spoken language.

In the West grammar study begins with the Greeks. At first it was informal and speculative, entirely within the realm of philosophy. Plato (427?–347 B.C.), in the dialogue *Cratylus*, discussed whether there was a connection between physical objects and the names given to them or whether names are merely conventions. While Plato seemed to believe that words had a "real" or predetermined meaning, his pupil Aristotle (384–322 B.C.) taught that language is conventional.

Our most immediate progenitor of grammar study, however, is Dionysus Thrax, whose *Technē Grammatikē*, a slender work written about 100 B.C. in Alexandria, was to set the pattern for grammar studies for hundreds of years to come. The title itself refers to the art of understanding letters *(grammata)*, that is, reading and writing. Thrax's grammar omits any statement about syntax except to define sentence as expressing a complete thought and to define the word as the minimal unit of a sentence. Its chief concern, after describing the eight classes of words, is pronunciation. The book is decidedly descriptive and empirical—Thrax admits in a preface that grammar is the practical knowledge of the written language of poets and prose writers and that the study of grammar should be undertaken to help the student read aloud, understand, and appreciate the literary works of those writers.

Latin grammarians followed essentially the same grammatical analyses to describe the Latin language, using almost the same terminology for parts of speech and cases of nouns. The most productive, a contemporary of Thrax, was named Marcus Terentius Varro, whose *De Lingua Latina* contained twenty-five volumes (six of which survive), treating etymology, morphology, and syntax.

The work of Varro and his followers culminates in two late Latin grammarians, Aelius Donatus (fl. 400 A.D.), and Priscianus Caesariensis (fl. 500 A.D.), more commonly referred to as Donatus and Priscian. Long after the breakup of the Roman empire, they continue to be the most influential grammarians for the study of Latin, a study still necessary because of the importance of Latin as a language of both religion and commerce.

In England William Lily wrote a Latin grammar (1540) modeled on

Donatus and Priscian, which had the official sanction of Henry VIII for use in the schools. The first English grammar, entitled *Pamphlet for Grammar*, was written by William Bullokar in 1586. From then on a series of grammar books appear both in English and in Latin, describing English in terms of Latin, among them Ben Jonson's *The English Grammar* (1640) and John Wallis's *Grammatica Lingua Anglicanae* (1653), which formulated rules for the use of *shall* and *will*.

Wallis, however, did confess in a prefatory statement that English ought to be studied as English and not forced to fit a Latin mold. His attempt in the book to teach foreigners to pronounce English is one of the important early studies of English phonology, the earliest one of importance being John Hart's *Orthographie* (1569). Like Hart, Wallis describes the organs of speech and classifies both vowels and consonants. Unlike Hart, Wallis includes examples from French, Welsh, German, Greek, and Hebrew in an attempt to establish some universal categories of sound.

A fellow scientist and fellow member of the Royal Society was Bishop John Wilkins, whose *Essay Towards a Real Character and a Philosophical Language* has already been mentioned in Chapter I in connection with Swift's satire on the vague speculations of the Royal Society. Wilkins came up with a system of thirty-four letters that he felt could represent the sounds of all the languages "which are commonly known and used in these parts of the world." Besides the sounds of European languages Wilkins includes references to Arabic, Japanese, Chinese, Mexican, and Armenian as well. (Gimson: 59–61.)

These attempts to discover a universal system of sounds and structure for all languages have their roots in the work of Réné Descartes (1596–1650) and other French rationalist philosophers of the seventeenth century whose ideas on linguistic universals are being reconsidered today and, indeed, form a significant basis for transformational-generative theory. (Chomsky, 1966.) They failed because they did not have at their disposal the descriptive apparatus, the mathematical and logical systems, necessary for describing and classifying their data. Modern technology has made such apparatus available to the present-day linguist; hence the new interest in language universals.

Prescriptive Grammar

By the eighteenth century, grammarians, in their reverence for the linguistic excellence of Latin and Greek and in their contempt for the debased descendents of those languages as well as distantly related languages like English and German, attempted to refine, purify, and permanently fix modern languages and save them from decay. Thus the need for language academies and more grammar books. These grammar books were highly prescriptive in tone, prescribing what the language ought to be rather than describing what it is; hence the eighteenth century is often called the Age of Prescriptivism.

These and other books give rise to American "school grammar," often called TRADITIONAL GRAMMAR, in which English is studied as if it were structured like Latin, which was considered a more logical, less corruptible language. The emphasis was on sentence analysis in which sentences were parsed through the identification of parts of speech or were diagrammed according to an elaborate system developed by Alonzo Reed and Brainerd Kellogg. A great part of these grammar books was devoted to "proper" usage with countless exercises in which students picked the correct answer according to a set of "rules" they had memorized. Because their "rules" for "correct English" are related to matters of usage, these books will be described in more detail in a later chapter, Chapter VII.

Unfortunately these highly prescriptive school grammars were attempting to modify linguistic behavior with what we now regard as a false set of assumptions: (a) language should be logical; (b) change is a sign of decay; (c) language can be legislated; (d) speech should imitate writing; (e) a standard exists which can be defined; finally, (f) the ability to label parts of the sentence enables the speaker to use "better" English.

Additionally, the authoritarian stance of prescriptive grammars and handbooks is subject to question. Such a stance might be illustrated by the conventional handbook comment on the active and passive versions of sentences. The active voice is prescribed by composition teachers (or should we say "Composition teachers prescribe the active voice"?) because it is presumably "more forceful" and less vague than the passive. However, are the active sentences below really any more forceful than the passive (and just what constitutes "forcefulness" anyway)?

(1)   Pablo underwent surgery at the hands of a doctor. (Active)
(2)   The doctor operated on Pablo. (Active)
(3)   Pablo was operated on by the doctor. (Passive)

A chief weakness of school grammars is their division of grammatical categories into eight (and sometimes a few more) parts of speech, which for English is an awkward division as well as an oversimplified one. Furthermore, the categories overlap in that some of the parts are defined notionally (noun, verb, interjection), others are defined functionally (adjective, adverb, conjunction, preposition), and some are a mixture of both (pronoun). The semantic definitions are essentially translations of Latin definitions and add little insight to our knowledge of nouns and verbs.

A sizeable portion of most school grammars is devoted to sentence diagraming, which, as one grammar put it, will help the student see at a glance the complete syntactic make-up of a sentence. (Pence and Emery, 1965:45.) Actually diagraming shows only a linear arrangement of syntactic relationships and very often obscures the two-dimensional structure of a sentence. A sentence like "The cow the boy my father knew bought died" defies traditional diagraming, yet native speakers understand it because they understand the hierarchical arrangements of its parts: "My father knew the boy"; "the boy bought the cow"; "the cow died." "The mooing of cows" and "the milking of cows" are diagramed alike, yet the diagrams do not reveal a lower level of structure and meaning—"cows moo" and "X milks cows." Still other examples of sentences presumably the same in structure are these:·

(4) George is easy to please.
(5) George is eager to please.
(6) We expected Bill to accept the offer.
(7) We persuaded Bill to accept the offer.

We can change (4) to one of these two constructions without changing the meaning:

(4a) To please George is easy.
(4b) It is easy to please George.

If (5) has the same structure we should be able to do the same thing with it. Obviously we can't without getting un-English sentences. Likewise we can change (6) to "We expected the offer to be accepted by Bill," but (7) will not allow the same change. School grammars simply cannot show why these pairs are not similar in structure.

Traditional school grammar is not able to deal adequately with ambiguity either, as its analysis of the following sentences indicates:

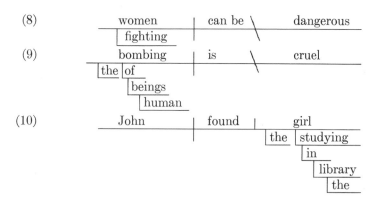

Each of the above sentences has at least two meanings, yet the diagrams indicate only one.

One reason school grammars cannot handle sentences like these is that the grammars are actually very incomplete grammars not meant to be full descriptions of the language. Rather they are therapeutic manuals written to teach people of the lower socioeconomic groups certain niceties of speech which will prove acceptable to their presumed superiors. Consequently they are restricted to certain problems of usage. Furthermore, school grammarians assumed that the grammatical system of the language was quite simple and tended to underanalyze their data. In a sentence like "Covered with ice, the highway was dangerous," the phrase "covered with ice" is simplistically labeled "adjective phrase modifying *highway*." Thus "Covered with ice, the highway was resurfaced last summer," should also be grammatical since it has the same structure. The truth of the matter is that "covered with ice" is either a truncated adverbial of time ("When(ever) it is covered with ice, the highway is dangerous") or a truncated adverbial of reason ("Because it is covered with ice, the highway is dangerous"). Thus the surface reading of the sentence is much more complex than it appears at first glance.

School grammars might also be censured for giving the impression that there is some absolute standard of correctness which can be described and subsequently learned. As Paul Roberts suggests, "Correctness is an accident of history, which bestowed power and prestige on certain groups and not on others, which made one city the capital of a country and not another. There are no *linguistic* reasons for preferring 'Jim and I saw it' to 'Me and Jim seen it,' though there are very powerful social reasons." (Roberts: 408.)

Finally school grammars have not attempted to explain why or how languages change. Indeed, change was considered a corrupting influence which should be stopped if possible. Nor have they attempted to explain how humans master the grammatical system of their language. These and other weaknesses mentioned above result from the lack of a clearly defined theory of language and language description.

The term "traditional" has also been used to include other grammars, grammars which are much more complete and much more scholarly, especially those of Etsko Kruisinga, Henrik Poutsma, and Otto Jespersen. Certainly their grammars are more honest and realistic in their attempts to describe the living language as something more than a fixed set of "rules." Unfortunately the scholarly grammarians did not go much beyond taxonomy, or labeling and classifying. Their classifications tend to proliferate without providing insight into the nature and structure of human language. Under the general heading of adverbs ("words which modify verbs, adjectives, or other adverbs") we have ad-

verbs of degree, manner, place, time, etc. *ad infinitum*, an endless list
which gives us no insight into the nature of adverbs or how they are
formed.

Like the school grammars, the scholarly traditional grammars focus
too closely on written English, usually of an academic or literary variety.
Such a misplaced emphasis leads to another weakness, the lack of any
clearly defined theory. To cite Paul Roberts again, traditional grammar
"never faced such fundamental questions as the following: What is the
purpose of a grammar? How does one determine what is grammatical
and what isn't? What is the basis of grammatical definition? How does
one show that one classification is better than another? What is the
nature of correctness? What is the relationship between writing and
speech?" (p. 406.)

In its theory a grammar should provide a description of any and all
sentences in the language. If it does this, then it has shown what grammaticality is, not by listing sentences in the language, but by its ability
to produce ("generate") an infinite number of sentences from a finite
number of rules for forming words and sentences. Thus a linguistic
grammar is a grammar of competence, i.e., what the speaker knows about
his language, whereas the traditional grammars are performance grammars which describe the appropriateness or acceptability of a particular
word or sentence. As we shall see in Chapter IV, these rather trivial
surfaces differences (*domicile* vs. *house; isn't* vs. *is not* vs. *ain't; Babdist*
vs. *Baptist*) are mostly matters of dialect or style and belong instead to
a theory of performance.

Structural Grammar

Unlike the comparative philologists of the nineteenth century who tried
to trace the history of certain modern languages to their Indo-European
beginnings, the linguists of the twentieth pursued a different course.
They sought the complete description of languages as they exist today,
especially those exotic languages which might someday become extinct.
Anthropologists in particular became interested in the vanishing American Indians and were instrumental in compiling some rather detailed
descriptions of their languages. Since these languages had no writing
system, linguists had to rely upon the spoken language. They first
isolated and described the discrete sounds they heard, thus developing
the science of PHONEMICS, the technique of reducing sounds to writing.
Next they noted how these sounds were combined into meaningful units
(morphemes) and described their arrangement in sentences. Such independent descriptions of phonology, morphology, and syntax based on

the actual structure of a given language came to be called STRUCTURAL GRAMMAR, or STRUCTURAL LINGUISTICS, and was held in great favor for several years. Indeed, these studies are good inventories of the sounds, word units, and syntactic patterns of those languages.

The following books focused primarily on phonology and morphology. Kenneth Pike's *Phonetics* (1942) and *Phonemics* (1947) reflect his interest in American Indian languages and in "reducing languages to writing." Eugene Nida, Executive Secretary of the American Bible Society, was interested in translating the Bible into other languages, many of which had no writing system, and published *Morphology: The Descriptive Analysis of Words* in 1946. *An Outline of English Structure* (1951), by George L. Trager and Henry Lee Smith, Jr., is one of the most thorough early studies of modern English phonology with some attention given to morphology and syntax. Zellig Harris's *Structural Linguistics* (1951) is the first textbook on structural linguistics with heavy emphasis on methodology and distributional analysis.

Leonard Bloomfield, whose *Language* first appeared in 1914 and later in revised form in 1933, is considered the father of structural grammar in America. His techniques are essentially those of Boas and Sapir; his theory is based partly on that of the Swiss linguist Ferdinand de Saussure, who suggested a division of language into *langue*, the idealized form of a language, and *parole*, the spoken form, terms which loosely correspond to deep structure (competence) and surface structure (performance).

Bloomfield's greatest influence on later language study was related to syntax, particularly his division of the sentence into immediate constituents, where levels of structure are separated into units, each having its key word and modifiers. Thus in a given sentence like "The crew should man the guns," the first division would separate the two binary units, "The crew" and "should man the guns." Then each of these constituents would be divided again; *should* is more closely related to *man* than to *the* and *guns*, and *the* is more closely related to *guns* than to *man*:

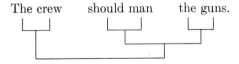

The same kind of division can be made within words, as in the word *unavailable*:

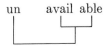

Other studies have used the same or a similar structural approach to English. In 1952 Charles C. Fries published *The Structure of English: An Introduction to the Construction of English Sentences*, a work based on several hundred hours of recorded telephone conversations. He rejected traditional terms for the parts of speech, substituting instead the terms Class 1, Class 2, Class 3, and Class 4 for the four form classes (nouns, verbs, adjectives, and adverbs) and Class A through O for fifteen different groups of function words. Thus nouns fall into the Class 1 category and are defined as words which fit the following testing frames:

(The) _____ is/are good.
The _____ remembered the _____.
The _____ went there.

Other descriptions of Modern English soon followed: *Patterns of English*, by Paul Roberts (1956); *An Introduction to Descriptive Linguistics*, by H. A. Gleason (1955); *American English in its Cultural Setting*, by Donald J. Lloyd and Harry R. Warfel (1956); *The Structure of American English*, by W. Nelson Francis (1958); *An Introduction to Linguistic Structures: from Sound to Sentence in English*, by Archibald A. Hill (1958); *A Course in Modern Linguistics*, by Charles F. Hockett (1958); *A Short Introduction to English Grammar*, by James Sledd (1959); and *A Synopsis of English Syntax*, by Eugene A. Nida (1960).

Like traditional grammar, structural grammar has certain glaring weaknesses. Unlike traditional grammar it gives increased attention to actual speech rather than to some idealized form of written language. Even so, it is limited to language *already* spoken or written and is unable to describe fully all of the possible utterances in a language, i.e., to generate new sentences not included in the body of material on which the grammar is based. Structural grammars were "generative" in the weak sense that, given a lexicon of 50,000 nouns, they could generate 50,000 different sentences from the testing frame "(The) _____ is/are good." However, they cannot generate another 50,000 of the type "The good _____. . . ." or still another 50,000 of the type "The _____ which is/are good. . . ." with the same meaning.

Furthermore, structural grammar dealt superficially with ambiguity, analyzing it as a matter of contrasting stress:

Fíghting wómen can be dangerous. (It is dangerous to fight women).
Fíghting wòmen can be dangerous. (Women who are fighting are dangerous).

The differences in such contrastive pairs as *fíghting wómen* vs. *fíghting wòmen* and *briéfcàse* vs. *briêf cáse* were explained by structuralists only in terms of concrete phonetic pronunciations rather than in terms of abstract syntactic makeup. The transformationalist can relate these forms with their meanings in very revealing ways by working from the syntax, which determines the spoken form. In as much as structural theoreticians did not (and to some extent still do not) recognize the concept of the transformation, such obvious relationships between form and meaning have been left unstated until now.

In addition to the weakness of a too limited scope, structural grammars, as it were, not only put the proverbial cart before the horse, but insisted upon the separation of the so-called levels of the grammar as sketched below:

$$
\text{Grammar}
\begin{cases}
\text{1. Phonetics} \\
\text{2. Phonemics}
\end{cases} \text{Sound System} \\
\begin{aligned}
&\text{3. Morphemics} && - && \text{Meaning System} \\
&\text{4. Syntax} && - && \text{Sentence Types}
\end{aligned}
$$

Additionally, as Andreas Koutsoudas has indicated (1963: 160-170), structural theoreticians never did clearly settle on a sound theory and follow it to its logical conclusions. Thus after discarding the traditional and typical foreign language word and paradigm grammar, these theoreticians failed to develop the two remaining theories, namely, item and arrangement grammar and item and process grammar.

Word and paradigm grammar, as the name implies, consists of awesome lists of noun, verb, and adjective declensions and conjugations with great attention given to a myriad of so-called grammatical cases such as nominative, genitive, dative, accusative, and vocative.[1] Item and arrangement descriptive grammars (labeled as IA grammars) rely heavily on the statement of the distribution of syntactic and phonological forms with great attention given to accurate statements of the contexts in which items occur. Item and process grammar (labeled as IP grammar), as we will see in this text, is essentially transformational-generative grammar (frequently labeled as T-G grammar).

Item and process theoreticians suggest that there can be no rigid separation of levels of a grammar. Additionally, grammatical processes called TRANSFORMATIONS are posited which relate abstract syntactic forms, or the DEEP STRUCTURE of language, to concrete phonetic forms, or the SURFACE STRUCTURE of utterances. The organization of an item and process grammar is roughly as follows:

---

[1]Several studies have appeared which treat Old and Middle English from a transformational-generative viewpoint, among them, Morton W. Bloomfield and Leonard Newmark, *A Linguistic Introduction to the History of English* (New York: Knopf, 1963); John C. McLaughlin, *Aspects of the History of English* (New York: Holt, Rinehart and Winston, 1970); and Robert A. Peters, *A Linguistic History of English* (New York: Houghton Mifflin Company, 1968). Our short history of English (Chapter II) is an example of a word and paradigm grammar, whereas our description of Modern English (Chapter IV) is transformational-generative.

MEANING   FORM
(Deep Structure)   (Surface Structure)
Syntax   Transformations
Semantics
Systematic Phonemics   Systematic Phonetics

The organization of a typical item and arrangement or structural-descriptive grammar might be sketched as follows; but the reader must bear in mind that each of the numbered levels of the grammar is considered in the main to be an independent level:

Grammar of a   4. Syntax (tagmemics)
limited corpus 3. Morphology (morphemics)
               2. Phonemics (contrastive sound units)
               1. Phonetics (unanalyzed sound units)

Thus, the usual procedure of a structural-descriptive linguist is to record a limited corpus of a language in phonetic characters. In his laboratory, so to speak, he then analyzes the raw phonetic data into an inventory of contrastive sound units called PHONEMES on the bases of complementary distribution, phonetic similarity, and overall pattern. After (and only after!) the phonemes of a language are arrived at, the structural linguist attempts to discover the minimal meaningful units or MORPHEMES of a language. The arrangement of morphemes into units of phrases and sentences constitutes what one might call the SYNTAX of a language. Thus, phonemes are abstract sound units which consist of ALLOPHONES that are phonetically similar and that are distributed complementarily in a systematic overall (and presumably non-overlapping) pattern. Morphemes, in turn, consist of sequential combinations of phonemes. Phrases and sentences, then, consist of sequential combinations of morphemes. By proceeding from phonetics to phonemics to morphemics to tagmemics, the structural-descriptive linguist constructs a grammar of a limited corpus of a language.

Since it is not our purpose to foster or champion the study of natural languages in a structural-descriptive framework, we content ourselves with extremely sketchy and highly simplified characterization above.[2]

---

[2]For the details of typical item and arrangement (IA) grammars, see Gleason (1955), Francis (1958), Hockett (1958), Sledd (1959), and Nida (1960). The variety of IA grammar called "stratificational" is the subject of Lamb (1966). For a scholarly criticism and comparison of item and arrangement (IA) and item and process (IP) grammars, consult Hockett (1954), Koutsoudas (1963), and Postal (1964). A rehashing and somewhat recent defense of IA grammar may be found in Hockett (1968) and Householder (1970). A derivative type of IP grammar called "case grammar" is treated in Fillmore (1968) and Langendoen (1970). For an integrated psychological-philosophical-linguistic theory of grammar, in an essential IP framework, compare Steinberg and Jakobovits (1971) and Chomsky (1968, 1972).

Generative-Transformational Grammar

Structural theory became the basis for another approach to grammar study, that suggested by Noam Chomsky in *Syntactic Structures* (1957), a study which provides the data for a later modification of his theory in *Aspects of the Theory of Syntax* (1965). To the transformational-generative grammarian the term *grammar* means all three of the definitions at the beginning of this chapter: the language system as a whole; the description of that system; plus a theory about how to describe that system. The grammar of a natural language like English is the system itself whereby sounds are combined into words that in turn are combined to form sentences, the basic universal units of all languages. It also means an explicit description not only of this system but also of the way we can utter an infinite number of grammatical sentences with a finite number of rules for word formation and word arrangement in sentences. Hence the term *generative*.

In generating novel utterances we make use of numerous TRANSFOR-MATIONS whereby sentences with transitive verbs can be made passive, declarative statements can be transformed into negative statements or questions, etc. A transformational model of a generative grammar may use one or more of three processes common to all languages—insertion, substitution, and deletion.

To illustrate INSERTION let us embed sentence 2 into sentence 1:

(1) X surprised Clyde.
(2) X = Bonnie kissed the sheriff.

We may add a factive particle *that*, the infinitive particles *for . . . to*, or the gerundive particles using the possessive with . . . *-ing* to get three different surface structures, all with an identical meaning:

(3) *That* Bonnie kissed the sheriff surprised Clyde.
(4) *For* Bonnie *to* kiss the sheriff surprised Clyde.
(5) Bonnie'*s* kiss*ing* the sheriff surprised Clyde.

Transformational SUBSTITUTION may be illustrated by the inversion of elements in a declarative sentence to form a question:

(6) Overfamiliarity can breed contempt.
(7) Can overfamiliarity breed contempt?

Another instance of substitution is the replacement of an entire phrase by a single word:

(8) The ice was *in this place* and the ice was *in that place*.

(9) The ice was *here* and the ice was *there*.

Transformational DELETION occurs as indicated below:

(10) She wants *for* you to drive the car.

(11) She wants you to drive the car.

(12) Blake refuses *for Blake* to compromise.

(13) Blake refuses to compromise.

A transformational-generative (T-G) grammar of a language, then, is not a psychological model of performance but is rather a description of an idealized speaker-hearer's intuitive language competence, i.e., his implicit knowledge of his native language. A T-G grammar is an attempt on the part of the linguist, in his role as a cognitive psychologist, to characterize what a person knows, for the most part unconsciously, about his language. It does not try to describe how he goes about forming sentences in his language, i.e., performance. It is therefore appropriate for the term "grammar" to refer both to the theory the linguist constructs for a language and to the speaker-hearer's competence, or implicit knowledge of a language.

If we define sentence as a structure which pairs a semantic interpretation (a concept, a meaning) with a phonetic interpretation (pronunciation), then our grammar becomes a description of that system of rules which specifies this correspondence between sound and meaning. Since sentences have both an abstract underlying structure, or a DEEP STRUCTURE, and one or more superficial variations, or SURFACE STRUCTURES, TRANSFORMATIONS are necessary to relate one to the other. The very abstract deep structure of a sentence determines its meaning, whereas its surface structure determines its pronunciation (and its spelling for those languages which have writing systems). The following sentences differ only on the surface:

(14) The musician who has long hair resigned.

(15) The musician with long hair resigned.

(16) The long-haired musician resigned.

At the abstract level the speaker has two messages: "The musician resigned" and "The musician has long hair." These the speaker may combine in any number of ways to arrive at the surface variations above (which also may differ in pronunciation from one region of the country to another).

Because native speakers have internalized a rich system of rules (a grammar) for pairing meaning with pronunciation, they are thus able to produce and understand an infinite number of sentences they have never heard before. The sentences you are now reading are probably ones you have never encountered before, nor do you understand them by dint of some kind of system of linguistic habit. It would seem, as we noted in Chapter I, that human beings exclusively are born with a predisposition for language. However, in order to acquire a language, a child must come in contact with other human beings using language. This contact apparently serves as a catalyst. Thus the task for the child learning a language is not so much to memorize and mimic what adult speakers do as it is for him to form hypotheses about whatever human language is in use in his environment. While it is seemingly true that the capacity for language is genetically transmitted, clearly the vocabulary of a particular language must be transmitted culturally. It is at this level that human languages are somewhat arbitrary and conventional, as we noted in Chapter I. Hence there is no necessary inherent relation between a particular lexical item or word and the concept it symbolizes.

In their general linguistic theory, transformational-generative grammarians have attempted not only to account for the acquisition of language but also to provide some insight into language change, or linguistic evolution. For example, Morris Halle (1962:54–73) has conjectured that sound changes in a language are in fact changes in the grammar brought about in at least two ways: 1) a conscious addition of rules to the grammar by adult speakers (as when non-New Yorkers attempt a Brooklyn accent), and 2) an unconscious reformulation of the rules by succeeding generations (as illustrated by the Great Vowel Shift). Halle convincingly argues that the only way an adult speaker can change his grammar is for him to add new rules consciously, which may result in less than an optimum grammar, or an awkward competence in certain language features. However, since language is re-created by each child and since children still have the ability to form hypotheses about the language they are learning, they are able to change the ordering of the rules and can thus construct what for them is an optimum grammar. Concerning sound change, Paul Postal has remarked (1968:283):

> It seems clear to the present writer that there is no more reason for languages to change than there is for automobiles to add fins one year and remove them the next, for jackets to have three buttons one year and two the next, etc. That is, it seems evident within the framework of sound changes as grammar changes that the "causes" of sound change without language contact lie in the general tendency of human cultural products to undergo "non-functional" stylistic change.

Of course it is also clear that functional or nonstylistic sound changes may occur in languages which are in contact with each other. English, for example, has borrowed heavily from the Romance languages in which there is a systematic surface-structure sound alternation between *k* and *s* in such words as *electric* and *electricity*. When these words were newly introduced into the English language, it was necessary for speakers to add a rule to their grammar that in certain words of Romance origin, deep structure *k* is realized as surface structure *k* only before low vowels as in *medical* or in final position as in *electric,* and as *s* before high vowels as in *electricity* and *medicine.* It seems reasonable to assume that succeeding generations reformulated the grammar so as to include this alternation as an automatic one; that is, the rule is now part and parcel an English rule and not an occasional one added to the end of the grammar. If this were not the case, *electric* and *electricity* might be better spelled *elektrik* and *elektrisity.*

We see now how the distinction between deep and surface structures is a useful as well as a necessary one, and how it may be applied to surface variations in both sound and syntax. To return to our examples of the passive used earlier in the chapter, we note that "The doctor operated on Pablo" and "Pablo was operated on by the doctor" mean the same because they have the same deep structure: doctor + operated on + Pablo. In hospital circles the particle *on* may be omitted to give another surface variation with exactly the same meaning: "The doctor operated Pablo." "The mooing of cows" and "The milking of cows," seemingly alike on the surface, have a different deep structure. *Mooing* and *milking,* traditionally called gerunds (or verbal nouns) function as intransitive and transitive verbs respectively in the deep structure and are derived from the sentences "Cows moo" and "X milks cows." In passive constructions the "by phrase," which contains the deep structure subject, can be omitted, and it might very well be in the sentence about Pablo: "Pablo was operated on."

Transformational-generative grammar can also explain quite easily why "George is easy to please" can be rearranged to give us "It is easy to please George" and why "George is eager to please" cannot result in "*It is eager to please George." In the first George is the one being pleased while in the second George is pleasing other people. (The formal rules for arriving at this conclusion will be given in the next chapter.) Likewise the deep structure gives the clue to the various meanings of the ambiguous sentences above. *Fighting,* for instance, can be the verbal portion of a relative construction "who are fighting" or the verbal portion of a truncated noun clause "X fights women" = "the fighting of women," as we shall see presently.

Speaking as college teachers who have used all three approaches to grammar study—traditional, structural, and transformational-generative —we feel that transformation-generative (T-G) grammar has the most to offer the student of language. Its focus on speech, even utterances as

yet unspoken, is clearly a mark in its favor. Its use of a deep structure–
surface structure dichotomy adds greatly to its explanatory and descriptive powers. These powers, coupled with its mathematical formalism,
explicitness, and precision, are very clearly appealing attributes. Its
attempt to explain a speaker's knowledge of his language is a new and
welcome dimension to the study of grammar, as is the attention given
to language acquisition and language change, areas heretofore untouched
by most grammarians.

Finally we feel that T-G grammar comes closer to DESCRIPTIVE ADE-
QUACY than any other school of grammar study. If the same grammar can
explain the specific innate abilities that make language acquisition possible, it would be exhibiting EXPLANATORY ADEQUACY. Linguists hope
ultimately to be able to construct a grammar which *is* adequate on
both the internal grounds of description and the external grounds of
explanation. But at the moment the greatest strides are being made
only in the area of description, although it is encouraging to note that
progress in the one domain often provides insights into the other. Contrary to popular belief, the final word about grammar has not been said.
Indeed, grammar study has just begun.

Exercises

1. A native speaker of English, because he has internalized the grammatical system of his language, is able both to speak and to understand
sentences he has never encountered before. His linguistic competence,
however, goes beyond this ability to produce and understand single
sentences and into the larger framework in which the sentence is ut-
tered. A study of the contextual framework of speech is called DISCOURSE
ANALYSIS. For example, "Yes, I did," while it is a common enough
utterance in English, is one which is dependent on a previous statement
of some kind. Likewise, "Thank you" and "You're welcome" assume a
certain order which native speakers have no trouble with. For example,
if Speaker A says, "You have a beautiful dress" and Speaker B says
"Thank you," Speaker A will not add, "You're welcome," unless he is
being deliberately perverse, or cute, or provocative.

    (a) Can you make an analysis to define an appropriate and
        inappropriate context for "You're welcome"?

    (b) Select a short passage of prose; then note what proportion
        of sentences are dependent on context for their meaning.
        How will the proportion vary in different contexts?

2. *Further reading.* An early influential study of discourse analysis was
made by Zellig Harris ("Discourse Analysis," *Language*, 28 (1952), 1–30).

Two succeeding schools of linguistics called TAGMEMICS and STRATIFICA-
TIONAL GRAMMAR, as developed by Kenneth Pike and Sydney Lamb respectively, aim specifically at language in context. Because Pike views
language as "purposive behavior," he is not interested in analyzing
sentences in isolation. His approach to language analysis has been
adopted by the Summer Institute of Linguistics, whose goal is the
translation of at least the New Testament into, ultimately, all the
languages of the world. Several studies are devoted to tagmemics:
Kenneth L. Pike, "A Guide to Publications Related to Tagmemic
Theory," *Current Trends in Linguistics*, 3 (1966), 365–94; Kenneth L.
Pike, *Languages in Relation to a Unified Theory of the Structure of Human
Behavior* (The Hague: Mouton, 1967); Benjamin Elson and Velma
Pickett, *An Introduction to Morphology and Syntax* (Santa Ana, California: Summer Institute of Linguistics, 1965); Sven Jacobson, "The
Problem of Describing Syntactic Complexity," *Studia Neophilologica*,
40 (1968), 144–29, reprinted in Clark, Eschholz, and Rosa, pp. 209–222;
and Peter Fries, "Tagmemics," in the Clark, Eschholz, and Rosa
anthology cited above.

Lamb's stratification grammar has allegedly been used successfully
in the field of machine translation. His full-length study is entitled
Outline of Stratificational Grammar (Washington, D.C.: Georgetown
University Press, 1966). A quick overview is John White's *"Stratificational Grammar: A New Theory of Language,"* *College Composition
and Communication*, 20 (October 1969), 191–97, also reprinted in the
Clark, Eschholz, and Rosa anthology, pp. 185–93.

Still another linguistic approach to discourse analysis is currently
emerging called GENERATIVE SEMANTICS in which linguists hope to deal
more precisely and formally with such notions as presupposition, topic
and comment, emphasis and focus. Cf. Danny D. Steinberg and Leon
Jakobovits, (eds.), *Semantics: An Interdisciplinary Reader* (London:
Cambridge University Press, 1971).

References

Bach, Emmon, and Robert T. Harms, eds. *Universals in Linguistic Theory.* New
    York: Holt, Rinehart, and Winston, 1968.

Chomsky, Noam. *Cartesian Linguistics.* New York: Harper and Row, 1966.

——. *Language and Mind*, enlarged edition. New York: Harcourt, Brace,
    Jovanovich, 1968, 1972.

Dykema, Karl W. "Where Our Grammar Came From." *College English*, 22
    (April 1961), 455–65. Reprinted in *Readings in Applied English Linguistics*,
    Second Edition, edited by Harold B. Allen. New York: Appleton-Century-
    Crofts, 1958.

Fillmore, Charles J. "The Case for Case." Pp. 1–88 in *Universals in Linguistic Theory*, edited by Emmon Bach and Robert Harms. New York: Holt, Rinehart and Winston, 1968.

Gimson, A. C. *An Introduction to the Pronunciation of English*. London: Edward Arnold, 1962.

Gleason, H. A., Jr. *Linguistics and English Grammar*. New York: Holt, Rinehart, and Winston, 1965.

Halle, Morris. "Phonology in Generative Grammar." *Word*, 18 (1962), 54–72.

Hockett, Charles F. "Two Models of Grammatical Description." *Word*, 10 (1954), 210–31. Reprinted in *Readings in Linguistics*, edited by Martin Joos. New York: ACLS, 1963.

————. *The State of the Art*. The Hague: Mouton, 1968.

Householder, Fred. "Review of *The State of the Art*." *Journal of Linguistics*, 6, No. 1 (1970), 129-34.

Koutsoudas, Andreas. "The Morpheme Reconsidered." *IJAL*, 29, No. 2 (April 1963), 160–70.

Lamb, Sydney M. *Outline of Stratificational Grammar*. Washington, D.C.: Georgetown University Press, 1966.

Langendoen, D. Terence. *Essentials of English Grammar*. New York: Holt, Rinehart, and Winston, 1970.

Liles, Bruce L. *An Introductory Transformational Grammar*. Englewood Cliffs, New Jersey: Prentice-Hall, 1971.

Pence, R. W., and D. W. Emery. *A Grammar of Present-Day English*, Second Edition. New York: The Macmillan Company, 1963.

Postal, Paul. *Constituent Structure: A Study of Contemporary Models of Syntactic Description*. *IJAL*, 30, No. 7 (January 1964).

Roberts, Paul. *English Syntax*, Alternate Edition. New York: Harcourt, Brace, and World, 1964.

Robins, R. H. *A Short History of Linguistics*. Bloomington, Indiana: Indiana University Press, 1968.

Steinberg, Danny, and Leon Jakobovits. *Semantics: An Interdisciplinary Reader*. London: Cambridge University Press, 1971.

Waterman, John T. *Perspectives in Linguistics*. Chicago: The University of Chicago Press, 1963.

IV

English Grammar Today: A Transformational-Generative Approach

The preceding chapter attempted to demonstrate that traditional and structural grammars have failed as a mechanism for studying language because they lacked a basic, far-ranging scientific theory of description and explanation. Thus, in our view, traditional and structural grammars are little more useful than catalogues or inventories which resemble grocery and laundry lists in their incompleteness and their limited, ephemeral application to language. We object not only to the limited taxonomy of traditional and structural grammars but also to the confounding of the concepts "grammatical sentence, acceptable sentence," and "statistically probable sentence."

Transformational-generative grammars are based on a linguistic theory in which the goal is adequate description of natural human languages such as English, French, German, Chinese, Russian. Adequate description results in adequate explanation of the so-called linguistic competence of human beings; hopefully, it will also provide insight into the nature of language acquisition.

In brief, transformational linguistic research is carried out for two reasons or with two goals in mind: (1) the transformational linguist is searching for the ideal set of descriptors for human languages, and (2) once the set of descriptors has been found, the transformational linguist applies it to an arbitrary human language such as English, French, German, etc. The task of the linguist, then, is to discover a procedure which will allow him to describe and explain a human speaker's ability to make infinite use of finite means. The linguist must find a way to relate the infinite set of concrete phonetic signals with the infinite set of abstract meanings. The description of the relationship must necessarily be abstract, since the linguist cannot detect it entirely from the concrete, physical data emanating from a human speaker or impinging on the ear of the human listener. Thus, the linguist is attempting to describe the abstract knowledge or competence that human speakers possess, or as some would have it, are possessed by!

The approach of the transformationalist to this descriptive task (as explained at the end of chapter III on p. 51 ff.) is one of positing hypothetical syntactic DEEP STRUCTURES, which by certain processes called TRANSFORMATIONS are related to SURFACE STRUCTURES. In essence, the grammarian constructs these formal descriptors, or RULES, to generate or enumerate the set of sentences which constitute a natural language. The deep syntactic structures which the linguist posits are, of course, actually intangible. They and the transformational rules are simply an algorithm or procedural statement.

Transformational descriptions, then, exist for the purpose of describing human language and explaining human language. As with any scientific material, there are no necessary pedagogical implications. The formal study of language may be a necessary prerequisite, but it is not a determiner of approaches for teaching language. On this point, the words of Peter S. Rosenbaum are instructive (1965:342):

> It remains not with the linguistic theory or description, but with the informed educator, whether he is a teacher, linguist, or specialist informed in both areas, to determine the applicability of valid linguistic results to the teaching of English.

The "valid results" to the transformationalist concern what is grammatical. Traditional grammarians attempted to define what is acceptable. The two terms are not the same.

Grammaticality and Acceptability

A native speaker of a natural language possesses several abilities which might be termed linguistic competence. Generally speaking, one is scarcely aware of this ability, which includes the following knowledge about sentences and the relationship between and among sentences:

    (a) the ability to recognize WELL-FORMED as well as ILL-FORMED sentences in his native tongue.

    (b) the ability to recognize sentence SYNONYMY.

    (c) the ability to recognize sentence PARAPHRASE.

    (d) the ability to recognize sentence AMBIGUITY.

Let us examine the first of these, the recognition of sentence form. In the list below, an asterisk (*) marks non-sentences for native English speakers. A question mark (?) indicates marginal sentences. Consider now the following data.

    (1)   John is to sing tomorrow.

    (2)   *Johann soll morgen singen.

    (3)   *Jean a à chanter demain.

    (4)   *Juan ha de cantar mañana.

    (5)   ?Flavorless, red iotas laugh raucously.

    (6)   Her aunt smiled.

    (7)   *Her ant smiled.

    (8)   Her aunt seemed to smile.

    (9)   Her ant seemed to smile.

Even though (2), (3), and (4) respectively make relatively close analogues in German, French, and Spanish for sentence (1), for a monolingual English speaker they are non-sentences, and are therefore marked with the asterisk. The string of words in (5) is structurally well-formed but lexically anomalous, as is (7). That is, the dictionary or LEXICAL word-items do not fit the structure of the sentence under normal grammatical circumstances. One might encounter (5) and (7) and the like in a Disney movie or in a story or poem by Lewis Carroll.

    Human beings can and do recognize relative scales of grammaticality. For example, all Modern English speakers will perhaps understand but reject "*Liked Gottlieb old wine and cheese?" and "*Babies the themselves cried sleep to"; and all will accept "Did Gottlieb like old wine and cheese?" and "The babies cried themselves to sleep." Similarly, if we use different words (or "lexical items") in (5) above (i.e., "relexify" it), it is no longer anomalous: "Dauntless, new grammarians write continuously."

    Recognizing SYNONYMY is a second basic human linguistic competence. As we shall demonstrate in a later section (p. 105), the sentences below numbered (10) through (13) all derive from a common deep structure; that is, they are synonymous. Likewise, (15) is derived from (14); they too share a common deep structure.

(10)   It is clear that it is unnecessary for grammar to be dull.
(11)   That for grammar to be dull is unnecessary is clear.
(12)   That it is unnecessary for grammar to be dull is clear.
(13)   It is clear that for grammar to be dull is unnecessary.
(14)   The crew should man the guns.
(15)   The guns should be manned by the crew.

The third linguistic ability of humans involves recognition of sentence PARAPHRASE. The following will illustrate:

(16)   Dr. Seewell is an ophthalmologist. = Dr. Seewell is an oculist. = Dr. Seewell is an eye-doctor.
(17)   Weak-Eyes Smith is myopic. = Weak-Eyes Smith is nearsighted.
(18)   George is a farmer. = George is someone who farms.
(19)   J. C. was a bachelor. = J. C. was an unmarried male.

Recognition of lexical and structural AMBIGUITY is a fourth kind of linguistic competence. This phenomenon is illustrated in these sentences:

(20)   The cannibals thought Reverend Tastewell was too hot to eat.
(21)   I'm looking for a bachelor. (One can find at least four meanings for *bachelor* in an unabridged dictionary.)
(22)   Hans found Lisa studying in the library.
(23)   Reverend Bibulous had the parish plastered by ten.
(24)   Fighting women can be dangerous.
(25)   Gottlieb liked old wine and cheese.
(26)   Gunter broke the window with his sister.
(27)   Captain Seaworthy decided on the boat.
(28)   The frightened vandals tore up the street.
(29)   The bombing of human beings is cruel.

A central thesis of transformational analysis is that grammaticality is a matter of linguistic competence in such matters as these, while acceptability is a matter of performance. ACCEPTABILITY or APPROPRIATENESS of sentences, then, is more a matter for the rhetorician, the communications specialist, the literary critic, or the composition teacher. There is a very crucial distinction here. As almost any writing teacher will admit, assembling a theory of performance is as back-breaking a task as is constructing and discovering a theory of competence.
Consider now this human microdrama:

(30)   The boy bought the cow.

(31)   My father knew the boy.

(32)   The cow died.

The three acts of this supershort play may be compressed into a single scene in at least five different ways, all equally grammatical:

(33)   My father knew the boy who bought the cow which died.

(34)   The boy who(m) my father knew bought the cow which died.

(35)   The cow which the boy who(m) my father knew bought died.

(36)   The cow the boy my father knew bought died.

(37)   The boy bought the cow and my father knew the boy and the cow died. (And isn't this dull?)

If the criterion for acceptability is rapid comprehension, then (33) and (34) are acceptable over (35) and (36), which possibly require paper and pencil analysis. If tight construction is the criterion for acceptability, then (35) and (36) are good candidates. A rhetorician might admire the balance of (33) and (34) and so on. It is unlikely that anyone would rank (37) over the others.

Clearly the performance grammarian must find the golden mean between the admirable brevity of Finnegan, the proverbial loquacious railroad conductor whose superintendent requested that he shorten his accident reports, and the lament of the unrequited man at the vending machine:

(38)   Off again, on again, gone again, Finnegan.

(39)   Although I deposited the required coin in the aperture designated by the extremely lucid and pithy directions, I was not rewarded with the least vestige of a sweetmeat. Thus the laws of compensation are lacking in expression.

A final notion concerning sentences is that there is no longest sentence; that is, one can, at least in theory, add elements endlessly, as is exemplified below.

(40)   This is the fish that swam in the pond that stood in the pasture, that was baked by the sun, that warms us all . . . .

(41)   Call the police, notify the sheriff, alert the fire department, man the guns . . . .

(42)   Let's see, I'd like the one, two, three, four, five, six, seven, eight, nine, ten, eleven, twelfth one from the end, around the corner, in the box, above the sealing wax.

(43)   Nitram and Nolur are able, acute, clear-sighted, discerning, intelligent, judicious, keen, perspicacious, sage, shrewd, wise, and, one hopes, entertaining linguists.

Before we begin a formal analysis of the English sentence, we would suggest that you review the preceding concepts by doing all or some of the exercises below.

Exercises

1.   Comment on the level of formality or informality in these sentences. Do they represent varieties in grammaticality or in acceptability?

    a.   *Although* he was ill, Santa delivered the goods.
    b.   *Though* he was ill, Santa delivered the goods.
    c.   *In spite of* his illness, Santa delivered the goods.
    d.   *Despite* his illness, Santa delivered the goods.

2.   Resolve the ambiguity of these sentences:

    a.   The sneaky lawyer tried to break the young girl's will.
    b.   The woman fell down the stairs and hurt her behind and bruised her somewhat.
    c.   Strephon looked up Cecilia's dress in the catalogue room.
    d.   Claudius appeared to love the Queen in public but did he underneath?

3.   Which sentence, if any, is not well-formed?

    a.   Ulysses asked should he go.
    b.   Ulysses asked if he should go.
    c.   Ulysses asked whether he should go.
    d.   Ulysses asked whether or not he should go.

4.   Rank the following sentences in order of acceptability.

    a.   He don't be here on Saturday(s).
    b.   He is not here on Saturday(s).
    c.   He isn't here on Saturday(s).
    d.   He doesn't be here on Saturday(s).
    e.   He ain't here on Saturday(s).

5. Rank these sentences in order of acceptability.

    a. Ivan called the publisher up who put out the book Heinrich told Elsabeth about.
    b. Ivan called up the publisher who put the book out Heinrich told Elsabeth about.
    c. Ivan called the publisher who put out the book which Heinrich told Elsabeth about up.
    d. Ivan telephoned the publisher who printed the book which Heinrich described to Elsabeth.

6. Comment on the structure of the following sentences.

    a. The man who was on the corner had a hat which the wind blew off.
    b. The man on the corner had a hat which the wind blew off.
    c. The wind blew off the hat of the man (who was) on the corner.
    d. The wind blew off the man on the corner's hat.
    e. The man on the corner's hat was blown off by the wind.

Grammar I
An Overview of T-G Grammar

Both Grammar I and Grammar II which follow are this book's linguistic attempts to grapple with the sometimes gossamer notion of sentencehood and the constituents of a sentence. They are distinguished from each other here as a way of discussing basic concepts at different levels of complexity. Grammar I differs from traditional grammar in that it consists of a set of rules which, if applied in order, generates the basic structure of a rather large number of English sentences. Grammar I differs from structural grammars in assuming a set of transformations which convert deep structures into surface structures. Like Grammar I, Grammar II produces a large number of English sentences; the main difference between the two, however, is one of formalism. Thus, many of the basic concepts only clumsily expressed in Grammar I find more adequate treatment in Grammar II where a feature analysis on a binary, computerlike basis is used to good advantage. Not inappropriately, Grammar II is an adaptation of *English I.B.M. Grammar II* (1968), by Peter S. Rosenbaum.[3]

---

[3]By permission of I.B.M. Corporation, Yorktown Heights, New York.

Major Sentence Types

There are three major types of sentences in Modern English: DECLARATIVE (simple statement), QUESTION (interrogative), and IMPERATIVE (command). Each of these sentence types may be NEGATIVE or POSITIVE (non-negative) as well as PASSIVE or ACTIVE (non-passive). An illustrative list of major sentence types is included below.

(1)   The crew should man the guns.
(2)   The guns should be manned by the crew.
(3)   The crew should not man the guns.
(4)   The guns should not be manned by the crew.
(5)   Should the crew man the guns?
(6)   Should the guns be manned by the crew?
(7)   Should the crew not man the guns?
(8)   Should the guns not be manned by the crew?
(9)   Man the guns!
(10) Do not man the guns!
(11) Let us man the guns!
(12) Let us not man the guns!
(13) Let the guns be manned by us!
(14) Let the guns not be manned by us!

An English speaker is aware of the similarity in meaning of the sentences above, and he is also aware of the similarity in structure. For example, all of the sentences in the list contain the unit *man*, which functions as a verb, and the unit *the guns*, which functions as a direct object. Further, a speaker of English knows that sentences (9) through (14) differ markedly from sentences (1) through (8) in which the unit *the crew* functions as the subject and the agent. One infers that the grammatical person which *you* represents is being enjoined in sentences (9) and (10), and one can clearly see that *us* is manning the guns in (11) through (14).

For the sake of exposition, let us assume that the basic form of sentences (1) through (8) is a declarative, positive (non-negative), active (non-passive) sentence which we repeat as (15) below.

(15) The crew should man the guns.

Let us also assume that this sentence is related to the other seven by grammatical processes known as the PASSIVE TRANSFORMATION, the NEGATIVE TRANSFORMATION, and the QUESTION TRANSFORMATION, as the case may be. In (16) below, the basic structure of "the crew should man the guns" is illustrated in the form of a branching ("tree") diagram.

(16)

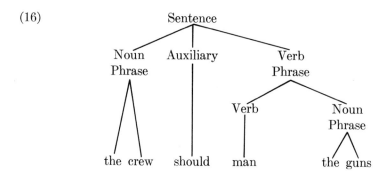

The passive transformation converts "the crew should man the guns" into "the guns should be manned by the crew"; thus, in effect the branching diagram in (16) is converted into the one below in (17).

(17)

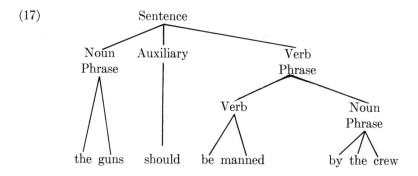

The differences between (16) and (17) are that the noun phrases have exchanged positions, that *be* and *-ed* have been added to the verb, and that *by* has been added to the subject noun phrase which has been shifted to object position. This process may be expressed in a formula, as in (18) below.

(18)   The passive transformation:
    (a) NP-1 Aux V NP-2 $\Rightarrow$ NP-2 Aux BE (*-ed*) V BY NP-1
    (b) *-ed* V $\Rightarrow$ V *-ed*

In this formula the copular verb (BE) and the verb suffix (*-ed*) are inserted as a unit. In (18b) the verb suffix is moved to the immediate right of the main verb (*man*). In tabular form the entire operation is as follows.

(19) (a) The crew should man the guns ⇒ (basic form)
      (b) The guns should BE *-ed* man by the crew ⇒ (18a)
      (c) The guns should BE man *-ed* by the crew ⇒ (18b)
      (d) The guns should be manned by the crew. (Surface structure)

The transformational process which accounts for sentence negation is as straightforward as passivization, albeit somewhat simpler. The sentence negator in English, of course, is the form *not*. The syntactic symbol for *not* and *n't* as well is "Neg(ative)." In the deep structure form of sentences, the "Neg" symbol appears in the left-hand domain of the tree diagram. Below in (20) is the informal underlying form of sentences (3), (4), (7) and (8).

(20)

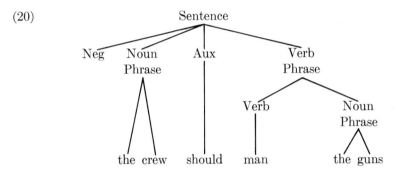

The NEGATIVE PLACEMENT transformation moves the "Neg" symbol to the immediate left of the "Verb Phrase" as is indicated in (21) below.

(21)

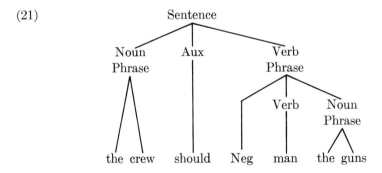

Other rules convert "Neg" into either *not* or into the contracted form *n't*. Negative placement and negative contraction are displayed in tabular form below.

(22) (a) Neg The crew should man the guns (Underlying form)
      (b) The crew should Neg man the guns (Neg placement)

    (c) The crew should not man the guns   (Surface structure)

    (d) The crew should n't man the guns   (Contraction)

    (e) The crew shouldn't man the guns   (Auxiliary Incorporation)

The reader has no doubt noticed that the contracted form of the negative is suffixed to the auxiliary verb, which in this particular sentence is *should*.

    Questions which can be answered simply *yes* or *no* are called YES/NO QUESTIONS in contrast to those which require more information, such as "Who went?" and "Where did they go?" Sentences (5) through (8) above (in this section) are yes/no question sentences. Question sentences are considered transforms of declarative sentences which in the deep structure are marked with the Q (uestion) symbol. The QUESTION TRANS-FORMATION (Q) reverses the order of the initial noun phrase and the auxiliary (Aux) constituent, as outlined below.

(23) (a)

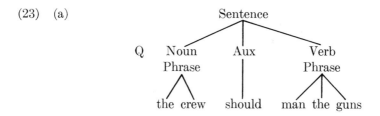

    (b)

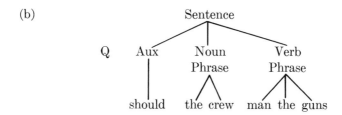

In many instances it is necessary for transformations to apply in a certain order to obtain a desired result. In the transformational deriva-tion of "Shouldn't the crew man the guns?" it is obvious that NEGATIVE PLACEMENT (Neg) and NEGATIVE CONTRACTION must precede question (Q) formation:

(24) (a) Q Neg the crew should man the guns   (Underlying form)

      (b) Q the crew should Neg man the guns   (Neg placement)

      (c) Q the crew should not man the guns

      (d) Q the crew should n't man the guns   (Contraction)

      (e) Q the crew shouldn't man the guns   (Auxiliary Incorporation)

(f) Q shouldn't the crew man the guns   (Question formation)

(g) Shouldn't the crew man the guns?   (Surface structure)

In transformational terms, it is fairly easy to see the relationship between two stylistically different but semantically equivalent sentences as (25a) and (25b) below.

(25) (a) Should the guns not be manned by the crew?

(b) Shouldn't the guns be manned by the crew?

The difference between the sentences transformationally is that NEG-ATIVE CONTRACTION and AUXILIARY INCORPORATION have occurred in (25b) but not in (25a).

The conventional formulation of the imperative sentence derives it from a declarative sentence which is marked with an "Imp(erative)" marker, just as negative sentences are marked with "Neg(ative)" and question sentences with "Q(uestion)." Additionally, it is assumed that the underlying subject is *you* and that the modal verb *will* appears as the auxiliary. Thus the underlying structure of "Man the guns" is that indicated in (26).

(26)

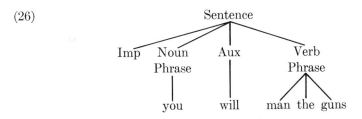

The IMPERATIVE TRANSFORMATION deletes *you* and *will* from the structure leaving "Man the guns!" If the negative (Neg) marker is present as well as the imperative (Imp) marker, then another transformation supplies the form *do* (a sort of dummy element) to which the negative particle may or may not attach, as in "Do not man the guns!" and "Don't man the guns!" Two other imperative-like structures are possible, namely, a positive "tag" question such as "Man the guns, will you?" or a negative "tag" question such as "Man the guns, will you not?" or more likely "Man the guns, won't you?" Of course, "Will you man the guns?" and "Won't you man the guns?" are ordinary yes/no questions as are "Will the guns not be manned by you?" and "Won't the guns be manned by you?"

The sentence "Let the crew man the guns!" is an ordinary imperative sentence as are "Let the crew man the guns, will you not?" and "Let the crew man the guns, won't you?" In light of the above, their derivation is clear; however, the derivation of "Let us man the guns!" and "Let's man the guns!" is an unsolved problem at the moment. These last sentences are called "jussives." We simply note their existence and point out that they are paralleled by similar problem forms in French and German, for example, as in "Let us go," which is equivalent to French "Allons!" and German "Gehen wir!" or "Lasz uns gehen!" Similar problems exist in deriving such Spanish forms as the following:

(27) (a) Vámonos = Let's go!

  (b) Vamos allá ahora = Let's go there now!

  (c) No nos vayamos = Let's not go!

Presumably yes/no question sentences and imperative sentences are mutually exclusive if our transformational formulation is accurate. Thus the YES/NO QUESTION TRANSFORMATION converts such a basic sentence as "Q you will read the book" into "Q will you read the book," whereas the imperative transformation converts such a basic sentence as "Imp you will read the book" into "Imp read the book." To our basic formulation for the sentence (Sentence → NP + Aux + VP) we need to add information which will allow us to know whether we are dealing with a negative sentence, a question sentence, or both, or with an imperative sentence. We can do this by using parentheses and braces as abbreviatory devices:

(28) Sentence → (Neg) $\left\{ \begin{matrix} Q \\ Imp \end{matrix} \right\}$ NP + Aux + VP

(29) (a) NP + Aux + VP: The crew should man the guns.

  (b) Neg + NP + Aux + VP: The crew shouldn't man the guns.

  (c) Q + NP + Aux + VP: Should the crew man the guns?

  (d) Imp + NP + Aux + VP: Man the guns!

  (e) Neg + Q + NP + Aux + VP: Shouldn't the crew man the guns?

  (f) Neg + Imp + NP + Aux + VP: Don't man the guns!

Exercises

1. Use the phrase structure rule numbered (28) above and draw deep structure tree diagrams of these sentences:

  a. The Widow Douglas couldn't civilize Huck Finn.

  b. Couldn't the Widow Douglas civilize Huck Finn?

  c. Could the Widow Douglas civilize Huck Finn?

  d. The rain must fall.

  e. Must the rain fall?

2. Use the formula (Sentence → NP + Aux + VP) and draw surface structure diagrams of these sentences:

    a.   Huck Finn couldn't be civilized by the Widow Douglas.

    b.   Huck Finn wasn't civilized by the Widow Douglas.

3. Assume that a grammatical transformation converts the sequence NP + Aux + VP into Aux + NP + VP. Draw surface structure diagrams of these sentences:

    a.   Couldn't Huck Finn be civilized by the Widow Douglas?

    b.   Could Huck Finn be civilized by the Widow Douglas?

    c.   Didn't Huck Finn admire Tom Sawyer?

    d.   Did Huck Finn admire Tom Sawyer?

    e.   Had Huck Finn admired Tom Sawyer?

    f.   Hadn't Huck Finn admired Tom Sawyer?

4. Convert, in prose, the following strings into well-formed surface structure sentences in your dialect:

    a.   Q Squire Booby might chase Pamela.

    b.   Neg Squire Booby might chase Pamela.

    c.   Neg Q Squire Booby might chase Pamela.

Sentence Constituents

By now it should be apparent that all sentences in the language share a common form in what we have been calling deep structure representation; that is, at this level all sentences consist of at least three major constituents: a NOUN PHRASE (NP), an AUXILIARY (Aux), and a VERB PHRASE (VP). We stated this in a formula as (Sentence → Noun Phrase + Auxiliary + Verb Phrase), which may be abbreviated as (S → NP + Aux + VP).

The Noun Phrase Constituent

Just as a sentence consists minimally of three constituents, so a noun phrase consists minimally of a NOUN. As a matter of fact, linguists have isolated three basic types of noun phrases which are exemplified in these sentences:

(1) *Time* flies.

(2) *The fact that time flies* worried Prufrock.

(3) *Time which flies* worried Prufrock.

Without bothering about details for the moment, we can display the italicized noun phrases above in the following diagrams:

(4) (a)

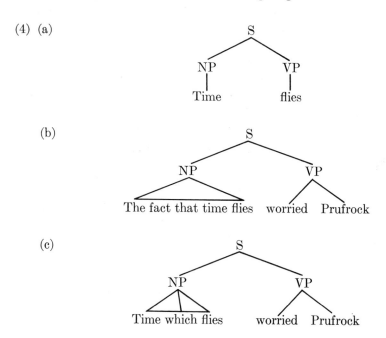

    (b)

    (c)

Conventionally, the difference between and among the three basic types of noun phrases may be expressed in branching diagrams:

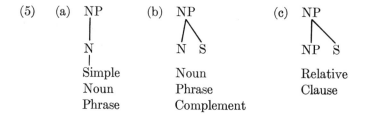

The essential difference between (5b) and (5c) is that in the former a simple ABSTRACT noun (fact, idea, notion, belief) is followed by a sentence, and that in the latter a noun phrase is followed by a sentence which repeats the noun phrase. This may be indicated thus:

(6)

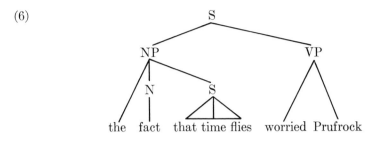

(7)

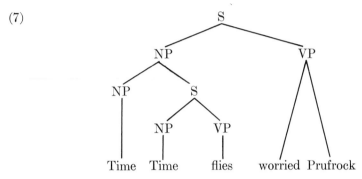

Needless to say, the second instance of *time* in (7) must be replaced by either the relative pronoun *which* or *that*.

(8) (a) Time *which* flies worried Prufrock.
    (b) Time *that* flies worried Prufrock.

To recapitulate, we have observed three different types of basic noun phrase constituents: the SIMPLE NOUN PHRASE, the NOUN PHRASE COMPLEMENT, and the RELATIVE CLAUSE STRUCTURE, all illustrated in the following formula:

(9)
$$NP \rightarrow \begin{cases} \text{Noun} \\ \text{Noun + Sentence} \\ \text{Noun Phrase + Sentence} \end{cases} \begin{matrix} (a) \\ (b) \\ (c) \end{matrix}$$

By using parentheses and braces we may compress the information in (9) into a single observation. Cases (a) and (b) can be compressed by means of parentheses:

(10) $NP \rightarrow N\ (S)$

In the formula below, braces enclose (a) and (b), which have been collapsed, and (c). Also, the plus (+) symbols have been omitted:

$$(11) \quad NP \rightarrow \begin{Bmatrix} N \ (S) \\ NP \ S \end{Bmatrix} \begin{matrix} (a) \\ (b) \end{matrix}$$

The rules which enumerate sentence types and noun phrase types are called expansion rules, since a single symbol to the left is expanded into one or more symbols to the right. The common term for these rules is PHRASE STRUCTURE EXPANSION RULES or, more simply, phrase structure rules. We repeat the two which we have examined in detail as PSR-1 and PSR-2.

$$(PSR\text{-}1) \quad S \rightarrow (Neg) \ (\begin{Bmatrix} Q \\ Imp \end{Bmatrix}) \ NP + Aux + VP$$

$$(PSR\text{-}2) \quad NP \rightarrow \begin{Bmatrix} N \ (S) \\ NP \ S \end{Bmatrix}$$

Exercises

1. a. Give a prose translation of this formula: $S \rightarrow NP + Aux + VP$
    b. Convert this phrase structure rule into three branching (tree) diagrams:
$$NP \rightarrow \begin{Bmatrix} N \ (S) \\ NP \ S \end{Bmatrix}$$
    c. Convert the following sentence into its passive transform: Andrew marveled at the coy mistress.
    d. Convert the following sentence into its yes/no question transform:
        A gentle knight was pricking on the plain.
    e. Convert this sentence into its negative transform; then form a negative yes/no question:
        Clough rewrote the decalogue.

2. a. Identify the different *that*'s in the following sentences:
        (1) The fact *that* the Pearly Gates opened surprised Lord Byron.
        (2) *That* the Pearly Gates opened surprised him.
        (3) The Pearly Gates *that* opened pleased Southey.
        (4) *That that that* the Pearly Gates opened frightened King George. (Is this sentence ungrammatical?)
    b. How does a relative clause differ in structure from a noun phrase complement?
    c. Draw deep structure diagrams of these sentences:
        (1) Go!
        (2) Don't go!

The Verb Phrase Constituent

Just as the noun phrase constituent consists of three basic types of noun phrases, so the VERB PHRASE CONSTITUENT consists of three types of verb phrases. The "VP" constituent consists minimally of a VERBAL, abbreviated "VB." The formula for the "VP" is this.

(1) VP → VB (NP) (NP)

Traditional grammarians recognized these three basic types of "VPs" and gave them the following labels:

(2) (a) Time *flies*. (Intransitive Verbal)
     (b) The crew should *man the guns*. (Transitive Verbal)
     (c) The dowager *offered some tea to Pip*. (Transitive Verbal)

These "VP's" may be illustrated in the following diagrams:

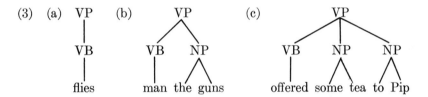

In the parlance of traditional grammar *flies* is an intransitive verb, *man* a transitive verb with *the guns* as direct object, and *offered* a transitive verb with *some tea* as the direct object and *to Pip* as indirect object. Other "VPs" to which we will return later are as follows:

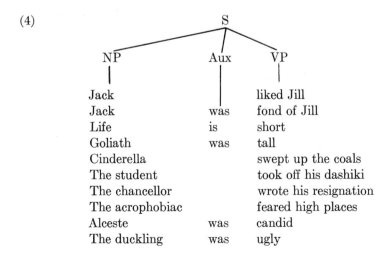

If we now add the rule for the formulation of the verb phrase to the other phrase structure rules, we get the following:

(PSR-1) $S \rightarrow (\text{Neg}) \ (\begin{Bmatrix} Q \\ \text{Imp} \end{Bmatrix})\ NP + Aux + VP$

(PSR-2) $NP \rightarrow \begin{Bmatrix} N\ (S) \\ NP\ S \end{Bmatrix}$

(PSR-3) $VP \rightarrow VB\ (NP)\ (NP)$

The Auxiliary Constituent

The concept of the AUXILIARY CONSTITUENT might be better grasped if we were to use the fuller term "auxiliary verb phrase," since typically an auxiliary ("helping") verb occurs here.

(1)   The astronaut *does* walk on the moon.
(2)   The astronaut *can* walk on the moon.
(3)   The astronaut *has* walked on the moon.
(4)   The astronaut *is* walking on the moon.

As we saw earlier when dealing with yes/no question formation, it was the auxiliary constituent which exchanged position with the subject noun phrase, as is indicated below for sentences (1) through (4):

(5)   *Does* the astronaut walk on the moon?
(6)   *Can* the astronaut walk on the moon?
(7)   *Has* the astronaut walked on the moon?
(8)   *Is* the astronaut walking on the moon?

Unlike main verbs, auxiliary verbs may have the negative particle suffixed to them: *doesn't, can't, hasn't, isn't.* Further, auxiliary verbs may be subcategorized into MODAL (mood indicating) and non-modal. Modal auxiliary verbs in turn may be either primary or secondary.

(9)

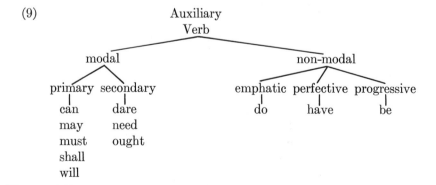

Modal verbs differ from main verbs in that modals are not marked for grammatical person ("*he cans," "*he mays") as the latter are in some, though not all, dialects ("he speak*s*," "he walk*s*"). Also, modal verbs have no perfect or present participial form: "*he has could," "*he has should," "*he is shalling," "*he is musting." It is germane to point out here that *dare* and *need* are both main and auxiliary verbs.

(10) (a) Prufrock *dares* to eat a peach.   (main verb)

      (b) Prufrock *needs* an antiacid tablet.

      (c) *Need* Prufrock come and go? (auxiliary verb)

      (d) *Dare* he eat a peach?

Syntactic Tense and Aspect

For many speakers of English a three-way contrast exists between and among verbs and suffixes as in (1):

(1) (a) George *speaks* Albanian. (present tense)

     (b) Georgia *spoke* Roumanian. (past tense)

     (c) Peggy *has spoken* Twi for several years. (perfective aspect)

Surprising as it may seem, a two-way contrast suffices for a large segment of the population:

(2) (a) George *speaks* Albanian. (present tense)

     (b) Georgia *spoke* Rumanian. (past tense)

     (c) Peggy *has spoke* Twi for several years. (perfective aspect)

There is even a fourth possibility in some dialects:

     (d) Peggy *have spoke* Twi for several years. (perfective aspect)

ASPECT in English is either PERFECTIVE (have + EN) OR PROGRESSIVE (be + ING). Both types may occur in the same sentence:

(3) (a) Peggy *has spoken* Twi for several years. (present tense, perfective aspect)

     (b) Peggy *had spoken* Twi for several years. (past tense, perfective aspect)

     (c) Peggy *is speaking* Twi now. (present tense, progressive aspect)

(d) Peggy *was speaking* Twi then.   (past tense, progressive aspect)

(e) Peggy *has been speaking* Twi for several years.   (present tense, perfective and progressive aspect)

(f) Peggy *had been speaking* Twi for several years.   (past tense, perfective and progressive aspect)

The tree diagrams below show the positions of the verbs and affixes we have been discussing.

(4)   (a)

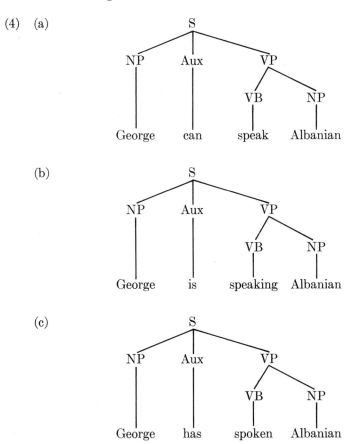

Let us recall that auxiliary verbs exchange places with subject "NP's" to form yes/no questions:

(5)   (a) *Can* George speak Albanian?

    (b) *Is* George speaking Albanian?

    (c) *Has* George spoken Albanian?

A first approximation of the phrase structure rule for the English auxiliary might be stated as (6) below:

(6)   Aux→ tense (modal) (perfective) (progressive)

This generalization or rule states that the auxiliary constituent consists of at least TENSE and may further consist of a MODAL or of PERFECTIVE ASPECT or PROGRESSIVE ASPECT or both. In other words, "tense" is the only part of the auxiliary which is obligatory; the other elements are optional. Let us now add (6) to our earlier list of general phrase structure rules for English:

(PSR-1)   S → (Neg) ($\begin{Bmatrix} Q \\ Imp \end{Bmatrix}$) NP + Aux + VP

(PSR-2)   NP → $\begin{Bmatrix} N\ (S) \\ NP\ S \end{Bmatrix}$

(PSR-3)   VP → VB (NP) (NP)

(PSR-4)   Aux → tense (modal) (perfective) (progressive)

In order to indicate the particular syntactic tense, modal, or aspect in question, we must add phrase structure rules and several "lexical" or "dictionary" entries.

(PSR-5)   Tense → $\begin{Bmatrix} Past \\ Non\text{-}Past \end{Bmatrix}$

The rule above states that "tense" consists of either a "past tense form" or a "non-past tense form" as in the difference between *walk* and *walked*. Some necessary lexical rules are these:

(LR-1)   Modal → can, may, must, shall, will, dare, need, ought
(LR-2)   Perfective → have + EN
(LR-3)   Progressive → be + ING

We should notice that only one form of the modals is given in Lexical Rule 1, namely, the non-past forms (except for *ought*). The reason for this is that a phonological rule will apply and, as it were, will produce the past tense forms. In simple terms these phonological rules are of this form:

(PR-1)   past tense → ED
(PR-2)   can + ED → could
(PR-3)   may + ED → might

(PR-4)   shall + ED → should
(PR-5)   walk + ED → walked
(PR-6)   eat + ED → ate
(PR-7)   hit + ED → hit

We have now examined at least one illustrative rule of the major components of a transformational-generative grammar of English. The four kinds of rules with examples which we encountered were:

(7)   (a) Phrase Structure Rules: S → NP + Aux + VP
      (b) Transformational Rules:
           NP-1 + Aux + V + NP-2 ⇒ NP-2 + Aux + BE + EN + V + by + NP-1
      (c) Lexical Rules: Modal → can
      (d) Phonological Rules: can + ED → could

Exercises

1.   Consider the italicized data which follows:
      a.   You *walk/walked.*
      b.   You *can/could* walk.
      c.   You *have/had* walk*ed.*
      d.   You *are/were* walk*ing.*
      e.   You *can/could have* walk*ed.*
      f.   You *can/could be* walk*ing.*
      g.   You *can/could have been* walk*ing.*

Notice that the basic sentence here is "you walk," which linguistically, as it were, is modified in a systematic pattern by the addition of past tense, the modal verb *can* and perfective aspect (HAVE + EN) and progressive aspect (BE + ING). Notice also that the syntactic "tense" marker suffix attaches to the first occurring verb and that the order of the affixes and verbs is always the same: tense (modal) (perfective aspect) (progressive aspect). The following transformational formula expresses or accounts for the surface order of these various affixes and verbs:

affix + verb ⇒ verb + affix
where: affix = ED, EN, ING
and where: verb = modal, HAVE, BE, or a main verb such as *walk*

For example, consider the deep structure of (1c), "you had walked":

you + ED + have + EN + walk ⟹

you + have + ED + walk + EN →

you hav + d + walk + ed

      had   walked

In the list below, perform the affix transformation on the following strings of symbols.

    a.   you + ED + walk ⟹
    b.   you + ED + can + walk ⟹
    c.   you + ED + have + EN + walk ⟹
    d.   you + ED + be + ING + walk ⟹
    e.   you + ED + can + have + EN + walk ⟹
    f.   you + ED + can + be + ING + walk ⟹
    g.   you + ED + can + have + EN + be + ING + walk ⟹

2. Many students of the English language are troubled and confused by the use of abstract symbols such as ED for past tense and EN for the perfective affix inasmuch as there are competing (or different) surface structure manifestations. While the trouble and confusion are natural, they should not be long-lived, since the common abstract symbols are really constants which bring order to the data. An everyday example of an abstraction that has several manifestations is the concept of "trinity," which may be symbolized as: 3, III, iii, three, five minus two (base ten) and so on. In the examples below, write the surface structure realization of the abstract form that is natural for your dialect, where ED = past and EN = perfect.

    a.   can + non-past →
    b.   can + past →
    c.   may + non-past →
    d.   may + past →
    e.   shall + non-past →
    f.   shall + past →
    g.   will + non-past →
    h.   will + past →
    i.   pat + past →
    j.   pad + past →
    k.   hug + past →

l. kiss + past →

m. go + past →

n. hit + past →

o. sing + past →

p. bring + past →

q. beat + past

r. have + past →

s. be + past →

t. pat + perfect →

u. sing + perfect →

v. beat + perfect →

w. have + perfect →

x. go + perfect →

y. be + perfect →

z. hit + perfect →

3. Briefly discuss the formal properties of auxiliary verbs which set them apart from main verbs. Also, explain how modal auxiliary verbs differ from non-modal auxiliary verbs.

4. As you discovered if you did Exercise 2, the past tense forms of the modal verbs *can, may, shall, will* are respectively *could, might, should, would*. Observe that the past tense form *could* has an orthographic *l*, which is not present in the form *can* and that *should* and *would* contain orthographic *l*, which is no longer pronounced in Modern English but was at one time when the past tense forms were something like *colde* and *sholde*. Observe also that the modal *must* has no past tense form in Modern English inasmuch as it is historically a past tense form with the older usual spelling of *moste*. In the examples below, add the negative particle *not* in its contracted form *n't* to the following modal verbs and observe what happens to the pronunciation of the modal verb:

a. can + not →   can + n't →   : _____

b. may + not →   may + n't →   : _____

c. shall + not → shall + n't → : _____

d. will + not →   will + n't →   : _____

e. must + not →   must + n't →   : _____

5. Many traditional grammar books denounce such historically valid expressions as *had ought* and *should ought* and *might could*, preferring instead simply *ought* and *could* and *should* and *might* as in:

a. He had ought to go. (He *ought* to go.)
b. He should ought to go. (He *should/ought to* go.)
c. He might could get hurt. (He *might/could* get hurt.)

Assume that the double auxiliary verb forms are valid and grammatical and discuss the possible negated forms in Modern English such as *hadn't ought* as opposed to *oughtn't* and so forth.

The Notions "Subject of" And "Object of"

Most traditional grammars seek to make the distinction between *subject of* and *object of* for sentences in general and in particular for sentences that are in the passive voice and sentences which contain a direct object and an indirect object.

(1) The dowager gave some tea to Pip.
(2) Some tea was given to Pip by the dowager.
(3) The dowager gave Pip some tea.
(4) Pip was given some tea by the dowager.
(5) The dowager gave some tea to him.
(6) The dowager gave him some tea.
(7) He was given some tea by the dowager.
(8) ? To him some tea was given by the dowager.
(9) *Him was given some tea by the dowager.

Let us assume that the informal underlying structure of this sentence paradigm is that indicated below. The noun phrases are numbered for convenience of reference: NP-1 is the underlying subject, NP-2 is the direct object, and NP-3 is the indirect object.

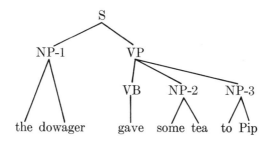

It is important to observe that, with this underlying sentence diagram as a reference for any and all sentences in the language, we can define the notions "subject of," "direct object of," and "indirect object of" as follows:

   a. The UNDERLYING SUBJECT of a sentence is that N(oun) P(hrase) which is immediately dominated by the S(entence) node.

   b. The UNDERLYING DIRECT OBJECT of a sentence is that N(oun) P(hrase) which is immediately dominated by the V(erb) P(hrase) node and which occurs immediately to the right of VB.

   c. The UNDERLYING INDIRECT OBJECT is that N(oun) P(hrase) which is immediately dominated by VP and which occurs to the right of the direct object.

Even though transformational processes may rearrange the order of the underlying form of such a sentence as "the dowager gave some tea to Pip," the relationship between the noun phrases remains constant. As a matter of fact, the underlying subject of a sentence can be deleted if the sentence occurs in the passive voice, in which case it will be marked overtly with the so-called "agentive" marker *by:* "The dowager gave some tea to Pip ⇒ Some tea was given to Pip by the dowager ⇒ Some tea was given to Pip."

Traditional grammarians used the terms "LOGICAL" and "GRAMMATICAL" subject in analyzing the sentences above. Thus, *the dowager*, no matter what its position, would be the "logical" subject. When passivization takes place, then the direct object *some tea* or the indirect object *(to) Pip* becomes the "grammatical" (first-occurring) subject.

No doubt, the reader has already noted for himself that when the direct object and the indirect object change positions (in the INDIRECT OBJECT INVERSION), then the form *to* is deleted. Also, when pronouns occur in these noun phrases, they behave in special ways:

(10) The dowager gave *some tea to Pip.*

(11) The dowager gave to Pip some tea. ⇒ The dowager gave Ø Pip some tea.

(12) The dowager gave *some tea to him.* ⇒ The dowager gave to him some tea. ⇒ The dowager gave Ø him some tea.

(13) The dowager gave *it to him.*

(14) The dowager gave to him it. ⇒ The dowager gave Ø him it.

In the generation of the sentence "Pip was given some tea by the dowager," the INDIRECT OBJECT TRANSFORMATION must apply before the passive transformation, as indicated below.

(15)　The dowager gave *some tea to Pip.* ⇒ (indirect object inversion transformation)

The dowager gave *to Pip some tea.* ⇒ ("to" deletion transformation)

The dowager gave Ø *Pip some tea* ⇒ (passive transformation)

Pip was given *some tea* by the dowager.

As we demonstrate on a number of occasions, the ordering of transformations is very important. Additionally, in this section, we have seen that one must make a distinction between deep structure subject and object and surface structure subject and object; that is, noun phrases may function as subjects, direct objects, and indirect objects. We have also seen that only in a deep structure does a constituent have a stationary position.

Inasmuch as the noun phrase, which is dominated by the "S(entence)" node in the deep structure, is always the logical subject of a sentence, it is appropriate to mark it as such, and to mark all other noun phrases as non-subject. We will then mark the logical subject as ⟨+subject⟩ and all other noun phrases as ⟨−subject⟩ as indicated below:

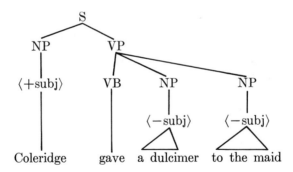

It is also possible to mark a noun plural ⟨+ plural⟩ or singular ⟨− plural⟩, as in (16) and (17):

(16)　Beowulf and Naegling faced the *monster.*
(17)　Beowulf and Naegling faced the *monsters.*

The two sentences immediately above differ only in number, not in meaning. Thus in the deep structure *monsters* will occur without plural -*s* but with the feature ⟨+ plural⟩. Similarly *monster* will be marked ⟨−plural⟩. A phonological rule will attach -*s* to those regular nouns which are marked ⟨+ plural⟩. For (16) and (17) the deep structure of *monster* and *monsters* is this:

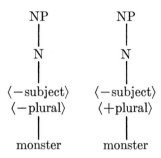

When a phonologically regular noun is marked ⟨+ plural⟩, a transformation creates a place to which this affix can attach itself:

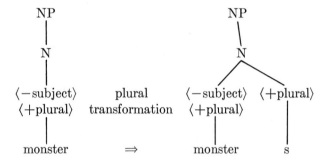

In effect, we are saying that it is not necessary to include the plural affix in the deep structure representation of nouns since any noun which may be counted (hence having the ⟨+ count⟩ feature) can be either singular or plural. For example, let us assume that all nouns are marked as ⟨+ N(oun)⟩. Now, all ⟨+ N(oun)⟩ segments are either *countable* ⟨+count⟩ or non-countable ⟨−count⟩. Those ⟨+ N(oun)⟩ segments which are also ⟨+ count⟩ can be either ⟨+ plural⟩ or ⟨− plural⟩. This arrangement may be expressed in the following formula:

$$\text{Noun} \to \begin{array}{l} \langle +\text{N (oun)}\rangle \text{ (henceforth } +\text{N)} \\ \langle +/-\text{count}\rangle \end{array}$$
$$+\text{count} \to \langle +/-\text{plural}\rangle$$

That is, all nouns are marked with the feature ⟨+N⟩ and either ⟨+count⟩ or ⟨− count⟩. Those nouns which are ⟨+ count⟩ may be either ⟨+ plural⟩ or ⟨− plural⟩. This formulation then predicts that there are at least three types of nouns:

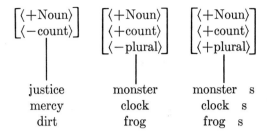

$$\begin{bmatrix} \langle+\text{Noun}\rangle \\ \langle-\text{count}\rangle \end{bmatrix} \quad \begin{bmatrix} \langle+\text{Noun}\rangle \\ \langle+\text{count}\rangle \\ \langle-\text{plural}\rangle \end{bmatrix} \quad \begin{bmatrix} \langle+\text{Noun}\rangle \\ \langle+\text{count}\rangle \\ \langle+\text{plural}\rangle \end{bmatrix}$$

justice	monster	monster s
mercy	clock	clock s
dirt	frog	frog s

Lexical Representation

In a transformational description of a natural language it is necessary to have a LEXICON (dictionary) that contains the items (formatives) which make up a particular language. However, instead of listing the forms alphabetically as an ordinary dictionary does, the linguist lists the lexical items by such syntactic classes as nouns and verbs. All nouns are marked "+N(oun)" and (in principle) all non-nouns are marked "−N(oun)," just as all verbs are marked "+V(erb)" and all non-verbs are marked "−V(erb)." In like manner the so-called "definite article" is marked ⟨+Article⟩ and ⟨+Definite⟩. Individual grammatical features are enclosed in angle brackets, and simultaneously occurring features are arranged in columns and enclosed in square brackets. Thus the individual elements of "the man smiled" are listed lexically as:

$$\begin{bmatrix} \langle+\text{Article}\rangle \\ \langle+\text{Definite}\rangle \end{bmatrix} \quad \begin{bmatrix} \langle+\text{Noun}\rangle \\ \langle+\text{Common}\rangle \end{bmatrix} \quad \begin{bmatrix} \langle+\text{Verb}\rangle \\ \langle-\text{Affix}\rangle \end{bmatrix} \quad \begin{bmatrix} \langle+\text{Verb}\rangle \\ \langle+\text{Affix}\rangle \\ \langle+\text{Past}\rangle \end{bmatrix}$$

the	man	smile	−d

Features of the Noun Segment

The term SEGMENT in transformational analysis is synonymous with "occupying space"; that is, a ⟨+Segment⟩ is what occurs between, say, periods of silence or between blank spaces on a printed page. Either silence or a blank space then is ⟨−Segment⟩. For example, the spoken English word *at* consists of initial silence followed by the ⟨+Segment⟩ *a* followed by the ⟨+Segment⟩ *t* followed by silence:

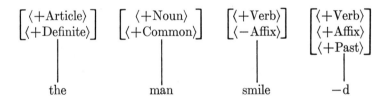

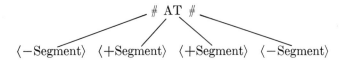

Things like nouns, verbs, and adjectives are termed ⟨+Segments⟩ by many transformational grammarians. Segments in turn are made up of an aggregate or collection of grammatical features. As we have seen, noun segments in part consist of such features or characteristics as ⟨+Noun⟩, ⟨+Count⟩, ⟨+Plural⟩.

Traditionally, nouns have been placed in one of three categories (proper, mass, and count) and numerous subcategories (common, concrete, animate, human, masculine, feminine, etc.). We propose the following feature description of the first three categories above.

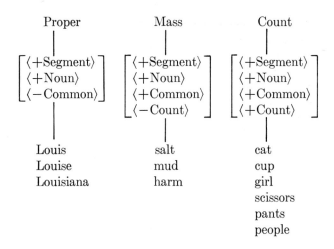

By convention, PROPER NOUNS are capitalized in English: *Louis, Louise, Louisiana, Richard-the-Lion-Hearted, David-the-Brave, Poor Richard.* These nouns may be masculine or feminine (*Louis/Louise*) and human or non-human (*Louisiana*).

MASS NOUNS have no plural forms: **mercies, *hates, *justices.* Mass nouns may be preceded by definite articles: *the mercy, this hate, that justice.* Mass nouns may also be concrete (*mud*) or non-concrete (*harm*).[1]

It is necessary to distinguish between two kinds of count nouns. There are those that have only ⟨+Plural⟩ forms: *pants, trousers, pliers, scissors, mumps, measles, people;* and also those that have both ⟨+Plural⟩ and ⟨−Plural⟩ forms: *cup(s), orange(s), apple(s), girl(s).* However, both

---

[1]Some mass mouns may also exist in more specific, countable senses, and hence as plurals, as in *mercies*, indicating plural blessings or good wishes.

types may be preceded by articles: *the pants, these trousers, some pliers, the cups, an orange.*

COUNT NOUNS may be either concrete (*cup*) or non-concrete (*assertion*). Also, count nouns may be animate (*cat*) or non-animate (*cup*). What is more, these nouns may be human (*woman*) and non-human (*wombat*). Finally, these nouns may be masculine (*boy, man*) or non-masculine (*girl, woman*).

Typically, *much* precedes ⟨−Count Nouns⟩ (*much mud, much salt, much sugar*) whereas *many* precedes ⟨+Count Nouns⟩ (*many men, many oranges, many apples*).

As Katz and Fodor (1963:186) indicate, semantic and lexical information can be schematized for a polysemous word of multiple meanings, such as *bachelor*, in the manner below:

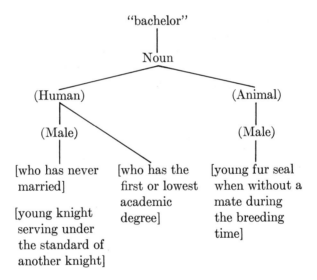

In this scheme, "noun" is a grammatical marker, "human," "animal," and "male" are semantic markers, and the prose descriptions are distinguishers. In feature notation, these four nouns may be described as follows:

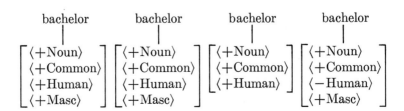

Co-occurrence Restrictions within Lexical Rules

It is still an open empirical question as to how ultimately one should state semantic restrictions between subjects and verbs on the one hand and objects on the other; i.e., certain verbs require direct objects, whereas others may be followed by a complement, etc. One method in current use is to make the statement in terms of the contextual framework below.

(1) +____ : NP → N : *Clouds* bring *rain.*

(2) +____ : VP → VB : Clouds *bring* rain.

(3) +____ NP : VP → VB + NP : Clouds *bring rain.*

(4) +____ NP NP : VP → NP + NP : Clouds *bring us rain.*

The formulations above describe the environment in which the restriction occurs: *Noun Verb Noun Noun.* For example, if we wished to indicate that *bring* is a TRANSITIVE VERB inasmuch as it must be followed by a noun phrase, and if we wished to indicate that *vanish* is NONTRANSITIVE, we could do so as follows:

(5) Clouds *bring rain*: bring : ⟨+____NP⟩

(6) The clouds *vanished*: vanish : ⟨−____NP⟩

Moreover, the restriction between subjects and verbs and verbs and objects may be stated negatively in the following form.

(7) (a) Her aunt smiled.
     (b) *Her ant smiled.
     (c) The verb *smile* requires a ⟨+Human⟩ subject noun (except in figurative usage).
     (d) smile: [− [⟨−Human⟩]____]

(8) (a) The man drank up the coffee.
     (b) *The cup drank up the coffee.
     (c) The verb *drink* requires a ⟨+Animate⟩ subject noun.
     (d) drink: [− [⟨−Animate⟩]____]

(9) (a) The water boiled.
     (b) *Justice boiled.
     (c) The verb *boil* requires a ⟨+Concrete⟩ subject noun.
     (d) boil: [− [⟨−Concrete⟩]____]

(10) (a) Time elapsed quickly.
     (b) *Silas elapsed quickly.

(c) The verb *elapse* requires a ⟨−Concrete⟩ subject noun.

(d) elapse: [− [⟨+Concrete⟩]____]

(11) (a) Oatmeal frightens Michael.

(b) *Michael frightens oatmeal.

(c) The verb *frighten* requires a ⟨+Animate⟩ object noun.

(d) frighten: [−____[⟨−Animate⟩]]]

Of course, it goes without saying that speakers often violate co-occurrence restrictions purposely to produce metaphors and other literary devices. To be sure, anthropomorphism enhances children's literature. It would be a rather dull language that did not allow a dish to run away with a spoon, or a rag to drink up spilled coffee.

Exercises

1. By using plus (+) and minus (−), describe the following nouns according to these features: Common; Count; Concrete; Human; Animate; Masculine; Feminine. Note that some features are redundant; for example, the features Masculine and Feminine are not germane to the classification of such ⟨−Animate⟩ nouns as *salt, mud, cup, justice*. Nouns that are ⟨+Human⟩ are predictably ⟨+Animate⟩.

> *Louis, Louise, Louisiana, salt, mud, justice, cat, cup, girl, boy, bull, cow, calf, pliers, scissors, song, people.*

2. State the anomalies, if any, in the following sentences.

(a) The test confirmed that Hector was pregnant.

(b) The walls have ears.

(c) The computer has a stomachache.

(d) The heart of the building cracked.

(e) Rex barked a command, and Roxanne obeyed.

Summary of Grammar I

In this section we have stressed the crucial difference between an understanding of the *grammaticality* and the *acceptability* or appropriateness of sentences in a natural language such as English. We have also suggested that it is useful for the linguist, the teacher, and the layman to recognize the dichotomy of linguistic performance and linguistic competence. The latter includes such abilities as recognition of sentence *paraphrase*, sentence *synonymy*, and recognition of sentence or phrasal *ambiguity*.

Another purpose of this section was to define, discuss, and exemplify the notion of sentencehood as well as to determine the three major constituents of sentences: the *noun phrase*, the *auxiliary*, and the *verb phrase*. Some discussion was given over to the function of such a constituent as the noun phrase, and in this vein we cited noun phrases functioning as *subjects*, *direct objects*, and *indirect objects*. Also, reference was made to the *logical* subject versus the *grammatical* subject.

We also gave some attention to the question of *lexical* or dictionary representation of the so-called formatives or *morphemes* of a natural language. In order to accomplish this, we alluded to the concept of *feature* representation on a binary (plus/minus) basis, and some coverage was given to co-occurrence restrictions between and among noun and verb formatives or morphemes.

An overall purpose of Grammar I was to identify major sentence types such as *declarative*, *question*, and *imperative*, along with such modifications as sentence *negation* and *passivization*. Mention was made of the theoretical notion that *transformations* convert or relate *deep structures* to *surface structures*. In addition to transformational *rules*, we identified three other types of grammatical rules: *phrase structure* rules, *lexical* rules, and *phonological* rules.

GRAMMAR II
A Feature Analysis of English Syntax

In Grammar I we listed the following phrase structure rules:

(PSR-1) S $\rightarrow$ # (Neg) ($\left\{ \begin{array}{c} \text{Q} \\ \text{Imp} \end{array} \right\}$) NP + Aux + VP #

(PSR-2) NP $\rightarrow$ $\left\{ \begin{array}{c} \text{N (S)} \\ \text{NP S} \end{array} \right\}$

(PSR-3) VP $\rightarrow$ VB (NP) (NP)

(PSR-4) Aux $\rightarrow$ Tense (Modal) (Perfective) (Progressive)

(PSR-5) Tense $\rightarrow$ $\left\{ \begin{array}{c} \text{Past} \\ \text{Non-Past} \end{array} \right\}$

We may update these rules by eliminating PSR-4 and PSR-5 and replacing them in part with what are known as SEGMENT STRUCTURE

RULES for the AUXILIARY CONSTITUENT or, in other words, AUXILIARY
SEGMENT STRUCTURE RULES. Just as we assumed previously that a
⟨+Noun⟩ was a ⟨+Segment⟩, so we will now assume that a ⟨+Aux(il-
iary)⟩ is a ⟨+Segment⟩:

$$\text{Aux} \rightarrow \text{Segment}$$
$$\text{Segment} \rightarrow \begin{array}{l} \langle+\text{Aux}\rangle \\ \langle\pm\text{Modal}\rangle \\ \langle\pm\text{Past}\rangle \end{array}$$

All we have done here is to incorporate PSR-5 into PSR-4 by replacing
"Past" with ⟨+Past⟩ and "Non-Past" with ⟨−Past⟩. Also, instead of
having "Modal" in parentheses, we now indicate that a modal is in a
structure by ⟨+Modal⟩ and that it is not in a structure by ⟨−Modal⟩.
For the moment, we will disregard perfective and progressive (analyzed
separately below). Tree diagrams now take on this appearance:

(1)   The boy can walk.

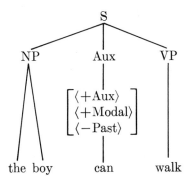

(2)   The boy could walk.

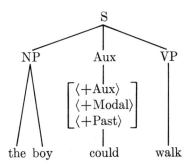

(3)   The boy walks.

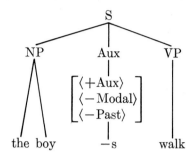

(The agreement transformation adds the −*s* to *walk* for those dialects which mark this phenomenon.)

(4)   The boy walked.

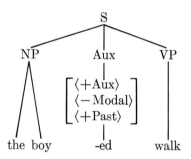

(The verb suffix transformation adds the -*ed* to *walk*.)

Exercise

1.   Analyze the auxiliary of the following sentences:

    a.   The rain must fall.
    b.   Batman should help Robin.
    c.   Donne caught the falling star.
    d.   A stitch in time saves nine.

2.   Analyze the auxiliary and aspect of these sentences:

    a.   The rain must have fallen.
    b.   Batman should be helping Robin.
    c.   Donne will have caught the falling star.
    d.   Donne would have been catching the falling star.

The Features of Aspect: Perfective and Progressive

We return now to the feature analysis of PERFECTIVE and PROGRESSIVE ASPECT, which were eliminated from rule PSR-4 above. Once again, let us assume that VB (verbal) is a segment and that perfective and progressive aspect appear as features of this segment:

VB → Segment
Segment → ⟨+VB⟩
⟨+Perfective⟩
⟨+Progressive⟩

Tree diagrams of sentences with aspect will now have this form:

(1) The boys have walked.

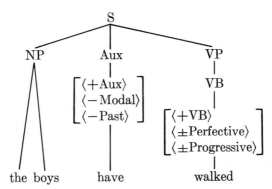

(2) The boys are walking.

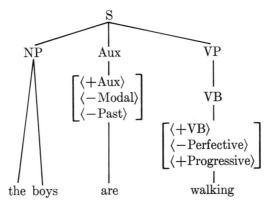

(3)   The boys have been walking.

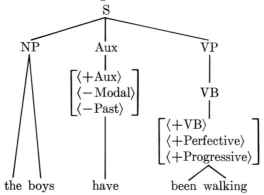

(4)   The boy shall be walking.

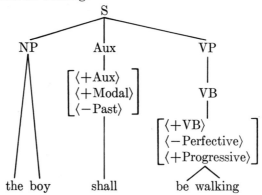

(5)   The boy should have walked.

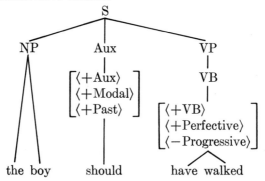

Exercise

Construct a chart which exemplifies the sixteen possible combinations
of TENSE + MODAL + PERFECTIVE + PROGRESSIVE. Organize it in the

following manner. Use the Modal *shall* and the verb *walk* and assume a subject of *he/she/it*.

		PAST	MODAL	PERFECTIVE	PROGRESSIVE
1.	walks	–	–	–	–
2.	walked	+	–	–	–
3.	shall walk	–	+	–	–
4.	is walking	–	–	–	+

Features in the Verbal Segment

Many traditional grammars state that a verb expresses an "action" or a "state of being." Let us reword this slightly and say that a verbal expresses an action or a state of being. Further, let us again observe that verbals may be transitive or non-transitive:

(1) Jack *liked Jill.*
(2) Jack was *fond of Jill.*   (transitive)
(3) Time flies.
(4) Life is short.   (non-transitive)

Thus, we are using the term "verbal" to refer to the class of items known traditionally as "verb" and "adjective." Let ⟨+Verb⟩ refer to the class of verbals that are marked for syntactic tense (⟨−Past/+Past⟩) and ⟨−Verb⟩ refer to the class of verbals that are marked for degree (*more/most; -er/-est*):

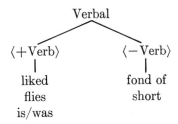

Transformational grammarians are not being intentionally perverse or esoteric when they suggest that such wellworn American traditions as "verb" and "adjective" be replaced by ⟨+Verb⟩ and ⟨−Verb⟩ respectively. The intent, rather, is to provide insight into the structure of language. For example, with this analysis one can explain the distribution that is shared by certain classes of verbs and adjectives. In brief, there is a class of verbals which co-occurs with progressive aspect and a class which does not. Let us use the dichotomy ⟨−Stative/ +Stative⟩. The distribution is this: ⟨+Stative⟩ verbals do not co-occur with progressive aspect (be + ing), while ⟨−Stative⟩ verbals can and do co-occur with progressive aspect. Inasmuch as progressive aspect in general is a mark of states of being which are subject to change ("honest/ candid" vs. "tall/short"), the distribution is what one would expect. By the same token, one would not expect such states as "tallness/short-ness" to be subject to either direct or indirect command:

(5)   *Pepin was being short.
(6)   *Goliath was being tall.
(7)   *The Franks urged Pepin to be tall.
(8)   *The Philistines urged Goliath to be tall.
(9)   *The Franks said, "Be tall, Pepin!"
(10) *The Philistines urged, "Remain tall, Goliath!"
(11) *The Franks said for Pepin to be tall.
(12) *The Philistines urged Goliath to remain tall.

On the other hand, exhortations to be "honest" or "candid" are not strange at all.

(13) The patient said to the physician, "Be candid and honest!"
(14) The patient said for the physician to be candid and honest.
(15) The physician was being honest and candid when he said, "I can neither save you nor heal myself!"

Finally, we may observe that statives must be conjoined with statives and non-statives with non-statives:

(16) Keats was being candid and honest when he wrote: "Here lies one whose name was writ in water!"
(17) *Keats was being neither tall nor short when he wrote: "Here lies one whose name was writ in water!"
(18) Pepin was short and Bertha was broad of foot.
(19) Pepin the Short and Bertha Broadfoot produced Charles the Great.

In summary, then, there are at least four subtypes of verbals, whose feature analysis may be illustrated as follows:

$$\begin{bmatrix} \langle+\text{Verbal}\rangle \\ \langle+\text{Verb}\rangle \\ \langle-\text{Stative}\rangle \end{bmatrix} \quad \begin{bmatrix} \langle+\text{Verbal}\rangle \\ \langle+\text{Verb}\rangle \\ \langle+\text{Stative}\rangle \end{bmatrix} \quad \begin{bmatrix} \langle+\text{Verbal}\rangle \\ \langle-\text{Verb}\rangle \\ \langle-\text{Stative}\rangle \end{bmatrix} \quad \begin{bmatrix} \langle+\text{Verbal}\rangle \\ \langle-\text{Verb}\rangle \\ \langle+\text{Stative}\rangle \end{bmatrix}$$

write	appear	honest	sad
hit	happen	candid	tall

Exercises

1. Explain the anomalies, if any, of the following sentences.

   a. The weather is seeming strange today.
   b. An analyst told the patient to be neurotic.
   c. Herr Oberessen had been being fat deliberately.
   d. In "My Last Duchess" the Duke was commanding and the smiles were stopping.

2. Write feature descriptions of the following verbals.

   a. long, linger, lengthen, lunge, lounge
   b. vicious, erotic, sensuous, titillate, scintillate
   c. petulant, snotty, supercilious, droll, dry, dead, die

We can now revise the segment structure rule for the verbal so as to include our observations about the stative feature:

VB → Segment
Segment → + VB
+VB → ⟨±Verb⟩
⟨±Stative⟩
⟨±Perfective⟩
⟨±Progressive⟩ / [−Stative]

The notation of the last line means that a verbal segment may be marked ⟨+Progressive⟩ just in case it is also ⟨−Stative⟩.

Summary of PS Rules and SS Rules

At this point the phrase structure rules (PSR) and segment structure rules (SSR) look like this:

(PSR-1) $S \rightarrow \# \, (\text{Neg}) \, (\left\{ \begin{array}{c} Q \\ \text{Imp} \end{array} \right\}) \, NP + \text{Aux} + VP \, \#$

(PSR-2) $NP \rightarrow \left\{ \begin{array}{l} N \, (S) \\ NP \, S \end{array} \right\}$

(PSR-3) $VP \rightarrow VB \, (NP) \, (NP)$

(SSR-1) Noun → Segment

    a. Segment → $\langle +N \rangle$
                         $\langle \pm \text{Subject} \rangle$
                         $\langle \pm \text{Count} \rangle$
                         $\langle \pm \text{Concrete} \rangle$
                         $\langle \pm \text{Human} \rangle$
                         $\langle \pm \text{Common} \rangle$
                         $\langle \pm \text{Animate} \rangle$
                         $\langle \pm \text{Masculine} \rangle$
                         $\langle \pm \text{Feminine} \rangle$

    b. $\langle +\text{Count} \rangle \rightarrow \langle \pm \text{Plural} \rangle$

(SSR-2) VB → Segment

        Segment → $\langle +VB \rangle$
                         $\langle \pm \text{Verb} \rangle$
                         $\langle \pm \text{Stative} \rangle$
                         $\langle \pm \text{Perfective} \rangle$
                         $\langle \pm \text{Progressive} \rangle \, / \, \left[\begin{array}{c} \langle -\text{Stative} \rangle \\ \underline{\quad\quad} \end{array} \right]$

Feature Analysis of the Passive Voice

The formal expression of the conditions necessary for the PASSIVE
TRANSFORMATION can now be stated as a segment structure rule. We
should recall that passivization takes place when a transitive verb is
followed by one or more noun phrases:

(1) The crew should *man the guns.* (active)
(2) The dowager *offered some tea to Pip.* (active)
(3) *The guns* should be manned by the crew. (passive)
(4) *Some tea* was offered to Pip by the dowager. (passive)

The appropriate form of the rule stating the conditions for the passive
transformation is this:

(SSR-3) $\langle +\text{Verb} \rangle \rightarrow \langle \pm \text{Passive} \rangle \, / \, \left[\begin{array}{c} \langle +\underline{\quad}NP \rangle \\ \langle +\underline{\quad}NP \, NP \rangle \\ \underline{\quad\quad\quad} \end{array} \right]$

We should recall that by the rule of indirect object inversion (IOI) sentence (2) above is converted into (5).

(5)   The dowager offered *Pip some tea.*

The condition for IOI can be stated as a supplement to the SSR-3 rule above:

$$\pm\text{IOI} \rightarrow \quad / \quad \left[\left\langle \begin{array}{c} \langle+\text{N}\rangle \langle+\text{Aux}\rangle\underline{\quad}\langle+\text{N}\rangle \langle+\text{N}\rangle \\ \langle+\text{Preposition}\rangle \\ \langle+\text{to}\rangle \end{array} \right\rangle \right]$$

Transformations

Now that we have dealt with the major constituents of the deep structure of sentences, it is appropriate to turn our attention to those processes which relate deep structures to surface structures, namely TRANSFORMATIONS. Some transformations will be described in detail and with some formality. Others, like the PREPOSITION SEGMENTALIZATION transformation and the VERB PARTICLE MOVEMENT transformation, will be discussed sketchily.

As Peter S. Rosenbaum has suggested (1968:32–34), PREPOSITIONS may be analyzed in the deep structure as features of $\langle+\text{Noun}\rangle$ segments. In the same manner, VERB PARTICLES may be analyzed as features of $\langle+\text{Verbal}\rangle$ segments. Since there is no difference in form between prepositions and verb particles, it is necessary to differentiate them in sentences. We should observe that prepositions may be FRONT-SHIFTED, whereas verb particles may not. In the sentences immediately below, we may observe various shifting positions for particles, which are italicized, and for prepositions, which are in small capitals.

(1)   The biologist will peer INTO the microscope.
(2)   Cinderella will sweep *up* the coals.
(3)   Cinderella will sweep the coals *up.*
(4)   What will the scientist peer INTO?
(5)   INTO what will the scientist peer?
(6)   What will Cinderella sweep *up?*
(7)   **Up* what will Cinderella sweep?

Let us represent verb particles as features of the $\langle+\text{Verbal}\rangle$ segment in the deep structure and assume that a transformation creates a segment on the tree diagram to which the particle may attach itself in the surface structure.

(8)   Cinderella *swept up the coals.*

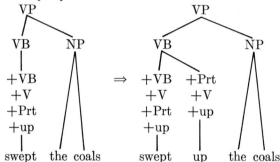

The optional PARTICLE MOVEMENT transformation shifts the particle to the right of the object noun phrase. If the sentence undergoes passivization, the particle cannot be moved. If the object noun phrase contains a pronoun, particle movement is obligatory:

(9)   Cinderella swept the coals *up.*   (particle movement)
(10)   The coals were swept *up* by Cinderella.   (passive voice)
(11)   Cinderella swept them *up.*   (The object is a pronoun.)
(12)   *Cinderella swept up them.   (But see the "Excursis" on verb prefixes after Exercise One below, citing *sweep up* in a different situation.)

Prepositions ("pre-posed" = placed before) become constituents by way of the PREPOSITION SEGMENTALIZATION transformation, the effect of which is to create a segment onto which relevant features of the noun segment are copied. After a preposition is introduced, a new noun phrase node is created which dominates the ⟨+Prep(osition)⟩ segment. One of the motivations for creating a new noun phrase node to dominate the preposition and the object noun phrase is that in certain grammatical processes the lower noun phrase may front-shift without the preposition:

(13)   The biologist will peer *into the microscope.*
(14)   *What* will the biologist peer *into?*
(15)   *Into what* will the biologist peer?

Consider now the following derivation of a preposition. The stages are as follows: (a) informal underlying structure; (b) preposition segmentalization; (c) introduction of a novel noun phrase node.

(a)

(b)

(c)

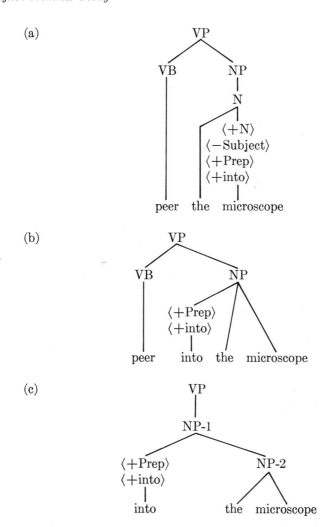

The motivation for marking the noun phrase above as ⟨−Subject⟩ is that, in general, ⟨+Subject⟩ noun phrases (underlying subjects) which occur in the initial position of a sentence do not contain prepositions in surface structures.

Exercise

Identify the italicized items as either verb particles or prepositions.

    a.   The student took *off* his dashiki.
    b.   The student took his dashiki *off*.

c. **Off* the student took his dashiki.
d. Alice advised the rabbit to slow *down*.
e. Alice advised the rabbit to slow himself *down*.
f. Strephon looked *up* Cecilia's dress *in* the catalogue room.
g. The plane took *off* at three.
h. What are you staring *at*?

Excursis

Separable and Inseparable Prefixes in Modern German. Inasmuch as many composition teachers as well as would-be grammarians (however well-intentioned) insist on "not ending a sentence with a preposition," it might be well to examine some constructions like *stand* UP and *sweep* UP, which are not redundancies with the same meaning as *stand* and *sweep*. Such a use of prepositions and particles has a long and stable history, both in English and in German.

Compound verbs in modern German are formed by prefixing certain elements (*be-, emp-, ent-, er-, ge-, ver-, zer-*) to a simple verb stem, thereby forming so-called inseparable verbs much like English UNDER*stand* and MIS*trust*. Notice how the following prefixes effect a semantic change on the verb stem. (In these items the main stress ( ) is on the verb.)

(1) be + stehen = bestéhen ("consist")
Sein Vermögen *bestéht aus* Geld. (His wealth *consists of* money.)
(2) ver + stehen = verstéhen ("understand")
Der Mann kann das nicht *verstéhen*. (The man cannot *understand* that.)

The principal parts of these two verbs are:

bestéhen, bestánd, bestánden ("consíst, consísted, consísted") verstéhen, verstánd, verstánden ("understánd, understóod, understóod")

On the other hand, when the prefix in Modern German receives the main stress, it is separable. Common separable prefixes are *ab-, an-, auf-, aus-, ein-, fort-, her-, hin-, los-, mit-, nieder-, vorbei-, weg-, weiter-,* and *zurück.* Thus, for example, *auf* plus *stehen* means something like "arise, get up from sleeping":

(3) auf + stehen = aúfstehen
Wir *stehen* jeden Morgen früh *aúf*. (We *get up* early every morning.)

As a final example consider the union of German *stehen* (stand) and *bleiben* (remain, stay), which means to "cease" from walking. Note too the *ge-* perfective prefix, also common in Old English.

(4) Der Mann *bleibt* jeden Morgen vor dem Hause *stéhen.* (The man stops every morning in front of the house.)

(5) Der Mann ist jeden Morgen vor dem Hause *stéhengeblieben.* (The man has stopped every morning in front of the house.)

The point, of course, is that rather than insisting that particles and prepositions are redundancies, why not view them as ways of enriching and modifying the basic meanings of verbs?

The Cyclic Principle

One may recall that it is possible to embed one sentence in another, the endless possibilities of which are exemplified in the poem "The House That Jack Built." Thus, sentences (1), (2), and (3) below may be arranged into (4) or (5):

(1) It is clear.

(2) It is unnecessary.

(3) Grammar is dull.

(4) It is clear that it is unnecessary that grammar be dull.

(5) It is clear that it is unnecessary for grammar to be dull.

What is more, (6), (7), and (8) below are synonymous with (4) and (5) above:

(6) That for grammar to be dull is unnecessary is clear.

(7) That it is unnecessary for grammar to be dull is clear.

(8) It is clear that for grammar to be dull is unnecessary.

The difference in the surface structure form of (4) through (8) is due precisely to the transformational processes called EXTRAPOSITION and IT-DELETION. Extraposition is the process whereby a subordinated or embedded sentence is wrested from its position in the left-hand field of a sentence and transported, as it were, to the right-hand field of a sentence. This is demonstrated in linear fashion below.

(9) The fact (that grammar is not dull) is clear $\Rightarrow$ extraposition

(10) The fact is clear that grammar is not dull.

It-deletion is the process whereby the pronoun *it* is deleted just in case it is contiguous with a subordinator or complementizer such as *that* or *for ... to* or *'s ... ing*. As should be clear from the examples below, if extraposition does not apply, then it-deletion will (if *it* is contiguous with a complementizer).

(11)   It (that grammar is not dull) is clear $\Rightarrow$ extraposition
(12)   It is clear that grammar is not dull.
(13)   It (that grammar is not dull) is clear $\Rightarrow$ it-deletion
(14)   Ø That grammar is not dull is clear.

The informal deep structure diagram below shows that sentence two (S-2) is embedded in sentence one (S-1). Traditionally, (S-2) has been called a dependent clause and (S-1) an independent clause. We refer to all instances of the "higher" sentence (or "highest" sentence when there are more than two) as the main sentence.

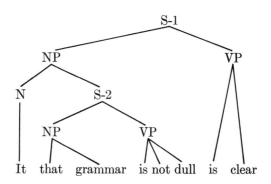

Extraposition and it-deletion are cyclic transformations, and extraposition precedes it-deletion. The concept of the TRANSFORMATIONAL CYCLE is that a transformation applies to an innermost or embedded sentence first. One can see very clearly how these tandem transformations operate by examining carefully the derivations below. Our demonstration sentences are (5) through (8), which we repeat:

(5)   It is clear that it is unnecessary for grammar to be dull.
(6)   That for grammar to be dull is unnecessary is clear.
(7)   That it is unnecessary for grammar to be dull is clear.
(8)   It is clear that for grammar to be dull is unnecessary.

We can assume that the informal deep structure of (5) through (8) is that in A. below in terms of a tree diagram and B. in the form of labeled brackets.

A. Informal Underlying Tree Diagram:

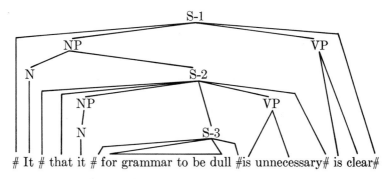

It # that it # for grammar to be dull #is unnecessary# is clear#

B. Labeled Bracketing:

s1[It s2[that it s3[for grammar to be dull]s3 is unnecessary]s2 is clear]s1

In the derivations below, a plus (+) means that the transformation has applied, and a minus (−) indicates that the transformation has not applied. In keeping with the notion that the transformations apply cyclically, the cycles are numbered from the bottom up:

S-1: Third Cycle
S-2: Second Cycle
S-3: First Cycle

Thus extraposition and it-deletion, in that order, apply first at the level of S-3, then S-2, then S-1, the abbreviations S-1, S-2, S-3 referring to the tree diagram or labeled brackets immediately above.

C. Surface Structure: It is clear that it is unnecessary for grammar to be dull.

Derivation:

S-1: Third Cycle:
   − It-deletion
   − Extraposition

It is clear *that it is unnecessary for grammar to be dull.*

S-2: Second Cycle:
   − It-deletion
   + Extraposition

It that it is unnecessary *for grammar to be dull* is clear.

S-3: First Cycle
   − It-deletion
   − Extraposition

It that it for grammar to be dull is unnecessary is clear

D. Surface Structure: That for grammar to be dull is unnecessary
    is clear.

Derivation:

S-1: Third Cycle:
   +It-deletion   Ø That for grammar to be
   −Extraposition   dull is unnecessary is clear.

S-2: Second Cycle:
   +It-deletion   It that Ø for grammar to
   −Extraposition   be dull is unnecessary is
                          clear.

S-3: First Cycle:
   −It-deletion   It that it for grammar
   −Extraposition   to be dull is unnecessary
                          is clear.

E. Surface Structure: That it is unnecessary for grammar to be dull
    is clear.

Derivation:

S-1: Third Cycle:
   +It-deletion   Ø That it is unnecessary
   −Extraposition   for grammar to be dull
                          is clear.

S-2: Second Cycle:
   −It-deletion   It that it is unnecessary
   +Extraposition   *for grammar to be dull*
                          is clear.

S-3: First Cycle:
   −It-deletion   It that it for grammar
   −Extraposition   to be dull is unnecessary
                          is clear.

F. Surface Structure: It is clear that for grammar to be dull is un-
    necessary.

Derivation:

S-1: Third Cycle:
   −It-deletion   It is clear *that for*
   +Extraposition   *grammar to be dull is*
                         unnecessary.

S-2: Second Cycle:
   +It-deletion   It that Ø for grammar
   −Extraposition   to be dull is unnecessary
                        is clear.

S-3: First Cycle:
— It-deletion   It that it for grammar
— Extraposition   to be dull is unnecessary
                    is clear.

One's inspection of the formal statement of extraposition and it-deletion should cement the understanding of these processes; at the very least, one should gain some insight into the type of formalism and explicitness the careful linguist exacts of himself. Transformations conventionally are stated in terms of a structural description (SD) and a structural change (SC). The former states the domain of the transformation; the latter, the actual change or process. The extraposition transformation and it-deletion transformation are stated immediately below in algebraic terms.

Extraposition (a substitution transformation):
$$X - {}_{NP}[\text{ it} - S]_{NP} - Y$$

S.D. $1 - 2 - 3 - 4 \Rightarrow$
S.C. $1 - 2 - \emptyset - 4 + 3$

It-deletion (a deletion transformation):
$$X - {}_{NP}[\text{ it} - S]_{NP} - Y$$

S.D. $1 - 2 - 3 - 4 \Rightarrow$
S.C. $1 - \emptyset - 3 - 4$

The surface structure diagrams below exemplify deep structures which have undergone extraposition and it-deletion.

(15)

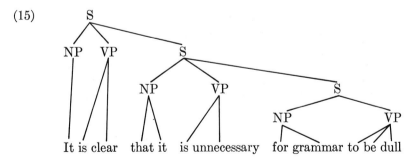

It is clear   that it   is unnecessary   for grammar to be dull

(16)

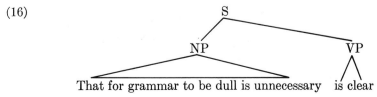

That for grammar to be dull is unnecessary   is clear

The tree diagram above displays the fact that English sentences may contain noun phrases of gigantic proportions.

Exercise

Derive at least four synonymous surface structures from this underlying string.

> s_1[It s_2[that it s_3[for Ahab to kill Moby Dick]s_3 was easy]s_2 was obvious]s_1

In what ways do the sentences below differ from your surface structures?

    a.   That for Ahab to be killing Moby Dick was easy was obvious.

    b.   That for Ahab to have killed Moby Dick was easy was obvious.

    c.   That for Moby Dick to be killed by Ahab was easy was obvious.

Extraposition and Pronoun Replacement

Certain types of sentences seem to defy grammatical analysis of an insightful and revealing type. Such is the case with such sentences as:

(1)   It was easy for Moby Dick to kill Ahab.

(2)   Ahab was easy for Moby Dick to kill.

The phenomena of EXTRAPOSITION and PRONOUN REPLACEMENT as formulated by Peter S. Rosenbaum (1968:48) explain the relationship of these two apparently semantically equivalent sentences. The derivation of (1) is straightforward:

(3)   It (for Moby Dick to kill Ahab) was easy. ⇒ Extraposition

(4)   It was easy (for Moby Dick to kill Ahab)

Pronoun replacement refers to the fact that the HEAD NOUN (*it*) may be replaced by a noun phrase from an embedded sentence. This process may be represented informally in this manner:

(5)   It (for Moby Dick to kill Ahab) was easy ⇒ Extraposition

(6) It was easy (for Moby Dick to kill Ahab) ⇒ Head Noun Deletion

(7) Ø was easy (for Moby Dick to kill Ahab) ⇒ Pronoun replacement

(8) Ahab was easy (for Moby Dick to kill)

Since *for Moby Dick* is deletable, two surface structures are possible:

(9) Ahab was easy for Moby Dick to kill.

(10) Ahab was easy to kill.

In example (3) above, a sentence ("for Moby Dick to kill Ahab") is embedded in the subject noun phrase *it*. In the examples which follow, the verb phrase contains a sentence.

(11) Satan expected Eve to eat an apple.

(12) Satan persuaded Eve to eat an apple.

The verbs *expect* and *persuade* are slightly dissimilar in that the former allows a clausal (*that*) complement whereas the latter does not:

(13) Satan expected that Eve would eat an apple.

(14) *Satan persuaded that Eve would eat an apple.

The fuller underlying forms of (11) and (12) are probably those below.

(15) Satan expected it for Eve to eat an apple.

(16) Satan persuaded Eve to it for Eve to eat an apple.

Exercise

Explain the synonymy of these surface structures.

    a. J. C. is hard to love.

    b. To love J. C. is hard.

    c. For one to love J. C. is hard.

    d. It is hard for one to love J. C.

Imperatives and Tag Questions

The conventional transformational derivation of imperative (command) sentences assumes that the underlying structure contains the imperative (Imp) constituent as well as "you + non-Past + will," which are subsequently deleted. One might formulate this transformation as follows:

Imperative Transformation:

Imp − you − non-Past − will − X

S.D. 1 − 2 − 3 − 4 − 5 ⇒
S.C. 1 − ∅ − 3 − ∅ − 5

Thus "Go and catch a falling star" may be derived in this manner:

(1) Imp − you − non-Past − will − go ⇒ Go
(2) Imp − you − non-Past − will − catch a falling star ⇒ Catch a falling star.

By the process of conjunction, we derive this surface structure:

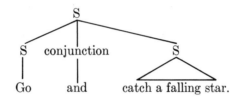

While the formulation above may be accurate, what is not clear is the relationship between imperatives and tag questions of the sort below. Observe in tag questions that if the main sentence is positive, the tag is negative, and vice versa.

(3) Dick the Shepherd will blow his nail, won't he?
(4) Greasy Joan would keel the pot, wouldn't she?
(5) Dick the Shepherd is blowing his nail, isn't he?
(6) Greasy Joan has keeled the pot, hasn't she?
(7) Dick the Shepherd blows his nail, doesn't he?
(8) Greasy Joan keeled the pot, didn't she?

Thus in the examples below, what is in question is the status or force of the sentence—are these imperatives or tag questions or a combination of both?

(9) Blow your nail, will you?/!
(10) Keel your pot, won't you?/!

Exercise

For those who are interested in the formal statement of tag questions, we include a first approximation in algebraic terms. The notation of braces enclosing the negative symbol (Neg) and the null symbol ($\emptyset$) with subscript numerals is intended to capture the positive/negative alternation mentioned earlier. The formulation below also assumes that if the auxiliary constituent does not contain a modal, "do" has to be incorporated into the auxiliary. Further, the negative affix (*n't*) is used rather than the negative particle (*not*). Observe also that the noun phrase in the tag must be a pronoun (+Pronoun) in the formulation below:

Tag Formation:

$$\begin{Bmatrix} \text{Neg} \\ {}_1\emptyset_1 \end{Bmatrix} - \begin{Bmatrix} \text{Q} \\ \text{Imp} \end{Bmatrix} - \text{NP} - \text{Aux} - \text{X}$$

S.D.   1   —   2   —   3   —   4   —   5 $\Rightarrow$

S.C.   1   —   2   —   3   —   4   —   5 + 4 + 1 + 3

$$\begin{Bmatrix} \emptyset \\ {}_1\text{Neg}_1 \end{Bmatrix} \quad [+\text{Pro}]$$

Apply the tag formation and imperative transformations to the following strings of symbols. A model is included below.

    a.   Q you non-Past will go

    b.   Imp you non-Past will go

    c.   Neg Q you non-Past will go

    d.   Neg Imp you non-Past will go

Model

    a.   Q you non-Past will catch a falling star $\Rightarrow$ tag formation
        You will catch a falling star, won't you?

    b.   Imp you non-Past will catch a falling star $\Rightarrow$ imperative
        Catch a falling star!

    c.   Neg Q you non-Past will catch a falling star $\Rightarrow$ tag question
        You won't catch a falling star, will you?

    d.   Neg Imp you non-Past will catch a falling star $\Rightarrow$ imperative
        Don't catch a falling star!

The surface structure diagram below may help one to understand the effect of the tag question transformation.

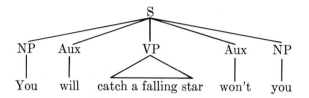

The Reflexive Transformation

In the underlying form of sentences, nouns are marked with the feature ⟨−Reflexive⟩. When two nouns with identity of reference occur within the same simple sentence, reflexivization takes place. The REFLEXIVE TRANSFORMATION converts ⟨−Reflexive⟩ to ⟨+Reflexive⟩. A segment transformation then creates a node to which the noun *self/selves* is attached. These processes may be sketched out as follows:

Underlying Form

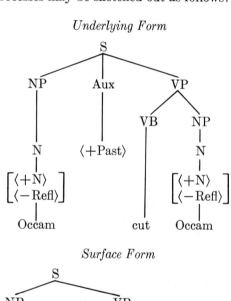

Surface Form

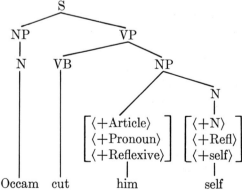

Algebraically, the reflexive transformation may be stated in this manner:

Reflexive Transformation:

$$X - NP - Y - NP - \qquad Z$$

S.D. $1 - 2 - 3 - 4 - \qquad 5 \Rightarrow$

S.C. $1 \qquad 2 \qquad 3 \qquad [+ \text{Reflexive}] \; 5$

It is appropriate to comment here that reflexive sentences such as "Be yourself" and "Be yourselves" are supportive evidence that *you* is in the underlying form of Imperative sentences. Thus "Imp you non-Past will be you" renders "Be yourself" and "Be yourselves."

The Complementizer Placement Transformation

We use the term COMPLEMENTIZER as a close parallel to the traditional term SUBORDINATOR. Our discussion is limited to these three complementizers:

(1) Clausal or Factive Complementizer: *that*
     The fact *that* mighty Casey struck out stunned Mudville.
(2) Infinitive Complementizer: *for . . . to*
     For mighty Casey *to* strike out stunned Mudville.
(3) Gerundive Complementizer: *'s . . . ing*
     Mighty Casey (*'s*) strik*ing* out stunned Mudville.

For many speakers of English the possessive (*'s*) part of the gerundive complementizer is deleted and thus does not appear in surface structures. As a matter of fact, the clausal complementizer (*that*) and the left-hand part of the tandem complementizers (*for*) and (*'s*) may be deleted for all speakers of English.

(4) The crowd knew *that* Casey would strike out.
(5) The crowd knew Casey would strike out.
(6) *For one* to swim is fun.
(7) To swim is fun.
(8) *One's* bathing should be done in private.
(9) Bathing should be done in private.

Peter S. Rosenbaum (1968:10) has pointed out that the appearance of a particular complementizer is apparently dependent upon the NOUN

HEAD. For example, the noun *opportunity* co-occurs with the infinitive (*for . . . to*) complementizer but not with the factive clausal (*that . . .*) complementizer.

(10)   The nation awaited the opportunity *to elect* a new president.

(11)   *The nation awaited the opportunity *that it elect* a new president.

Syntactic tense and number agreement are suppressed in infinitive and gerundive complements, but not in factive clausal complements:

(12)   The fact that Casey *strikes* out often annoys Mudville.

(13)   *For* mighty Casey *to strike* out often annoys Mudville.

(14)   Mighty Casey's *striking* out often annoys Mudville.

Both perfective and progressive aspect may occur in infinitive complements, but only perfective aspect occurs in gerundive complements.

(15)   *For* mighty Casey to *have struck* out often annoyed Mudville.

(16)   *For* mighty Casey to *be striking* out often annoyed Mudville.

(17)   Mighty Casey's *having struck* out often annoyed Mudville.

It has been observed by Rosenbaum (1968:11) that subjunctive (number suppressed) sentences occur with clausal (*that*) and infinitive (*for . . . to*) complements:

(18)   Marie Antoinette suggested *that* the prisoner *eat* nothing but cake. (subjunctive)

(19)   Marie Antoinette suggested *for him to eat nothing but cake*. (subjunctive)

Of course, clausal and infinitive complement sentences may be non-subjunctive:

(20)   Marie Antoinette suggested that he *eats* nothing but cake.

(21)   Marie Antoinette believes the prisoner *eats* nothing but cake.

(22)   Marie Antoinette believes the prisoner *to eat* nothing but cake.

The Question Transformation

Earlier we dealt with the tag question and the ordinary yes/no question. There are three other kinds of questions which we shall consider only in passing:

(a) Echo Questions: You don't say? He blew his cool?

(b) Direct WH-questions: *Who* will answer? *Where* have all the flowers gone? *Where* are the snows of yesteryear? *What* price glory? *When* will B.C. return? *Why* not peace, *why* war? *How* does a poem mean?

(c) Indirect Questions: Ulysses wondered *if he should go*. Ulysses wondered *whether he should go*. Ulysses wondered *should he go*?

Echo questions seem to have declarative structure but question intonation. They are often accompanied by raised eyebrows or a puzzled countenance.

In the derivation of DIRECT WH-QUESTIONS, we assume that the +WH feature replaces the Q(uestion) constituent. Notice the derivation of this surface structure: "Which toy would Christopher want?"

(1) Q Christopher would want +WH toy   (underlying form)
     Q would Christopher want +WH toy   (Aux-NP shift)
     +WH toy would Christopher want   (Q-replacement)
     Which toy would Christopher want?   (surface structure)

Now let us consider the derivation of this sentence: "Who would want the toy?"

(2) Q +WH would want the toy   (underlying form)
     Q would +WH want the toy   (Aux-NP shift)
     +WH would want the toy   (Q-replacement)
     Who would want the toy?   (surface structure)

This is an opportune time to digress briefly and examine the feature characterization of a number of WH-words. The forms *which* and *what* differ in what might be called their specificity. As we indicate below, *which* and *what* are non-definite articles whereas *who*, *where*, and *when* are nouns. Future analyses of English syntax will probably bear out our assumption that *what* is really a transformationally derived complex of *wh-* plus the preposition *-at*, and *which* is probably really a complex of *wh-* plus *-ilk* (the assumed underlying form of *each*). The Scots parallel form *whilk* and the German form *welch* tend to support this analysis. Moreover, closer future scrutiny needs to be given to the relationship between "what is he doing" and "he is a(t)-sleep" and "he is *at* work" and "he is *a(t)*-working." This interim feature analysis, however, is offered at the present time:

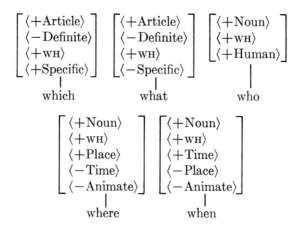

$$\begin{bmatrix} \langle+\text{Article}\rangle \\ \langle-\text{Definite}\rangle \\ \langle+\text{WH}\rangle \\ \langle+\text{Specific}\rangle \end{bmatrix} \quad \begin{bmatrix} \langle+\text{Article}\rangle \\ \langle-\text{Definite}\rangle \\ \langle+\text{WH}\rangle \\ \langle-\text{Specific}\rangle \end{bmatrix} \quad \begin{bmatrix} \langle+\text{Noun}\rangle \\ \langle+\text{WH}\rangle \\ \langle+\text{Human}\rangle \end{bmatrix}$$
$$\text{which} \qquad\qquad \text{what} \qquad\qquad \text{who}$$

$$\begin{bmatrix} \langle+\text{Noun}\rangle \\ \langle+\text{WH}\rangle \\ \langle+\text{Place}\rangle \\ \langle-\text{Time}\rangle \\ \langle-\text{Animate}\rangle \end{bmatrix} \quad \begin{bmatrix} \langle+\text{Noun}\rangle \\ \langle+\text{WH}\rangle \\ \langle+\text{Time}\rangle \\ \langle-\text{Place}\rangle \\ \langle-\text{Animate}\rangle \end{bmatrix}$$
$$\text{where} \qquad\qquad \text{when}$$

Embedded sentences as well as main sentences may be made into questions, the results being INDIRECT QUESTIONS. Note the difference between the sentence examples which follow.

(3)   Ulysses wondered, "Should I go?"

(4)   Ulysses wondered *if he should go.*

(5)   Ulysses wondered *whether he should go.*

(6)   Ulysses wondered *should he go.*

Rosenbaum (1968:12) has suggested that in (4) and (5) either *if* or *whether* has replaced the Q(uestion) constituent. In (6), of course, Q is deleted and ordinary Aux-NP shift has taken place. The form *whether* is most likely a complex of *wh-* plus *other*.

The Relative Clause Transformation

A "restricted" relative clause structure arises when a sentence is embedded into a noun phrase of this type:

This structure contrasts with sentence embedding of the "complement" type which we examined earlier:

To illustrate relative clause formation, let us embed (2) below into (1).

(1)   Icarus saw the comet.
(2)   The comet struck the earth.
(3)   *Icarus saw the comet which struck the earth.*

The underlying structure of (3) is that given below.

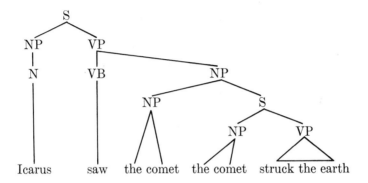

The RELATIVE CLAUSE transformation marks the repeated noun phrase (*the comet*) in the embedded sentence with +WH, which is the abstract form of a relative pronoun.

(4)   Icarus saw the comet (the comet struck the earth).
(5)   Icarus saw the comet (+WH comet struck the earth).

By a process unstated formally here, the repeated noun (*comet*) is deleted.

(6)   Icarus saw the comet (+WH Ø struck the earth).

A phonological process converts +WH into *which* rendering (7).

(7)   Icarus saw the comet *which* struck the earth.

By an alternate phonological process, the relative pronoun *that* is specified, and thus (7) is synonymous with (8).

(8)   Icarus saw the comet *that* struck the earth.

It is appropriate for us to mention here the fact that the relative pronoun *that* does not occur contiguous to the preposition *by* although the relative pronouns *which* and *who* do.

(9)   The comet *which* struck the earth was fiery red.
(10)   The comet *by which* the earth was struck was fiery red.
(11)   The comet *that* struck the earth was fiery red.
(12)   *The comet *by that* the earth was struck was fiery red.
(13)   The man *by whom* I was greeted smiled.

Many grammarians are of the opinion that relative clause structures are responsible for the so-called "attributive" adjective structures. Observe the synonymity of the following sentences:

(14)   The *old* leech-gatherer is plodding home.
(15)   The leech-gatherer *who is old* is plodding home.

The conventional transformational formulation for (14) and (15) is this:

(16)   The leech-gatherer (the leech-gatherer is old) is plodding home.
       (deep structure) ⇒

The leech-gatherer (+WH ∅ is old) is plodding home. (relativization and identical noun deletion)
       The leech-gatherer *who is old* is plodding home. (surface structure)

The relative pronoun (*who*) and the copula (*is*) can now be deleted, giving:
       The leech-gatherer *old* is plodding home.

The adjective transformation places *old* before the noun *leech-gatherer*.
       A complete grammar of English would illustrate in detail the difference between "non-interrogative" pronouns and "interrogative" pronouns. We have space only for a short but hopefully enlightening sketch. As is well known, these two types of pronouns are identical in pronunciation. Nonetheless, it is possible for one to distinguish between them. Let us assume with Jacobs and Rosenbaum (1968:209–10) that the Q(uestion) constituent is present in the deep structure of the interrogative sentence but not in the relative sentence. Thus (17) is the deep structure of (18), and (19) is the deep structure of (20).

(17) $_s$[the turkey who lived on the hill knew $_s$[Q the owl married the pussy cat TIME]$_s$]$_s$ (interrogative)
(18)   The turkey who lived on the hill knew *when* the owl married the pussy cat. (interrogative)
(19) $_s$[The turkey who lived on the hill wept TIME $_s$[the owl married the pussy cat]$_s$]$_s$ (non-interrogative)
(20)   The turkey who lived on the hill wept *when* the owl married the pussy cat. (non-interrogative)

The non-interrogative pronoun can be easily identified, since it and the embedded sentence in which it occurs may be front-shifted:

(21)   *When* the owl married the pussy cat, the turkey who lived on the hill wept.

On the other hand, the interrogative structure can be identified, too, since it is subject to the process of *clefting*:

(22)   W HAT the turkey who lived on the hill knew W AS *when the owl married the pussy cat.*

The CLEFT-PROCESS is a useful device for isolating noun phrases. Its general makeup can be seen by comparing the sentence pairs below.

(23)   (a) God created the world.
      (b) *What* God created *was* the world.
(24)   (a) Colderidge felt good vibes.
      (b) *What* Coleridge felt *were* good vibes.
(25)   (a) Amor vincit omnia.
      (b) *What* amor vincit *is* omnia.

Summary

The first part of Grammar II extended the notion of a feature analysis of English syntax in the form of *segment structure rules* that were introduced in Grammar I in connection with noun phrases. In Grammar II the *auxiliary constituent* and the *verb phrase constituent* were subjected to an extensive feature analysis, whereby the auxiliary constituent was marked with the feature $\langle +\text{Aux} \rangle$, which includes syntactic tense and auxiliary (helping) verbs, and whereby perfective aspect and progressive aspect as well as passive voice were included as features of the verb phrase constituent and the verbal constituent. Additionally, the traditional verb and adjective were collapsed under the heading *verbal*. We should recall that the traditional verb was marked as $\langle +\text{V} \rangle$ whereas the traditional adjective was marked $\langle -\text{V} \rangle$. Also, a division was made between *stative* and *non-stative* verbals.

The concept of a feature analysis of English syntax was extended to passive voice and to verb particles and prepositions. Next, several novel and some slightly familiar transformational processes were discussed: the *cyclic principle, extraposition, pronoun replacement, impera-*

*tives, tag questions, reflexivization, complementizer placement, question
formation, relative clause formation,* and the *cleft-process.*

Once the reader has grasped the order-making power of the feature
analysis of the first part of Grammar II, he will be ready to explore a
second, more novel part of Grammar II, which in the main extends into
the areas of pronouns and articles, predicate adjectives, conjunctions,
nonrestrictive relative clauses, comparatives, existential sentences, adverbs, and number agreement. The chapter then terminates in a sophisticated set of phrase structure and segment structure rules of a very
powerful and revealing nature.

Grammar II Amplified
Transformations and Formalism

In the preceding section of Grammar II we introduced the concept of
the cyclic principle for such transformations as extraposition and it-
deletion. We also provided a formal statement of these transformational
processes: extraposition, it-deletion, imperative, tag formation, and reflexivization. In addition we sought to differentiate relative pronouns from
interrogative pronouns, and we attempted to provide some insight into
the nature of wh-questions. Of course, we have by no means exhausted
the transformational study of English syntax; and, if the reader has a
fairly good grasp of the syntactic analyses presented thus far, he will
encounter little difficulty with the material which follows. We now
turn our attention to the noun phrase once again, specifically those
noun phrases which contain personal pronouns, definite and non-definite
articles, and demonstrative and possessive articles. These several forms
are generated by the pronoun and article transformations.

The Pronoun Transformation

In traditional grammar it was generally assumed that pronouns were
entities which replaced or stood for nouns; hence grammarians used the
term *pro* ("for") and *noun.* We suggest that pronouns replace entire
noun phrases; this is a key concept in this section.

Most English grammarians recognize at least three types of pronouns—ANAPHORIC, REFLEXIVE, RECIPROCAL:

(1) Anaphoric: Goliath thought *he* was invulnerable.
(2) Reflexive: Goliath thought *himself* to be invulnerable.

(3)   Reciprocal: The Gingham Dog and the Calico Cat ate *each other* (one another) up.

Anaphoric pronouns are derived from at least two sources. First, they may be present in the deep structure of a sentence. Secondly, they may arise through the pronoun transformation: ($-$Pronoun $\Rightarrow$ $+$Pronoun). If we examine (1) above, we notice that the anaphoric pronoun *he* is ambiguous, since it may refer to Goliath or to, say, Samson. If this were the case, there would be two different deep structures something like:

(4) ${}_s$[Goliath thought it ${}_s$[Goliath was invunerable]${}_s$]${}_s$

(5) ${}_s$[Goliath thought it ${}_s$[Samson was invulnerable]${}_s$]${}_s$

Ambiguous anaphoric pronouns can be clarified by the use of appositives:

(6)   Goliath thought that he, Goliath, was invulnerable.

(7)   Goliath thought that he, Samson, was invulnerable.

As we demonstrated earlier (p. 114), reflexive pronouns arise when two co-referential nouns appear within the same simple sentence, as when "Occam cut Occam" $\Rightarrow$ "Occam cut himself." The transformational processes of complementizer placement, complementizer deletion, pronoun replacement, and reflexivization are involved in the derivation of (2) above: "Goliath thought himself to be invulnerable."

(8) ${}_s$[Goliath thought it ${}_s$[for Goliath to be invulnerable]${}_s$]${}_s$
      Goliath thought it $\emptyset$ Goliath to be invulnerable
      Goliath thought $\emptyset$ Goliath to be invulnerable
      Goliath thought Goliath   to be invulnerable
      Goliath thought himself   to be invulnerable

Moreover, "Goliath thought himself to be invulnerable" may be further reduced to "Goliath thought himself invulnerable."

We will demonstrate in a later section (p. 136) that the derivation of reciprocal pronouns (*each other, one another*) hinges on processes of conjunction.

In an interesting and insightful analysis, Paul Postal (1966) has demonstrated that pronouns are nouns in underlying structures and articles in surface structures. What is more, pronouns replace entire noun phrases rather than just nouns. In addition, pronouns are $\langle+$Definite$\rangle$ articles. For example, in formulaic sentences such as "X $+$ BE $+$ Y" (Predicate nominative sentences), if "X" is $\langle+$Definite$\rangle$ then "Y" must be $\langle+$Definite$\rangle$:

(9)   *The key* is *Chuck's (key).*

(10)   *These pictures* are *David's (pictures).*

(11)   *That cat* is *Doug's cat.*

(12)   **A key* is *Chuck's (key).*

(13)   **Pictures* are *David's (pictures).*

(14)   **Cat* is *Doug's (cat).*

(15)   *It* is *Chuck's* (key).

(16)   *They* are *David's* (pictures).

(17)   *It* is *Doug's* (cat).

In essence we are claiming that articles and pronouns are features of nouns much like such features as animate/non-animate, human/non-human, etc. Thus, the underlying structure of the noun phrase *the man* would be:

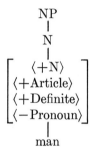

The ARTICLE SEGMENTALIZATION transformation creates an article segment to the left of the noun phrase:

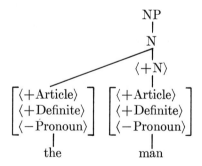

Articles may be subclassified into ⟨+Definite/−Definite⟩, ⟨+Demonstrative/−Demonstrative⟩ (pointing/non-pointing), ⟨+Proximal/−Proximal⟩ (near/far) and ⟨+Plural/−Plural⟩ (plural/singular). Non-definite articles may be ⟨+WH/−WH⟩. The chart below schematizes various kinds of articles.

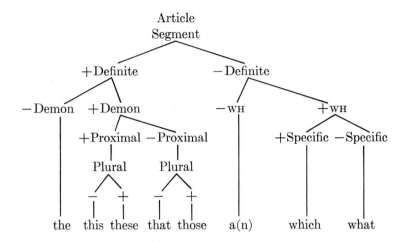

In the analysis of pronouns and articles made by Postal, some very convincing arguments are presented in favor of including the form *one* in the deep structure. To put it simply, the suggestion is, for example, that *he-one/they-ones/we-ones/you-ones* underlie *he/they/we/you*. This would explain *we-ones* and *you-ones* popularly spelled *we'uns* and *you'uns* or *youse*. What is more, such an analysis removes the cloak of mystery from the possessive form *mine* if it is to be derived from *my-one* or *me-one*. There is also a very good possibility that *my own* is a phonological variant of *my-one*.

Thus, the derivation of pronouns is really much like the derivation of articles. For example, *he* may be derived as follows.

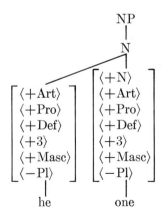

In the operation above, the article segment has been created, and the relevant feature information is copied from the +Noun segment. Below, the ⟨+Noun⟩ segment is deleted.

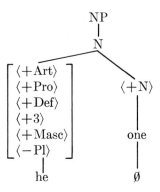

As we have demonstrated, then, pronouns are nouns in the deep structure and articles in the surface structure. Also, pronouns replace entire noun phrases. To further illustrate this last claim, notice that the possessive −s is suffixed not just to nouns but to noun phrases, as in:

(18) *The man on the corner's* hat blew off.

(19) *His* hat blew off. (he + -s → his)

The observation that pronouns are nouns in the deep structure and articles in the surface structure explains a number of hitherto obscure phenomena. For example, it provides a reason for mutual exclusiveness of forms like *the, this* and *he* within the same phrase; that is, English will tolerate only one ⟨+Definite⟩ form per phrase per noun. Hence, "*You students* should read more" occurs to the exclusion of "**The you students* should read more." The preceding analysis then accounts for data italicized below.

a. *You students* should read between the lines. (Article + Noun)

b. *We teachers* should lecture better. (Article + Noun)

c. Clark Kent was really a *he-man*.

d. The culprit was a *she-wolf*.

e. *We'uns* prefer store-bought bread. (we ones)

f. What do you'uns (youse) prefer? (you ones)

g. That's *his'n*, this is *her'n*, and *them('n)* are *your'n*. (his one, her one, them ones, your ones)

h. This is *my'n*. (my one, my own, mine)

i. He should do it *his own self*. (his one self)

j. They should do it *their own selves*.

k. They should do it *themselves*.

On the facing page is a feature description of the personal article-pronouns of modern academic English.

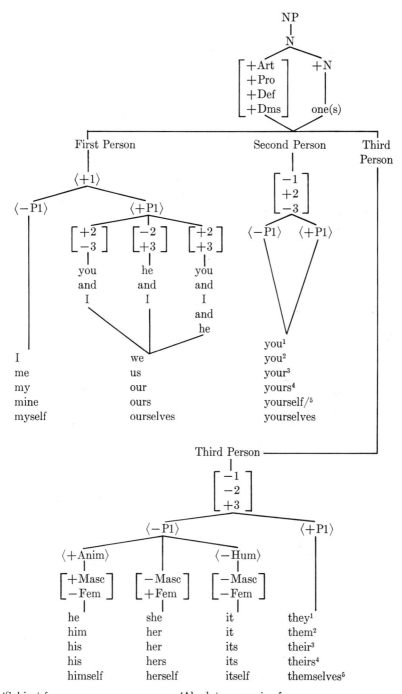

¹Subject forms
²Object forms
³Possessive forms

⁴Absolute possessive forms
⁵Reflexive forms

Exercises

1.   Interrogative noun phrases arise when an underlying sentence contains the Q(uestion) constituent and the noun phrase is marked ⟨+WH⟩. Let us suppose the existence of this prose description:

> There is a house in New Orleans, which is called the Rising Sun, which is run by Madame Bonte, and which opens promptly at six p.m.

Let us also suppose the existence of the following question sentences:

    a.   *Which house* is called the Rising Sun?
    b.   *What house* is called the Rising Sun?
    c.   *Who* runs the house called Rising Sun?
    d.   *Where* is the house called Rising Sun?
    e.   *When* does the Rising Sun open?

Match the feature descriptions below with the underscored interrogative descriptions above.

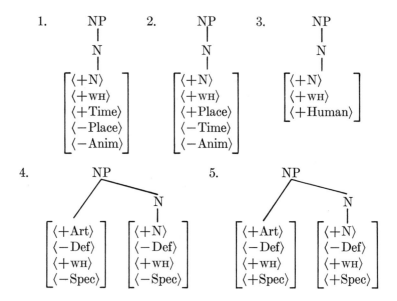

2.   Construct feature segments like those in Exercise 1 for these English formatives: *the, this, that, these, those.*

    Exercises 3 through 6 immediately below are fairly sophisticated and require the aid of someone who knows German or French or Spanish as well as English. A useful beginning might be to draw a surface structure diagram of the corresponding English analogue sentences and then to superimpose the foreign language examples upon them. For example, 3a, 4a, 5a, and 6a might be analyzed as follows:

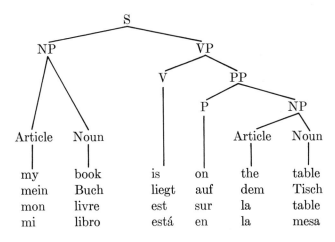

From this point on, the procedure must be determined by the individual instructor. However, let us suggest that the next step might involve, say, English "Mine is on the table" and German *Meines liegt auf dem Tisch* and French *Le mien est sur la table,* and a discussion of *mine* with *meines* and *le mien,* and so on.

3. Speculate on the transformational derivation of these English sentences.

    a. My book is on the table.
    b. My own book is on the table.
    c. Mine is on the table.
    d. The book which is my own is on the table.
    e. The book which is mine is on the table.

4. Speculate on the transformational derivation of these German sentences.

    a. Mein Buch liegt auf dem Tisch.
    b. Mein eigenes Buch liegt auf dem Tisch.
    c. Meines liegt auf dem Tisch.
    d. Das Buch das mir gehört liegt auf dem Tisch.
    e. Das mir gehörige Buch liegt auf dem Tisch.
    f. Das mir gehörende Buch liegt auf dem Tisch.

g. Das meine (Buch) liegt auf dem Tisch.

h. Das meinige (Buch) liegt auf dem Tisch.

5. Speculate on the transformational derivation of these French sentences.

    a. Mon livre est sur la table.

    b. Le mien est sur la table.

    c. Ce livre qui est le mien est sur la table.

    d. Ce livre, qui est à moi, est sur la table.

6. Speculate on the transformational derivation of these Spanish sentences.

    a. Mi libro está en (sobre) la mesa.

    b. El libro mío está en (sobre) la mesa.

    c. El mío está en (sobre) la mesa.

    d. El libro que es el mío está en (sobre) la mesa.

    e. Ese libro que es el mío está en (sobre) la mesa.

7. Assume that there is a so-called case transformation ($-$Case $\Rightarrow$ $+$Case) which relates the following pairs of pronouns: *I/me, you/you, he/him, she/her, it/it, we/us, they/them.* Construct feature segments for these various pronouns. Assume that the left-hand pronoun is $\langle -$Case$\rangle$ and the right-hand $\langle +$Case$\rangle$.

8. Assume that German *der* is made up of the $\langle +$Definite$\rangle$ article *d-* and the third person masculine pronoun *-er* and that *ein* is the equivalent of English *a(n)* and *one.* Comment on the article, pronoun, and inflectional endings in these German sentences.

    a. Der dumme Esel ist immer ein dummer Esel.

    b. The dumb (jack)ass is always a dumb (jack)ass.

    c. Der Dumme ist immer Ein Dummer.

    d. The dumb (one) is always a dumb (one).

The Predicate Adjective Transformation

In an earlier section we suggested that "attributive" adjectives (those which precede nouns) derive from embedded sentences which are rel-

ativized and which undergo "relative-be" deletion and adjective placement. For example, "The tall giant taunted David" is derived as follows.

(1) s[The giant s[The giant is tall]s   taunted David]s

     The giant +wh Ø is tall taunted David ⇒
     The giant who   is tall taunted David ⇒
     The giant Ø   is tall taunted David ⇒
     The giant   Ø tall taunted David ⇒
     The tall giant taunted David.

John Robert Ross (1966a) has suggested that at some stage in their
derivation predicate adjectives are noun phrases. In part, the fact that
predicate adjectives, like predicate nominatives, are both subject to
the "cleft" process suggests that such an analysis is tenable. You
will recall that the "cleft" process isolates noun phrases:

(2) Jack climbed *the beanstalk.* ⇒
(3) What Jack climbed was *the beanstalk.*
(4) Goliath was *haughty.* ⇒
(5) What Goliath was was *haughty.*

Let us assume that the underlying form of (4) is this:

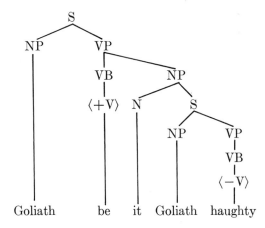

Notice that (4) has an underlying structure much like (6) below.

(4) s[Goliath be it s[Goliath haughty]s]s
(6) s[Goliath try it s[Goliath laugh]s]s

In the subsequent derivation of these sentences, the identical noun

(*Goliath*) is deleted along with the noun head (*it*). The *for* complementizer is deleted from (6). The two sentences above appear in their surface structure as:

(7)   Goliath was haughty.
(8)   Goliath tried to laugh.

After the deletion of *it* and *Goliath* from (4), the sentence has the intermediate structure below:

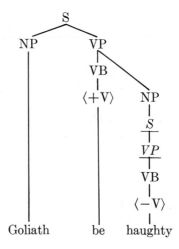

By a process known as tree-pruning, the underscored nodes above are deleted and the verbal (*haughty*) is adjoined under the VP node in the main sentence.

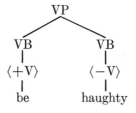

By other incidental processes, the surface structure below is achieved.

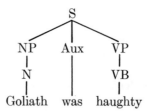

Exercises

1. Jacobs and Rosenbaum (1968:113) suggest that the copula (*be*) in sentences of the predicate nominative type is "a peculiar type of transitive verb." Paralleling German *Ich bin es* and French *C'est moi*, Old English had *Ic eom hit* = "I am it" as a response to "Who's there?" If the object forms of pronouns follow transitive verbs, then what is the natural response in Modern English to this question?

    a. It's me.
    b. It is I.
    c. It's us.
    d. It is we.

2. In Modern German, attributive adjectives agree in number and person with the article and noun. Adjectives as well may be nominalized (in effect, the noun is simply deleted) in which case they, like other nouns in German, are capitalized. However, predicate adjectives are not inflected. Speculate on the transformational derivation of these German sentences.

    a. Der Mann ist ehrlich.
    b. Der Mann ist ehrlich und bleibt ehrlich.
    c. Der ehrliche Mann steht jeden Morgen früh auf.
    d. Ein ehrlicher Mann steht jeden Morgen früh auf.
    e. Der Ehrliche steht jeden Morgen früh auf.
    f. Ein Ehrlicher steht jeden Morgen früh auf.
    g. Ein ehrlicher Mann ist ein guter Mann.
    h. Ein Ehrlicher ist auch ein Guter.

The Conjunction Transformation

In this section we distinguish between conjunction of full sentences and conjunction of constituents of sentences. Thus (3) is an example of sentence conjunction and (4) is one of phrasal conjunction.

(1) Jack went up the hill.
(2) Jill went up the hill.
(3) Jack went up the hill and Jill went up the hill.
(4) Jack and Jill went up the hill.

Surface structure diagrams of these sentences are handled in this manner:

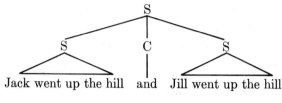

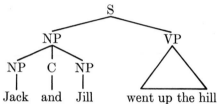

Of course, constituents other than subject noun phrases can be conjoined.

(5) Little Miss Muffett was *sitting on her tuffet* and *eating curds.* (Conjoined verb phrases)

(6) Little Boy Blue *could and would* not blow his horn. (Conjoined modals)

(7) Mary's garden grew with *silver bells and cockle-shells.* (Conjoined objects of a preposition)

(8) Jack the Candle Jumper was *nimble and quick.* (Conjoined predicate adjectives)

The conjoining of subsentence units has been called PHRASAL CONJUNCTION by Lakoff and Peters (1966). We present a simplified and abbreviated sketch of their analysis of conjunction.[1]

(9)   Jack and Jill went up the hill together.   phrasal

(10) Jack went up the hill with Jill.   conjunction

(11) Both Jack and Jill went up the hill.   sentence

(12) Jack went up the hill and Jill went up the hill. conjunction

It is instructive to observe the stages of derivation of (10) above. We assume by an unstated convention that the noun phrases to be conjoined are each marked by *and,* the second instance of which is replaced by *with.* Next, by conjunct movement *with Jill* is placed to the extreme right of the sentence. Finally, initial *and* is deleted:

[1]By permission of the authors and of the President and Fellows of Harvard College.

(13) (a) And Jack *and Jill* went up the hill

     (b) And Jack *with Jill* went up the hill

     (c) And Jack went up the hill *with Jill*

     (d) Ø Jack went up the hill with Jill

     (e) Jack went up the hill with Jill.

Let us recall that this grammar recognizes four distinct types of verbals:

(14) (a) go: +Verb, −Stative

     (b) recognize: +Verb, +Stative

     (c) honest: −Verb, −Stative

     (d) intelligent: −Verb, +Stative

In general, verbals which carry the feature ⟨+Stative⟩ do not appear in underlying conjoined noun phrases. Thus (17) and (18) are not paraphrases of (15) and (16).

(15) (a) Jack recognized the danger and Jill recognized the danger.

     (b) Jack was intelligent and Jill was intelligent.

(16) (a) Jack and Jill recognized the danger.

     (b) Jack and Jill were intelligent.

(17) (a) *Jack and Jill recognized the danger together.

     (b) *Jack and Jill were intelligent together.

(18) (a) *Jack recognized the danger with Jill.

     (b) *Jack was intelligent with Jill.

It is now necessary to restrict the generalization above as follows: ⟨+Stative⟩ verbs and adjectives do not occur with conjoined underlying subjects unless the verbal is a verb of possession (*have, own, possess*) or an adjective of measure (*heavy, light, slow, fast*). Some examples appear below.

(19) Peter and his wife own a house.

(20) Peter owns a house with his wife.

(21) Jack and his wife were heavy.

(22) Monsieur and Madame Curie were intelligent.

(23) How heavy were Jack and his wife?

(24) How intelligent were Monsieur and Madame Curie?

A certain class of ⟨−Stative⟩ verbs (*agree, confer, remonstrate*) obligatorily take conjoined noun phrases:

(25)   The professor agreed with the students.
(26)   The president conferred with the regents.
(27)   The regents remonstrated with the deans.

As we have already seen in this section, *and* is sometimes replaced by *with*. It seems likely that in the sentences below *and* is replaced by *to* to render a positive connotation and by *from* to render a negative connotation.

(28)   Sugar is similar to salt. (And sugar and salt be similar)
(29)   Cats are different from dogs. (And cats and dogs be different)
(30)   Cats differ from dogs. (And cats and dogs differ)

Presumably reciprocal pronouns (*each other, one another*) arise when a sentence with conjoined noun phrases is conjoined to a second sentence which states its converse, as in "Sugar and salt are similar and salt and sugar are similar" ⟹ "Sugar and salt are similar to each other (one another)." As Lakoff and Peters have observed, the reciprocal pronoun in the preceding sentence is redundant in a way that it is not in this sentence:

(31)   Johann and Guillaume slew each other.

Exercises

1.   How would you transformationally derive these surface structures?

   a.   Dallas is near (to) Ft. Worth.
   b.   Dallas is far from El Paso.

2.   How are these sentences related to (la) and (lb) above?

   a.   Dallas's nearness to Ft. Worth can be seen on a map.
   b.   Dallas's farness from El Paso can be seen on a map.

3.   Comment on the form and meaning of these sentences:

   a.   Salt's similarity to sugar is not surprising.
   b.   The fact that salt is similar to sugar is not surprising.

c. For salt to resemble sugar is not surprising.

d. Salt's resembling sugar is not surprising.

e. For salt to be similar to sugar is not surprising.

f. The fact that salt resembles sugar is not surprising.

4. Comment on the occurrence of *between* with *resemble* and *agree*.

a. The resemblance *between* Peter and Jane is what one would expect *between* brother and sister.

b. The agreement *between* parent and child is known as the generation gap.

The Nonrestrictive Relative Clause Transformation

The parenthetical nature of nonrestrictive relative clauses suggests that they be derived by conjunctive processes. For example, it seems reasonable to assume that "David, who was brave, slew Goliath" derives from two underlying independent sentences:

(1) David was brave.

(2) David slew Goliath.

(3) David, and David was brave, slew Goliath.   (Sentence conjunction)

(4) David, who was brave, slew Goliath.   (Relative clause formation)

One might assume that the relationship between (3) and (4) is as follows.

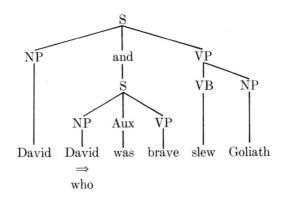

The Comparative Transformation

Earlier in this grammar we placed the traditional "verb" and "adjective" under the single label "verbal." Also we made a distinction between verbals which are marked for syntactic tense $\langle +\text{Past}/-\text{Past}\rangle$ and verbals marked for "degree" (*-er/-est, more/most*) with the features $\langle +\text{Verb}\rangle$ and $\langle -\text{Verb}\rangle$ respectively.

John Robert Ross (1966b) has suggested that the derivation of the comparative degree is something like the following.

(1)   Goliath was tall to a degree to which David was not tall.   (Informal underlying form) $\Rightarrow$

(2)   Goliath was taller than David was.

The steps of the transformation are these:

a.   The comparative affix *-er* is placed to the immediate right of *tall*.

b.   The string *to a degree to* is deleted.

c.   *Than* replaces *which*.

d.   *Not tall* is deleted.

e.   Optionally, the copula (*be*) is deleted.

Exercises

1.   What observations can be made about the following sentences, which might be called "iterative"?

a.   The earth got more and more polluted.

b.   The convalescent got better, and better, and better.

c.   The space capsule grew colder, and colder, and colder.

d.   The space capsule grew cold, and more cold, and more, and more, and more cold, until . . .

e.   The space capsule grew cooler, and cooler, and cooler . . .

2.   Comment on these surface structures.

a.   David was a youth than who(m) Goliath was taller.

b.   David was a youth who(m) Goliath was taller than.

c.   Goliath was a giant who(m) David was not as tall as.

d. Goliath was a giant who(m) David was shorter than.

e. Goliath was a giant than who (m) David was shorter.

The Existential It/There Transformation

The conventional transformational derivation for "existential" sentences assumes an underlying form with a subject noun phrase that is ⟨−Definite⟩ as in (1) and (2), which can be transformed into (3) and (4).

(1) No soap is in the bathroom.

(2) Five patients are in the waiting room.

(3) There is no soap in the bathroom/It is no soap in the bathroom.

(4) There is/are five patients in the waiting room/It is five patients in the waiting room.

Although modern German speakers make a distinction between a ⟨+/ −Plural⟩ form of the copula in existential sentences, not all modern English speakers do. The corresponding German analogues to (1–4) illustrate this.

(5) Keine Seife *ist* in dem Badezimmer.

(6) Fünf Patienten *sind* in dem Wartezimmer.

(7) *Es ist* keine Seife in dem Badezimmer.

(8) *Es sind* fünf Patienten in dem Wartezimmer.

As the examples above indicate, the *es ist/es sind* form is used in German to denote "existence" within limited confines. Existence of a more general type is indicated by *es gibt* (it gives) plus the accusative case.

(9) Es gibt Löwen in Afrika. (There are lions in Africa.)

(10) Es gibt Leute, die nicht lächeln. (There are people who don't smile.)

Exercises

1. Comment on the transformational derivation of these English and German sentences.

   a. There are only two chairs in this room.

   b. Nur zwei Stühle sind in diesem Zimmer.

    c. Es ist nur zwei Stühle in diesem Zimmer.

    d. The people came out of their houses.

    e. Die Leute kamen aus ihren Häusern.

    f. Es kamen die Leute aus ihren Häusern.

2. Compare the somewhat archaic English sentences with the modern German sentences:

    a. I am *loath* to do it.

    b. I am *lief* to do it.

    c. Es tut mir *leid*. (I am sorry.)

    d. Es ist mir *lieb*. (I am glad.)

    e. Es tut mir *leid* um die arme Frau. (I am sorry for the poor woman.)

    f. Die arme Frau tut mir *leid*. (I am sorry for the poor woman.)

3. Comment on the differences between the way German and English express *like*, *dislike*, *please*, and *displease*.

    a. Flowers please me.

    b. Blumen gefallen mir.

    c. I like flowers.

    d. Ich mag Blumen.

    e. Ich habe Blumen gern.

    f. Flowers displease me.

    g. Blumen gefallen mir nicht.

    h. I don't like flowers.

    i. Ich mag Blumen nicht.

    j. Ich habe Blumen nicht gern.

The Adverb Transformation

Perhaps we should state at the very outset that "adverbs" need not be marked with terminal *-ly* to be so classified. Conversely, not all words ending in *-ly* are adverbs.

(1) Mercury could run *fast*.

(2) A guillotine cuts the head *clean* off.

(3) Goethe said that he disapproved of *sickly* German romances.

(4) Jupiter and Juno were not *happily* married.

(5) Chanticleer did not listen to Pertelote *intently*.

(6) It was *hard* for Miles to know what to say to Priscilla.

(7) Miles *hardly* knew what to say to Priscilla.

This and other data have led many transformational linguists to believe that the great majority of so-called adverbs are most economically derived from underlying adjectives (+Verbal, −Verb) in complement sentences. Observe the data below.

(8) *It is fortunate* for Atlas that he did not drop the globe.

(9) *It is fortunate* for us that Atlas did not drop the globe.

(10) *Fortunately* for Atlas, he did not drop the globe.

(11) *Fortunately* for us, Atlas did not drop the globe.

(12) *Fortunately*, Atlas did not drop the globe.

(13) Atlas did not drop the globe, *fortunately*.

Sentences (12) and (13) are ambiguous and derive from either (8) or (9) depending on the interpretation one gives them.

One fact about adverbs marked with *-ly* is clear. The suffix *-ly* both historically and probably contemporaneously derives from *ilk* and its metathesized (cf. Chapter 5) variant *lik(e)*: *hard-like/hardly; quick like a rabbit/quickly as a rabbit; fortunate-like/fortunately*.

Exercises

1. Comment on the grammatical relationship between *valor, valiant, valiantly* on the one hand and *troops* and *Hannibal* on the other.

    a. The troops marched up the hill with valor.

    b. The valiant troops marched up the hill.

    c. The troops marched up the hill valiantly.

    d. Valiantly, the troops marched up the hill.

    e. Hannibal commanded the troops to march up the hill with valor/valiantly.

    f. Hannibal commanded the troops to valiantly march up the hill.

    g. Hannibal commanded the troops to march up the hill valiantly/with valor.

    h. With valor/valiantly Hannibal commanded the troops to march up the hill.

    i.   Hannibal valiantly commanded the troops to march up the hill.

2. Comment on the syntax of *(on) Monday* in these sentences.

    a.   They made it in the workroom (on) Monday.
    b.   (On) Monday, they made it in the workroom.
    c.   It was (on) Monday that they made it in the workroom.

3. Comment on the syntax of *good, well,* and *bad* in these sentences.

    a.   The naïve youth said that he didn't know how *good* girls felt.
    b.   The naïve youth said that he didn't know how *well* girls felt.
    c.   Shyly, the youth asked: "Do you feel *well*?"
    d.   Shyly, the youth asked: "Do you feel *good?*"
    e.   Bad girls feel good.
    f.   Good girls feel bad.
    g.   Bad girls feel bad.
    h.   Good girls feel good.
    i.   Bad girls feel, good girls don't.
    j.   Bad girls feel good girls don't.

The Number Agreement Transformation

This grammar of English accounts for number agreement transformationally by one or more of the following processes.

    a.   Auxiliary Number Agreement
    b.   Verbal Number Agreement
    c.   Verbal Affix Segmentalization
    d.   Auxiliary Incorporation

The AUXILIARY NUMBER AGREEMENT transformation copies (in many, though not all, dialects of English) grammatical person(+1, +2, +3) and number (+Plural/−Plural) information from the subject noun phrase onto the auxiliary segment just in case the auxiliary segment does not contain ⟨+Modal⟩.

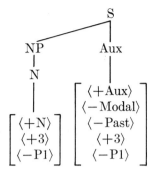

In the event that the auxiliary constituent contains no verb, the person, number, and tense features are copied onto the verbal segment.

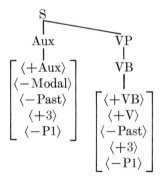

The VERBAL AFFIX SEGMENTALIZATION transformation creates a segment onto which the tense, person, and number information is copied, as in "The cow *jumps* over the moon."

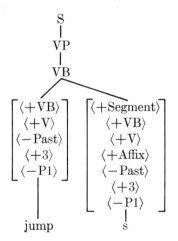

As the diagrams below indicate, the progressive and passive copula (*be*) and perfective *have* can be incorporated into the auxiliary constituent if there is no modal verb or emphatic verb (*do*) as in these sentences:

(1)   The   cow   *is jumping*   over   the   moon.

(2)   The cow *has jumped* over the moon.

(3)   The Milky Way *was created* by a comet-stricken cow.

(4)   The cow *do(es) jump* over the moon.

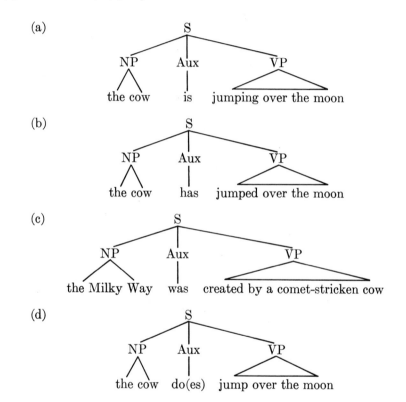

Exercises

1.   For some speakers of English the auxiliary agreement rule does not operate. Comment on the data below.

    a.   He is here on Saturday(s).

    b.   He does be here on Saturday(s).

    c.   He do be here on Saturday(s).

2.   Compare the transformational derivation of these sentences.

     a.   He does be being honest.
     b.   He do be being honest.
     c.   He do be tall.
     d.   He doesn't be being honest.
     e.   He don't be being honest.
     f.   He don't be tall.

3.   There is good reason to believe that certain dialects of modern English have developed a rule by which inflectional -*s* may be deleted from auxiliary verbs, just in case the auxiliary verb is contracted as when *is* or *has* become '*s*. Comment on the data below.

     a.   He'*s* tall, I know he *is*.
     b.   He'*s* honest, I know he *is*.
     c.   He'*s* being honest, I know he *is*.
     d.   He'*s* gone, I know he *has*.
     e.   He tall, I know he *is*.
     f.   He honest, I know he *is*.
     g.   He being honest, I know he *is*.
     h.   He gone, I know he *has*.

Summary

In this section, initially, we set out to suggest that personal pronouns and the several kinds of articles are most economically derived as features, such as ⟨+article⟩, ⟨+pronoun⟩, ⟨+demonstrative⟩ and so forth, on noun phrases. Such an analysis provides a partial explanation for one's natural inclination to consider such formatives as *the, that, this, my, our, your* as basic modifiers of nouns. Hence, the traditional terms "demonstrative adjective" or "limiting adjective" for *that, this* and the term "possessive adjective" for *my, our, your* are somewhat appropriate.

     Serious analysis was also given to the deep structure difference between attributive adjectives (+VB, −V) that precede nouns and predicate adjectives that follow some form of the copula (*be, is, are, was, am, been, being*). Our analysis suggested that attributive adjectives derive from truncated relative clauses, whereas predicate adjectives derive from truncated complement sentences. Unfortunately, at the present writing, knowledge of the derivation of predicate nominatives ("Lord Byron was *an alleged rake*") is lacking, so we were not able to provide insight into these somewhat parallel structures.

In the part of the chapter devoted to the conjunction transformation, we differentiated between the collocation (conjoining) of full sentences and the collocation of the constituents of sentences (phrasal conjunction). Special attention was given to conjunction of nouns and conjunction of verbals, and there was some brief speculation on the conjunctive nature of the nonrestrictive relative clause construction. This was followed by some brief comments on comparatives and the existential *it/there* transformation. The section closes with some comments on adverbs, which suggest that they are to be derived from underlying adjectives (+VB, −V). Last but not least, we presented an analysis of the number agreement transformation for modern academic English.

Conclusion

A *natural language* is a set of well-formed sentences. A *sentence* is a device for pairing a deep structure meaning with at least one and possibly many surface structure pronunciations. Typically, the sentences which human beings use are novel; that is, they are not linguistic generalizations of earlier sentences. This fact suggests that linguistic ability is very much like mathematical ability in that in both systems infinite use is made of finite means. For example, in mathematics, the cipher zero functions as a recursive element as in "1" versus "10" versus "100" versus 1000 and so on. In like manner, the notion "sentence" is recursive and can occur indefinitely. Since a sentence may have infinitely embedded elements within it, it follows that there is no longest sentence inasmuch as one can in theory make a sentence longer, and longer, and longer, and longer, and longer.

The knowledge that a speaker has about his native language is called *linguistic competence*, which among other things includes:

a. the ability to recognize an infinite number of well-formed sentences and the ability to reject ill-formed sentences.

b. the ability to recognize scales of *grammaticality*, as well as the ability to make judgments about the appropriateness or acceptability of utterances such as "Our father who art in heaven" versus "Our devil who art in hell."

c. the ability to recognize sentence *synonymy*.

d. the ability to recognize sentence *paraphrase.*

e. the ability to recognize sentence *ambiguity.*

A person's manifestation of his native language is called linguistic performance, which unlike competence is subject to certain physical limitations; that is, one must pause for food and sleep; furthermore, sore throats, larynectomies, missing teeth, and swollen tongues affect linguistic performance. Another limitation is memory span; hence, there is a limit on the depth of sentence embedding which one is allowed in oral discourse. Seemingly "The cow the boy my father knew bought died" overtaxes at first hearing even the most agile short-term memory.

The emphasis of transformational-generative grammar is on description and explanation rather than on prescription and parochialism. The term *generative* means that the grammar is self-interpretive; that is, nothing is left to the imagination of the user or reader of the description. It is all laid out in ordered fashion much like a mathematical algorithm.

Our discussion covered several aspects of a typical transformational-generative grammar. In part we found the grammar to consist of at least the following:

a. a set of *phrase structure rules* which assign a structural description to any and all sentences.

b. a set of *segment structure rules* which subcategorize major syntactic categories such as noun, auxiliary verb, and main verb.

c. a set of *transformations* which while preserving meaning convert *deep structures* into *surface structures.* What is more, we identified three elementary types of transformations which appear to be universal.

d. a set of *phonological rules* (examined in detail in the next chapter) which convert syntactic surface structures into pronounceable units for a single dialect or speech style or into a set of related pronunciations for a language.

e. a set of *lexical rules* which state the syntactic and semantic properties of all units (formatives, morphemes) of the language.

f. a set of *orthographic rules* for matching surface structure pronunciations with deep structure meanings.

Here is a schematic outline of the major components of a transformational-generative grammar.

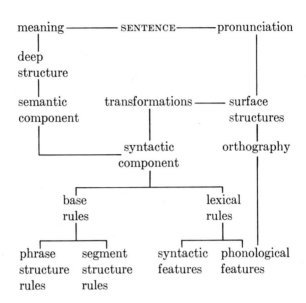

We conclude this chapter with a very sophisticated set of illustrative phrase structure and segment structure rules which have been adapted from *English IBM Grammar II*. These are a summary and to some extent a slight refinement of rules which we have mentioned and anticipated in this chapter.

References

Campbell, R. N., and R. J. Wales. "Comparative Structures in English." *Journal of Linguistics*, 5, No. 2 (1969), 215–51.

Chomsky, Noam. *Syntactic Structures*. The Hague: Mouton and Co., 1957.

_____. "Review of Skinner's *Verbal Behavior*." *Language*, 35, No. 1 (1959), 26–58.

_____. *Aspects of the Theory of Syntax*. Cambridge, Massachusetts: MIT. Press, 1965.

_____. *Cartesian Linguistics*. New York: Harper and Row, 1968.

_____. "Remarks on Nominalization." In Jacobs and Rosenbaum (1970).

_____, and Morris Halle. *The Sound Pattern of English*. New York: Harper and Row, 1968.

Fasold, Ralph. "Tense and the Form *BE* in Black English." *Language*, 45, No. 4 (1969), 763–76.

Hall, R. M. R., and Beatrice L. Hall. "The 'Double'-Negative: A Non-Problem." *The Florida Foreign Language Reporter*, 7, No. 1 (Spring/Summer 1969), 113–15.

Halle, Morris, and S. J. Keyser. *English Stress.* New York: Harper and Row, 1971.

Hasegawa, Kinsuke. "The Passive Construction in English." *Language,* 44, No. 2 (1968), 230–43.

Huddleston, Rodney. "More on the English Comparative." *Journal of Linguistics,* 3, No. 1 (1967), 91–102.

_____. "Some Observations on Tense and Deixis." *Language,* 45, No. 4 (1969), 777–806.

Jacobs, Roderick A., and Peter S. Rosenbaum. *English Transformational Grammar.* Waltham, Massachusetts: Blaisdell [Xerox] Publishing Company, 1968.

_____, eds. *Readings in English Transforational Grammar.* Waltham, Massachusetts: Blaisdell [Xerox] Publishing Company, 1970.

_____. *Transformations, Style, and Meaning.* Waltham, Massachusetts: Xerox Publishing Company, 1971.

Katz, Jerrold J., and Jerry A. Fodor. "The Structure of a Semantic Theory." *Language,* 39, No. 2 (1963), 170–210.

Labov, William. "Contraction, Deletion, and Inherent Variability of the English Copula." *Language,* 45, No. 4 (1969), 715–62.

_____. *The Study of Non-Standard English.* Champaign, Illinois: NCTE, 1970.

Lakoff, George, and Stanley Peters. "Phrasal Conjunction and Symmetric Predicates." Mathematical Linguistics and Automatic Translation, Harvard Computation Laboratory Report No. NSF-17 (1966), pp. VI-1 to VI-49. Reprinted in Reibel and Schane.

Langacker, Ronald W. *Language and Its Structure.* New York: Harcourt, Brace, and World, 1967.

Lees, R. B., and E. S. Klima. "Rules for English Pronominalization." *Language,* 39, No. 1 (1963), 17–28. Reprinted in Reibel and Schane.

Liles, Bruce. *An Introductory Transformational Grammar.* Englewood Cliffs, New Jersey: Prentice-Hall, 1971.

Postal, Paul. "On So-Called 'Pronouns' in English." *19th Monograph on Languages and Linguistics.* Washington, D.C.: Georgetown University Press, 1966. Reprinted in Reibel and Schane.

Reibel, David A., and Sanford A. Schane, eds. *Modern Studies in English.* Englewood Cliffs, New Jersey: Prentice-Hall, 1969.

Rosenbaum, Peter S. "On the Role of Linguistics in the Teaching of English." *Harvard Educational Review,* 35, No. 3 (Summer, 1965), 332–48.

_____. *English Grammar II,* RC 2070. Yorktown Heights, New York: IBM. Corporation, 1968.

Ross, John Robert. "Adjectives as Noun Phrases." Paper presented at the Winter meeting of the Linguistic Society of America, New York, December 28, 1966. Reprinted in Reibel and Schane.

_____. "A Proposed Rule of Tree Pruning." Mathematical Linguistics and Automatic Translation, Harvard Computation Laboratory, Report No. NSF-17 (1966), pp. IV-1 to IV-18. Reprinted in Reibel and Schane.

ENGLISH I.B.M. GRAMMAR II
A Mini-version and Adaptation

A. *Phrase Structure Rules*[2]

(1) $S \rightarrow \# (Neg)(\left\{ \begin{array}{c} Q \\ Imp \end{array} \right\})NP + Aux + VP \#$

    S = Sentence
    # = Sentence boundary
    Neg = Negative
    Q = Question
    Imp = Imperative
    NP = Noun Phrase
    Aux = Auxiliary
    VP = Verb Phrase

(2) $NP \rightarrow \left\{ \begin{array}{l} N\ (S) \\ NP + S \end{array} \right\}$ (a) (b)

(3) $VP \rightarrow VB\ (NP)\ (NP)$ (VB = Verbal)

B. *Segment Structure Rules*

(i)   N → Segment = (an aggregate of X-number of the features below)

Segment →	$\langle +N \rangle$ (Noun)
	$\langle \pm Subj \rangle$ (Subject)
	$\langle +\_\_\_ \rangle$ (+Segment)
	$\langle +\_\_\_ S \rangle$ (+Segment, Sentence)

(ii) $\langle +N \rangle \rightarrow$ $\langle \pm Def \rangle$ (Definite)
                          $\langle \pm Pro \rangle$ (Pronoun)
                          $\langle \pm Count \rangle$
                          $\langle -Case \rangle$
                          $\langle -Refl \rangle$ (Reflexive)

(iii) $\langle +Def \rangle \rightarrow$ $\langle \pm Demon \rangle$ (Demonstrative)
                          $\langle -\text{WH} \rangle$ (Non-WH form)

(iv) $\langle +Demon \rangle \rightarrow$ $\langle \pm Prox \rangle$ (Proximal)

(v) $\langle -Def \rangle \rightarrow$ $\langle \pm \text{WH} \rangle$

(v) $\langle -Def \rangle \rightarrow$ $\langle +\text{WH} \rangle$
                          $\langle \pm Spec \rangle$ (Specific)

(vi) $\langle -Count \rangle \rightarrow$ $\langle -Pl \rangle$ (Plural)

(vii) $\langle +Count \rangle \rightarrow$ $\langle \pm Pl \rangle$

(viii) $\langle +Subj \rangle \rightarrow$ $\langle -P \rangle$ (Preposition)

(ix) $\langle -Subj \rangle \rightarrow$ $\langle \pm P \rangle$

(x) $\langle+P\rangle \rightarrow$ $\left\{\begin{array}{l}\langle+\text{about}\rangle\\\langle+\text{at}\rangle\\\langle+\text{by}\rangle\\\langle+\text{for}\rangle\\\langle+\text{of}\rangle\\\langle+\text{on}\rangle\\\langle+\text{over}\rangle\\\langle+\text{through}\rangle\\\langle+\text{under}\rangle\\\cdots\end{array}\right\}$

(xi) $\langle+\underline{\quad}\rangle \rightarrow$ $\begin{array}{ll}\langle\pm\text{Conc}\rangle & \left[\dfrac{\langle+N\rangle}{\quad}\right] \\ \langle\pm\text{Human}\rangle & \\ \langle\pm\text{Com}\rangle & \left[\dfrac{\langle+N\rangle\;\langle-\text{Pro}\rangle}{\quad}\right]\end{array}$ (Concrete)

(Common)

(xii) $\langle-\text{Human}\rangle \rightarrow \langle\pm\text{Anim}\rangle$ (Animate)

(xiii) $\langle+\text{Human}\rangle \rightarrow$ $\langle+\text{Anim}\rangle$ $\left[\begin{array}{c}\langle\pm1\rangle\\\langle\pm2\rangle\\\langle\pm3\rangle\end{array}\right]$ $\left[\dfrac{\langle-\text{WH}\rangle\;\langle+\text{Pro}\rangle\;\langle+\text{Def}\rangle}{\quad}\right]$ (First person)
(Second person)
(Third person)

(xiv) $\langle-\text{Anim}\rangle \rightarrow \langle\pm\text{Time}\rangle$

(xv) $\langle-\text{Time}\rangle \rightarrow \langle\pm\text{Place}\rangle$

(xvi) $\langle+\text{Anim}\rangle \rightarrow \langle\pm\text{Masc}\rangle \quad / \quad \left[\dfrac{\langle-\text{WH}\rangle\;\langle-1\rangle\;\langle-2\rangle\;\langle+3\rangle}{\quad}\right]$ (Masculine)

(xvii) $\langle-\text{Masc}\rangle \rightarrow \langle\pm\text{Fem}\rangle$ (Feminine)

(xviii) Aux $\rightarrow$ Segment
Segment $\rightarrow$ $\langle\text{Aux}\rangle$ (Auxiliary)
$\langle\pm\text{Modal}\rangle$ (+can, +may, +must, etc.)
$\langle\pm\text{Past}\rangle$ (Tense)

(xix) VB $\rightarrow$ Segment   (Verbal)
Segment $\rightarrow$ +VB
$\langle+\underline{\quad}\rangle$
$\langle+\underline{\quad}NP\rangle$
$\langle+\underline{\quad}NP\;NP\rangle$

(xx) $\langle+\text{VB}\rangle \rightarrow$ CS / $[\langle\langle+N\rangle\;\langle+\text{Aux}\rangle\underline{\quad}\langle+N\rangle\;\langle+N\rangle\rangle]$ (Complex symbol)[3]

$\langle\pm\text{V}\rangle$ (Verb)
$\langle\pm\text{Stat}\rangle$ (Stative)
$\langle\pm\text{Perf}\rangle$ (Perfective aspect)
$\langle\pm\text{Prog}\rangle \quad / \quad \left[\dfrac{\langle-\text{Stat}\rangle}{\quad}\right]$ (Progressive aspect)

(xxi) $\langle +V \rangle \to$ $\langle \pm \text{Pass} \rangle$ / $\left[\left\{ \begin{array}{l} \langle + \underline{\quad} \text{NP} \rangle \\ \langle + \underline{\quad} \text{NP NP} \rangle \end{array} \right\} \right]$ (Passive)

$\langle \pm \text{IOI} \rangle \to$ /

$\left[\left\langle + \begin{array}{l} \langle +\text{N} \rangle \langle +\text{Aux} \rangle \underline{\quad} \langle +\text{N} \begin{array}{l} \langle +\text{N} \rangle \\ \langle +\text{P} \rangle \\ \langle +\text{to} \rangle \end{array} \right\rangle \right]$

(IOI = Indirect Object Inversion)

[2]These rules are an adaptation of *English IBM Grammar II* by Peter S. Rosenbaum. Permission for this adaptation was kindly granted by the International Business Machines Corporation and the Thomas J. Watson Research Center, P.O. Box 218, Yorktown Heights, New York 10598.

[3]The theoretical import and repercussions of the notion of "complex symbol" (CS) are discussed in *Aspects of the Theory of Syntax*, by Noam Chomsky (1965), pp. 91–111. In substance, positing the complex symbol allows the linguist to explain why, for example, the sentence "Oatmeal terrifies John" is grammatical while "*John terrifies oatmeal" is not.

V

English Phonology Today: A Feature Approach

Phonology is the study of the sound systems of natural languages. As in syntax, we recognize both a deep structure level of phonology and a surface structure level. We refer to deep structure phonology as SYSTEMATIC PHONEMICS. Surface structure phonology we refer to as SYSTEMATIC PHONETICS. In brief, the term SYSTEMATIC implies that we do not (as many structural phonologists did) consider phonology to be an independent level of investigation; that is, syntactic information is often used in determining both underlying and surface transcriptions.

Inasmuch as an English speaker is able to relate the phonetically abridged forms (*bike*) and (*trike*) to (bi*cycle*) and (tri*cycle,*) it would seem that the latter are likely candidates for underlying forms. Moreover, such words as (*column, solemn, hymn, damn,*) and the like have final sound segments that are deleted unless a suffix follows: (*column*al, *solemn*ity, *hymn*al, *damn*ation). Thus the underlying forms of these words must contain the -*n* just as (*sign*) and (*signify*) must contain underlying *g*.

Such deletion can also be observed in what are sometimes called "portmanteau words," or "word blends," such as *chortle* from *chuckle* and *snort* and *fantabulous* from *fantastic* and *fabulous*. Another good example of this is from French, where the masculine definite article (*le*) is modified following the preposition *à* ("to, from, on") and where the feminine definite article (*la*) is left intact as in *à la carte* ("from the menu") versus *à le contraire* which becomes the surface structure *au contraire* ("on the contrary"). In like manner, such a phrase as *in dem* ("in the") in German may be truncated to *im* as in *Der Mann steht* in dem *Zimmer* ("the man stands in the room"), which may be shortened to *Der Mann steht* im *Zimmer*.

By linguistic convention, phonemic forms are enclosed in parallel slant lines and phonetic forms are enclosed in square brackets: /phonemes/; [phones].

One can gain an understanding of systematic phonemics and systematic phonetics by examining the alternation of sounds which represent ⟨+Past⟩ and ⟨+Plural⟩ as in: "The lad*s*, lasse*s*, and parent*s* hugg*ed*, patt*ed*, and kiss*ed* the baby." There is good reason to believe that the underlying form of ⟨+Past⟩ is /d/ and the underlying form of ⟨+Plural⟩ is /z/. Let us focus attention for the moment on ⟨+Past⟩ = /d/. One can observe for himself that ⟨+Past⟩ is pronounced three different ways in (*hug*ged, *pat*ted, *kiss*ed.) In (*hug*ged) ⟨+Past⟩ is pronounced *d*. In (*patt*ed) ⟨+Past⟩ is pronounced *uh* plus *d*. In (*kiss*ed) ⟨+Past⟩ is pronounced *t*. These pronunciations are highly predictable and systematic.

The sound represented by the orthographic symbol *d* (shown phonemically as /d/) is said to be "voiced"; that is, the vocal cords in the Adam's apple (larynx) are vibrating. The sound represented by *t* is exactly the same as *d* except that the vocal cords are not vibrating for *t*. (Other voiced/voiceless pairs of sounds are those spelled as *b/p*, *v/f*, and *z/s*.) Let us symbolize the "uh" sound that occurs in (*patt*ed) as "ɨ" (barred i), represented [ɨ]).

The formation of past tense for verbs can be represented by the following formulae:

hug + Past → hug + /d/ = hugged
pat + Past → pat + /d/ = patted
kiss + Past → kiss + /d/ = kissed

These formulae represent the deep structure form of ⟨+Past⟩. The surface structure forms of ⟨+Past⟩ are sketched out below.

hug + /d/ → hug[d]
pat + /d/ → pat[ɨd]
kiss + /d/ → kis[t]

Our listing of the phonologically regular ⟨+Past⟩ forms of English verbs will be complete with the addition of an arbitrary verb such as (*pad*), whose ⟨+Past⟩ form is (*pad*ded).

pad + Past → pad + /d/
pad + /d/ → pad[ɨd]

Thus the underlying form of ⟨+Past⟩ is the systematic phoneme /d/ which surfaces as [ɨd] after the spellings *t/d*; [d] after such a voiced sound as that spelled *g;* [t] after such a voiceless sound as represented by the letter *s.*

Exercises

1. Write the ⟨+Past⟩ forms of the following English verbs. Arrange them into three sets which correspond to those in the text above.

> *mop, mob, cart, card, back, bag, latch, cage, pull, purr, bam, ban, bang, lay, die, caw*

2. Comment on these noun and verb pairs.

   a. life/lived
   b. safe/saved
   c. wreath/wreathed
   d. bath/bathed
   e. house/housed

3. Discuss the ⟨+Past⟩ forms of these English verbs.

   a. sing, ring, sling, swing
   b. hit, cost, bet
   c. lie, lay, sit, set
   d. spill, bend, blend
   e. rise, raise, rear
   f. dive, live, thrive
   g. slay, draw
   h. bake, make, take

4. Consult either an English grammar handbook or a dictionary and secure a list of so-called strong or irregular verbs. Survey either a class or a group of friends. What differences in ⟨+Past⟩ forms can you find? Comment on the impairment, if any, to communication which the differences cause.

The Noun Plural

There is good reason to believe that /z/ is the underlying form of ⟨+Plural⟩. Just as there are three surface structure forms of ⟨+Past⟩, so there are three surface structure forms of ⟨+Plural⟩: [z, iz, s]. The actual distribution of the surface structure forms of ⟨+Plural⟩ is this:

[ɨz] occurs after noun stems which terminate in [s/z, š/ž, č/ǰ] as in (*bus/buzz, bush/beige, church/judge*);

[z] occurs after voiced sounds other than [z, ž, ǰ];

[s] occurs after voiceless sounds other than [s, š, č].

The conversion of underlying /d/ and /z/ into surface structure [t] and [s] (as in *kiss* +/d/ and *parent* + /z/) is known as voicing assimilation; that is, /d/ and /z/ become like *t* and *s* as concerns vocal cord vibration (voicing). Since the terminal segment of the verb or noun affects the suffix, this process is called *progressive voicing assimilation*.

Exercises

1. Make an observation about the distribution of the ⟨+Plural⟩ suffix and the suffixes commonly called "possessive" and "third person singular" for the data below.

    a.   The guard*s* wore guns.

    b.   The sheriff guard*s* the county.

    c.   Luckily the guard'*s* gun did not have to be used.

    d.   Fred and Ginger performed three dance*s*.

    e.   Ginger dánce*s* as well as Fred.

    f.   The dance'*s* rhythm was exhausting.

    g.   Shelley watched the skylark*s*.

    h.   A blithe spirit seldom skylark*s*.

    i.   A skylark'*s* spirit is seldom blithe.

2. Comment on these ⟨+Plural⟩ forms.

    a.   oxen, children, oxen's, children's

    b.   stigmata, data

    c.   sheep, deer, fish

    d.   baalim, seraphim, cherubim

    e.   mice, lice, men, women, feet, geese, dice

    f.   six foot six/six feet six

    g.   twenty mile, forty mile

    h.   mumps, pliers, trousers, scissors

    i.   formulae/formulas, concerti/concertos

3. Some linguists suggest that the ⟨+Plural⟩ suffix attaches to nouns whereas the ⟨+Possessive⟩ suffix attaches to noun phrases. How do these data suggest this?

a. An ox*'s* tail is good for soup.
b. Ox*en's* tails are good for soup.
c. A cat*'s* tail tickles.
d. Cat*s'* tails tickle.
e. The man on the corner*'s* hat blew off.

Some Common Phonological Processes

All of the linguistic rules in this text reduce to three basic types: IN-SERTION, DELETION, and SUBSTITUTION. This is true both of syntactic rules and phonological rules. Below we refer to competing pronunciations of English words. It goes without saying that no one pronunciation is linguistically any better than any other.

The term EPENTHESIS refers to the internal insertion of a sound segment, whereas EPITHESIS refers to the terminal insertion of a sound segment as in *elm* versus *elum*, *athlete* versus *athelete*, and *chance, once, twice* versus *chanst, wunst, twyst.*

APHESIS is the deletion of an initial sound segment as in *above, afraid, alive* vis-à-vis *'bove, 'fraid, 'live.* The internal deletion of a sound is called SYNCOPE as in *regular, general* against *reg'lar, gen'ral.* Deletion of a terminal sound segment is called APOCOPE as in *bound, sound, finest* versus *boun', soun', fines'.*

Another type of phonetic deletion is called HAPLOLOGY, as when *simple* and *-ly* join to form *simply* rather than **simplely.* A modern Spanish example occurs when *haber* ("have") combines with *-e* to form *habré* ("will have") and *-ia* to form *habría* ("would have") rather than **haberé* or **habería.*

METATHESIS is a very common phonological process. The term refers to the inversion of one or more sound segments. There is historical metathesis in Modern English *ask, bird, curds, clasp* (Middle English *aks, brid, cruds, claps*). Metathesis is very common where the liquids *(l,r)* are concerned: *relevant, pervert, modern* over against *revelant, prevert, modren.* "Spoonerisms" are a special case of metathesis as when *well-oiled bicycle* and *crushing blow* become *well-boiled icycle* and *blushing crow.*

Two Janus-faced phonological processes that merit discussion are AS-SIMILATION and DISSIMILATION. Since we have already mentioned voicing assimilation, let us simply give another example of it as when *Baptist* in the South and Southwest is pronounced as if it were spelled *Babdist;* that is, the sequence *-pt-* assimilates to the voicing of the surrounding vowels.

Any English speaker who has struggled with the spelling of the military word (*colonel*) well knows that the word would not be quite so puzzling were it spelled (*coronel*) as it is in Modern Spanish. Even so, Modern French spelling retains the same two *l*'s in the word as in English. This alternation of *r* and *l* is known as dissimilation (becoming unalike). For example, it is alleged that English (*pilgrim*) is an analogue of *peregrine* or "wanderer.") The same kind of difference exists between English (*paper, azure*) and Spanish (*papel, azul.*) Within English, there is the interesting competition among *chimney, chimbley,* and *chimley.*

Exercises

1. Create or find three examples of Spoonerisms like *a swell foop* rather than *a fell swoop.*

2. Create or find two examples of the following.

    a. epenthesis
    b. epithesis
    c. metathesis
    d. aphesis
    e. syncope
    f. apocope
    g. assimilation
    h. dissimilation

3. Give some technical names for these phonological processes. (Hint: use the list above!)

    a. insertion
    b. deletion
    c. substitution

4. Write a formal linguistic rule describing each of the phonological processes below using this formula:
X A Y → X B Y (or, A → B/X ____Y).

    a. epenthesis, epithesis (excrescence)
    b. aphesis, syncope, apocope (loss)
    c. metathesis

Rudimentary Phonological Features

Most literate English speakers are aware of the traditional division of the alphabet into CONSONANTS, VOWELS, LIQUIDS, and GLIDES. These are known as the NATURAL CLASSES of English sound segments. For example, if we assign a binary valence to the concept "consonant" and the concept "vowel," we can describe the four natural classes above in this manner.

$$\begin{bmatrix} +\text{consonant} \\ -\text{vowel} \end{bmatrix} \quad \begin{bmatrix} -\text{consonant} \\ +\text{vowel} \end{bmatrix} \quad \begin{bmatrix} +\text{consonant} \\ +\text{vowel} \end{bmatrix} \quad \begin{bmatrix} -\text{consonant} \\ -\text{vowel} \end{bmatrix}$$

TRUE CONSONANT	VOWEL	LIQUID	GLIDE
p,t,k/c/q/x, b,d,g/j, f,s,v,z,m,n	a,e,i,o,u	l,r	y,w,h

While it is true that we can now refer unambiguously to any one of these four natural classes of sounds, it is not possible without further information to single out any one particular symbol. Thus, a natural class is one which may be described or referred to with fewer symbols and less notation than any member of the natural class. It is the concept of the DISTINCTIVE FEATURE which allows us to refer unambiguously to any member of a natural class. A distinctive feature, therefore, is one which differentiates one sound segment crucially from any other sound segment (once given the concept of the natural class). For example, the feature ⟨+nasal⟩ sets *m,n* apart from all other sound segments of Modern English or any language for that matter.

Nasal Assimilation

Phonetically, one must recognize three different nasal consonants as in (*ram, ran, rang,*) which are commonly transcribed as [m,n,ŋ] respectively. In the underlying form of words wherein a nasal consonant precedes a non-nasal true consonant we use the archisegment *N*, which stands for what the nasal consonants have in common, as in (*liNp, laNp, laNb, lyNph, liNt, leNd, leNs, teNse, teNth, piNch, tiNge, siNg, siNk,*) which parallel (*limp, limb, lamp, lamb, lymph, lint, lend, lens, tense, tenth, pinch, tinge, sing, sink.*)

In this position the nasal consonant is said to assimilate to the following consonant. For example, the underlying form of *singing* is

/siNgiNg/ in which both of the nasals assimilate to /g/, which is then deleted: [siŋiŋ]. Thus the *g* in this and other words is called "dropped *g*." Observe further that *g* is pronounced in *ginger, linger, longer* but not in *long* or *king*. In the Greek language our loanword *angel* (messenger) is spelled *aggel*, and here the *gg* indicates the velar nasal, [ŋ].

Nasal assimilation is dependent upon where the main stress occurs in a word as in *cóngress* with [ŋ] versus *congréssional* with [n]. Notice that the nasal segment is deleted from the negative prefix *in-* (/iN/) before *m, l, r*; this is indicated orthographically by doubling the consonant with which the stem begins:

$$/iN/ + legal \quad \rightarrow illegal$$
$$relevant \rightarrow irrelevant$$
$$modest \quad \rightarrow immodest$$
$$\text{-}nocent \rightarrow innocent$$
$$noxious \rightarrow innoxious$$

In words of Greek origin the negative prefix is *an-* as in *an + theist* and *an + hydrous*, which render *atheist* and *anhydrous*. Curiously enough, the negative form of *noble* is *ignoble* from *in-* plus *gnoble*. The form *gno-* is closely related to English *know*, Romance *(ac)quaint*, German *können* and *kennen*, French *connaître*, and Spanish *conocer*. Other related forms are *cognition, recognize,* g*nome,* g*nosis, prognosis, diagnosis.*

The distribution of the nasal consonants is such that [m, n] occur initially, medially, and finally whereas [ŋ] occurs only medially and finally. In Tagalog, a language of the Philippines, [ŋ] occurs in initial position as in *nguni at* which means "but, on the other hand": [ŋ]uniat.

A fourth type of nasal consonant called a palatal nasal and symbolized by [ɲ] occurs in such Spanish words as *cañon* ("canyon") and French words as *gagner* ("gain"). Physiologically, a nasal consonant may be articulated (formed) in four basic areas of the mouth: at the lips, [m]; at the teeth, [n]; at the hard palate, [ɲ]; at the soft palate, [ŋ]. If we divide the area of the mouth into anterior/non-anterior and if we indicate that the "blade" (crown = corona) of the tongue either is or is not involved in pronouncing the nasal consonant (coronal/non-coronal), we can chart these four nasals as follows.

$$\begin{bmatrix} \langle +anterior\rangle & \langle +anterior\rangle & \langle -anterior\rangle & \langle -anterior\rangle \\ \langle -coronal\rangle & \langle +coronal\rangle & \langle +coronal\rangle & \langle -coronal\rangle \end{bmatrix}$$

m	n	ɲ	ŋ
ra*m*	ra*n*	ra*nge*	ra*ng*

A minimal feature description of all nasal consonants is this:

$$
\begin{bmatrix}
\langle-\text{vowel}\rangle \\
\langle+\text{consonant}\rangle \\
\langle+\text{nasal}\rangle
\end{bmatrix}
$$

Let us now combine all of these feature descriptions to distinguish among the four nasal segments:

$$
\begin{bmatrix}
\langle-\text{vowel}\rangle & \langle-\text{vowel}\rangle & \langle-\text{vowel}\rangle & \langle-\text{vowel}\rangle \\
\langle+\text{consonant}\rangle & \langle+\text{consonant}\rangle & \langle+\text{consonant}\rangle & \langle+\text{consonant}\rangle \\
\langle+\text{nasal}\rangle & \langle+\text{nasal}\rangle & \langle+\text{nasal}\rangle & \langle+\text{nasal}\rangle \\
\langle+\text{anterior}\rangle & \langle+\text{anterior}\rangle & \langle-\text{anterior}\rangle & \langle-\text{anterior}\rangle \\
\langle-\text{coronal}\rangle & \langle+\text{coronal}\rangle & \langle+\text{coronal}\rangle & \langle-\text{coronal}\rangle
\end{bmatrix}
$$

m   n   ɲ   ŋ

Exercises

1. Explain the following generalizations.

     a. Nasal → [m] / ____: as in *liNp, liNb, lyNph*
     b. Nasal → [n] / ____: as in *liNt, leNd, teNth, teNse, leNs*
     c. Nasal → [ɲ] / ____: as in *piNch, tiNge*
     d. Nasal → [ŋ] / ____: as in *siNk, siNg*

2. Let the symbol alpha (α) range over the valence of the feature $\langle$anterior$\rangle$ and the symbol beta (β) range over the valence of the feature $\langle$coronal$\rangle$ in the formula below. Now, interpret this rule; that is, explain what it describes. It is called the rule for regressive (anticipatory) nasal assimilation.

$$
\begin{bmatrix}
\langle-\text{vowel}\rangle \\
\langle+\text{consonant}\rangle \\
\langle+\text{nasal}\rangle
\end{bmatrix}
\rightarrow
\begin{bmatrix}
\langle\alpha\text{anterior}\rangle \\
\langle\beta\text{coronal}\rangle
\end{bmatrix}
\Bigg/
\begin{bmatrix}
\langle+\text{vowel}\rangle \\
\langle-\text{consonant}\rangle \\
\langle+\text{stress}\rangle
\end{bmatrix}
\text{——}
\begin{bmatrix}
\langle-\text{vowel}\rangle \\
\langle+\text{consonant}\rangle \\
\langle-\text{nasal}\rangle \\
\langle\alpha\text{anterior}\rangle \\
\langle\beta\text{coronal}\rangle
\end{bmatrix}
$$

3. Above, we mention the distribution of the nasal consonants in English; we indicated that [m, n] occur in all positions (initial, medial, final) and that [ŋ] does not occur initially in English. Let the cross-hatch (#) stand for the left-hand boundary of English words as in #map and #nap. Interpret the rule below. *Hint:* two statements are being made at once; that is, there is one statement being made about words with initial nasal segments and another about what follows an initial nasal.

$$\# \begin{bmatrix} \langle -\text{vowel} \rangle \\ \langle +\text{consonant} \rangle \\ \langle +\text{nasal} \rangle \end{bmatrix} \begin{bmatrix} \langle +\text{segment} \rangle \end{bmatrix} \rightarrow \# \begin{bmatrix} \langle -\text{vowel} \rangle \\ \langle +\text{consonant} \rangle \\ \langle +\text{nasal} \rangle \\ \langle +\text{anterior} \rangle \end{bmatrix} \begin{bmatrix} \langle +\text{vowel} \rangle \\ \langle -\text{consonant} \rangle \end{bmatrix}$$

4. It is interesting to note with James Harris (1969:8–18) that before vowels, Spanish has three distinct nasals ([m, n, ɲ]) as in *cana* ("bed"), *cana* ("gray hair"), and *caña* ("cane"). In a slow speech style regressive nasal assimilation usually does not take place as in *un peso* ("a peso," [un pēsō]) and *un cacto* ("a cactus," [ūn kāktō]). However, in a rapid style of delivery assimilation does take place as in [ūm pēsō] (*un peso*) and [uŋ kāktō] (*un cacto*). Now, relate these Spanish words to their English confreres: *redimir, redención, redentor.*

5. In Modern French, nasal consonants assimilate to preceding vowels.

    a.   La musique est *un* art. [ɔ̃en] ("Music is an art.")
    b.   La patience est *une* vertu. [ün] ("Patience is a virtue.")
    c.   Ici *on* parle français. [ɔ̃] ("Here one speaks French.")
    d.   C'est *mon* frère. [ɔ̃] ("That's my brother.")
    e.   C'est *ma* soeur. [a] ("That's my sister.")
    f.   Le bonheur [ɔ] ("Happiness")
    g.   Bonjour [ɔ̃] ("Good day, hello")
    h.   Bonsoir [ɔ̃] ("Good evening")
    i.   La bonté [ɔ̃] ("goodness, kindness")
    j.   Bonne nuit [ɔ] ("Good night")

A wavy line (tilde) over a vowel in square brackets indicates nasalization. State the conditions under which a vowel is nasalized.

6. As we have said, the English rule of nasal assimilation is regressive or anticipatory. English also has a regressive rule of voicing assimilation. For example, when the suffix *-th*, which is ⟨−voice⟩, is added to a stem like *broad* or *wide*, the final *d* of the stems "devoices" giving *brea*[t]*th* and *wi*[t]*th*. The rule which accomplishes this devoicing is given below. Observe that the alpha (α) symbol is used instead of +/− on the feature ⟨Voice⟩. Either explain orally or write in ordinary prose what the rule "says."

Regressive Voicing Assimilation

$$\begin{bmatrix} -\text{vowel} \\ +\text{consonant} \\ -\text{nasal} \end{bmatrix} \rightarrow \begin{bmatrix} \alpha\text{voice} \end{bmatrix} / \underline{\hspace{2em}} \begin{bmatrix} -\text{vowel} \\ +\text{consonant} \\ -\text{nasal} \\ \alpha\text{voice} \end{bmatrix}$$

7. Below is the rule which insures that "ki*ssed*" and "paren*ts*" have surface structure voiceless clusters of final consonants even though +Past has the underlying form /z/.

Progressive Voicing Assimilation

$$
\begin{bmatrix} -\text{vowel} \\ +\text{consonant} \\ -\text{nasal} \end{bmatrix} \rightarrow \begin{bmatrix} \alpha\text{voice} \end{bmatrix} / \begin{bmatrix} -\text{vowel} \\ +\text{consonant} \\ -\text{nasal} \\ \alpha\text{voice} \end{bmatrix}
$$

Either explain orally or write in ordinary prose what the rule "says." You might find it useful to compare the two rules of voicing assimilation. Finally, you might find these two formulae helpful aids in your discussion.

a. $A \rightarrow B /$＿＿Y
    (A rewrites as B when A precedes Y)

b. $A \rightarrow B / X$＿＿
    (A rewrites as B when A follows X)

A Set of English Phonological Features

In *The Sound Pattern of English*,[1] Chomsky and Halle (pp. 176–77) use fourteen phonological features in their discussion of English phonology. We have already encountered at least four of these: vowel, consonant, nasal, and voice. Instead of using the terms "vowel" and "consonant," Chomsky and Halle use "VOCALIC" and "CONSONANTAL." Some phonologists prefer to use "syllabic" rather than "vocalic." Henceforth, we will use Chomsky-Hallean symbology.

Consider now a non-detailed list of phonetic features which Chomsky and Halle deem necessary to describe English phonology as found in *The Sound Pattern of English* (1968:293–329).

(1) sonorant/non-sonorant: ⟨+sonorant⟩ sound segments are characterized by involuntary vocal cord vibration (voicing).

(2) vocalic/non-vocalic: ⟨+vocalic⟩ sound segments are characterized by automatic vocal cord vibration and by a lack of radical constriction.

(3) consonantal/non-consonantal: ⟨+consonantal⟩ sound segments are a product of radical construction in the vocal cavity.

[1]Noam Chomsky and Morris Halle, *The Sound Pattern of English* (New York: Harper and Row, 1968). Reprinted with permission.

(4) anterior/non-anterior: ⟨+anterior⟩ sound segments are produced in front of the gum-ridge and hard palate (alveo-palatal) region of the mouth.

(5) coronal/non-coronal: ⟨+coronal⟩ sound segments are produced by raising the blade of the tongue.

(6) high/non-high: ⟨+high⟩ sound segments are made with the body of the tongue raised from neutral position. Neutral position is approximated when one pronounces the vowel of English *bet.*

(7) low/non-low: ⟨+low⟩ sound segments are made with the body of the tongue lowered from neutral position.

(8) voice/non-voice: ⟨+voice⟩ sound segments are attended by vibration of the vocal cords in the Adam's apple (voice box, larynx).

(9) nasal/non-nasal: ⟨+nasal⟩ sound segments are made with the nasal passages open; that is, they are not sealed off by the soft palate (velum).

(10) round/non-round: ⟨+round⟩ segments are made with narrowed (rounded) lips.

(11) continuant/non-continuant: ⟨+continuant⟩ sound segments are a product of a radically constricted vocal cavity.

(12) tense/non-tense: ⟨+tense⟩ sound segments are accompanied by appreciable tightening of the supraglottal and facial muscles.

(13) strident/non-strident: ⟨+strident⟩ sound segments are acoustically noisy and turbulent.

(14) back/non-back: ⟨+back⟩ sound segments are made with the body of the tongue retracted from neutral position.

Discussion Of The Fourteen Phonological Features

The feature ⟨+/− sonorant⟩ is used to distinguish resonant sounds such as nasals (*m, n*), vowels (*a, e, i, o, u*), liquids (*l, r*) and glides (*y, w, h*) from STOP consonants ([p/b, t/d, č/ǰ, k/g]) and FRICATIVE consonants ([f/v, θ/ð, s/z, š/ž]). Spontaneous vocal cord vibration characterizes ⟨+sonorant⟩ sound segments:

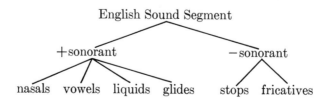

English Sound Segment

+sonorant   −sonorant

nasals vowels liquids glides   stops fricatives

In effect then, ⟨−sonorant⟩ sound segments are the non-nasal obstruents (cf. radical obstruction) which are commonly called stops and fricatives. As a class, stops and fricatives can be referred to by this redundancy formula:

$$-\text{sonorant} \rightarrow \begin{bmatrix} \langle -\text{vocalic} \rangle \\ \langle +\text{consonantal} \rangle \\ \langle -\text{nasal} \rangle \end{bmatrix}$$

As we saw in the section dealing with nasal assimilation, the features ⟨anterior⟩ and ⟨coronal⟩ are distinctive for the various nasals. In general, sounds which are produced anterior to the region where the initial segment of English (sh*i*p) is pronounced are ⟨+anterior⟩. When it is necessary to raise the blade of the tongue to make a sound, that sound is said to be ⟨+coronal⟩. Thus, the typical English liquids (*l*, *r*) are ⟨+coronal⟩. They are differentiated on the basis of the anterior feature.

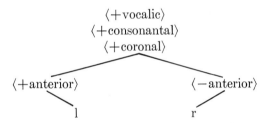

The features ⟨high⟩, ⟨low⟩, ⟨back⟩, ⟨round⟩ are especially useful in characterizing the vowel systems of languages. All languages make a distinction between vowels made in the region of the hard palate (palatal vowels) and vowels made in the region of the soft palate (velar vowels). Palatal vowels are ⟨−back⟩ and velar vowels are ⟨+back⟩.

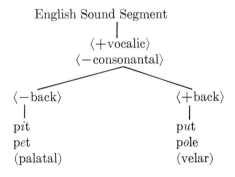

Vowels, additionally, may be pronounced ⟨high⟩, ⟨mid⟩, or ⟨low⟩ in the mouth; they may also be ⟨+round⟩ or ⟨−round⟩.

	⟨−back⟩ ⟨−round⟩	⟨+back⟩ ⟨+round⟩	
⟨+high⟩ ⟨−low⟩	p*i*t	p*u*t	(high)
⟨−high⟩ ⟨−low⟩	p*e*t	p*o*le	(mid)
⟨−high⟩ ⟨+low⟩	p*a*t	*ou*ght	(low)

The traditional term for ⟨+continuant⟩ sounds is FRICATIVE, or "sibilant"; that is, for these sounds, air is expelled from the lungs through a vocal cavity which is narrowed (constricted) in such a manner so as to cause friction. For fricatives, the vocal cavity is only incompletely closed or narrowed. For the ⟨−continuant⟩ sounds called STOPS, the vocal cavity is completely closed momentarily. Fricatives and stops may be either ⟨−voice⟩ (voiceless) or ⟨+voice⟩ (voiced).

CONSONANT

	⟨−voice⟩		⟨+voice⟩	
STOPS (−continuant)	[p]	*p*in	[b]	*b*in
	[t]	*t*in	[d]	*d*in
	[č]	*ch*in	[ǰ]	*g*in
	[k]	*c*oat	[g]	*g*oat
FRICATIVES (+continuant)	[f]	*f*at	[v]	*v*at
	[θ]	e*th*er	[ð]	ei*th*er
	[s]	*s*ue	[z]	*z*oo
	[š]	me*sh*	[ž]	mea*s*ure

It is now possible for us to construct a simplified yet revealing table or chart of English true consonants. The symbols used are surface structure phonetic ones found in *The Sound Pattern of English*. The first chart uses traditional articulatory terms. The second chart uses Chomsky-Hallean distinctive features.

TRADITIONAL CONSONANT CHART

	Labial	Inter- Dental	Dental	Palatal	Velar	Glottal	
Voiceless	p		t	č	k		STOPS
Voiced	b		d	ǰ	g		
Voiceless	f	θ	s	š		h	FRICATIVES
Voiced	v	ð	z	ž	γ		
	m		n	ɲ	ŋ		NASALS

FEATURE CONSONANT CHART*

	m	n	ɲ	ŋ	⟨+⟩ nasal
−vocalic +consonantal	p/b	t/d	č/ǰ	k/g	⟨−⟩ ⟨−⟩ continuant
	f/v s/z	θ/ð	š/ž	h/γ	⟨+⟩

+anter	+anter	−anter	−anter
−coron	+coron	+coron	−coron

*A slant line separates ⟨−voice⟩ from ⟨+voice⟩ segments. Underscored segments are ⟨+strident⟩.

Exercises

1. Which distinctive feature, in general, distinguishes Set 1 from Set 2 below?

Set 1	Set 2
keen	queen
hen	when
Ghent	Gwen
kick	quick
kite	quite
cake	quake
coat	quote
calm	qualm
kid	quid
cough	quaff

2. Consonant segments which exhibit extreme noisiness or turbulence are ⟨+strident⟩. In English the feature ⟨strident⟩ is germane to the classification of fricatives (f/v, θ/ð, s/z, š/ž) and affricates (č/ǰ, a combination of a stop plus a fricative). Observe that the class of English sound segments which are both ⟨+strident⟩ and ⟨+coronal⟩ (s/z, š/ž, č/ǰ) has special status, as it were, in the language; that is, as we noted early in this chapter, if a ⟨+Noun⟩ or ⟨+Verb⟩ stem terminates in a sound segment which is ⟨+strident⟩ and ⟨+coronal⟩, then an epenthetic vowel is inserted when the ⟨+Plural⟩, ⟨+Possessive⟩, or ⟨+Third Person Singular⟩ suffix is added as in (*buses, buzzes, bushes, garages, lunches, lunges*) and so on. Below is an informal rule for such vowel epenthesis. Convert this rule into feature formulation.

$$\text{null} \rightarrow \text{vowel} \ / \ \left\{ \begin{matrix} \text{s/z} \\ \text{š/ž} \\ \text{č/ǰ} \end{matrix} \right\} \underline{\quad\quad} \begin{matrix} /\text{z}/ \\ +\text{Plural} \\ +\text{Possessive} \\ +\text{Third Person Singular} \end{matrix}$$

3.   In like manner as above, construct a feature rule that describes vowel epenthesis between ⟨+Verb⟩ stems which terminate in *t* or *d* and the ⟨+Past⟩ suffix /d/.

$$\text{null} \rightarrow \text{vowel} \ / \ \left\{ \begin{matrix} \text{t} \\ \text{d} \end{matrix} \right\} \underline{\quad\quad} \begin{matrix} /\text{d}/ \\ +\text{Past} \end{matrix}$$

4.   There is good reason to believe that words such as (*right, light, bought, caught*) and the like contain an underlying ⟨+continuant⟩ segment, as the conventional spelling suggests. What is more, in certain Scottish dialects a ⟨+continuant⟩ segment occurs in the surface structure pronunciations of these and other words. Also, the fact that Modern German, a sister language, has ⟨+continuant⟩ analogous segments in such words as (*Recht, Licht, Nacht*) is supportive evidence for the view above. Many phonologists think that the segment in question is /x/, which seems to have at least this feature analysis: ⟨−vocalic⟩, ⟨+consonantal⟩, ⟨+high⟩, ⟨+back⟩, ⟨−anterior⟩, ⟨−coronal⟩, ⟨+continuant⟩, ⟨−round⟩. A ⟨+round⟩ version is /x^w/. In initial position, one might argue, /x/ and /x^w/ become phonetic [h] and [hw] as in (h*en*) and (wh*en*). If this is so, one must posit a rule which will insert *w* in the latter form. Another view is that the underlying form of *when* contains four segments: /xwen/. What then would be the underlying forms of *queen* and *Gwen*? On the supposition that *who* is a relativized form of *he*, is the underlying form of *who* /x^{w}e/? Would /xwe/ or /xwo/ be better candidates?

5.   Not all phonological rules are rules of change. Some rules simply express distributional statements or redundancies. A very simple example of this is the generalization that ⟨+high⟩ segments cannot be ⟨+low⟩ and that ⟨+low⟩ segments cannot be ⟨+high⟩:

(a)   ⟨+high⟩ → ⟨−low⟩
(b)   ⟨+low⟩ → ⟨−high⟩

Another example of a redundancy rule is one which states the characteristics that ⟨+nasal⟩ segments have in common:

$$\langle+\text{nasal}\rangle \rightarrow \begin{bmatrix} \langle-\text{vocalic}\rangle \\ \langle+\text{consonantal}\rangle \\ \langle+\text{sonorant}\rangle \\ \langle-\text{continuant}\rangle \\ \langle+\text{voice}\rangle \\ \langle-\text{strident}\rangle \end{bmatrix}$$

The next type of redundancy rule is a distributional one. It makes a statement about the type of clusters of sounds with which English words begin. The crosshatch (#) symbolizes initial word boundary as in *#speak, #steak, #sky, #small, #snail, #sled*, and the like. What sequences does the rule permit? Can you think of any exceptions? Is the rule stated in its most economical form?

$$\begin{bmatrix} \langle-\text{voc}\rangle \\ \langle+\text{cons}\rangle \end{bmatrix} \begin{bmatrix} \langle-\text{voc}\rangle \\ \langle+\text{cons}\rangle \end{bmatrix} \rightarrow \begin{bmatrix} \langle-\text{voc}\rangle \\ \langle+\text{cons}\rangle \\ \langle+\text{anter}\rangle \\ \langle+\text{coron}\rangle \\ \langle-\text{voice}\rangle \\ \langle+\text{strident}\rangle \end{bmatrix} \begin{bmatrix} \langle-\text{voc}\rangle \\ \langle+\text{cons}\rangle \end{bmatrix}$$

6. In Martin's dialect the word (shr*ed*) and the like are pronounced as [šred]. In Rulon's dialect either [sred] or [šred] is possible. One way to relate the two pronunciations is to consider the underlying form to be /sred/ and to posit a rule which converts [s] to [š] before [r] for certain dialects of English. The rule would be optional for Rulon and obligatory for Martin:

$$s \rightarrow š / \underline{\hspace{1cm}} r$$

That is, [s] is replaced by [š] when [s] precedes [r]. In light of the data below, why is this an attractive solution?

Data A	*Data B*
s*p*read	*shpread
s*tr*eet	*shtreet
s*pr*ite	*shprite
s*m*all	*shmall
s*n*ail	*shnail
s*l*ed	*shled
"sred"	shred

Spirantization, Palatalization, and Velar Softening

An understanding of spirantization, palatalization, and velar softening should help one to grasp more quickly the concept that the conventional English writing system is based on deep phonological structures rather than on surface structure. If the writing system is phonetic rather than phonemic in nature, it is indeed a poor system.

SPIRANTIZATION is the phonological process which relates the romanized alternations in (*mete/measure* and (*permit/permission*) as well as in (*evade/evasive/evasion*). PALATALIZATION is the process which accounts for the fact that the romanized segment in (*evasive*) is ⟨+anterior⟩ and that the romanized segment in (*evasion*) is ⟨−anterior⟩. The rule of VELAR SOFTENING relates the underscored −coronal segment in (*legal*) to the +coronal segment in (*legislate*).

A feature description of these three processes is clearly beyond the scope of the discussion in this text. Hopefully, it will suffice if we informally indicate the force of these rules in the following manner.

Spirantization:

(a) t → s / ＿＿ i as in (permi*t*/permi*s*sive)

(b) d → z / ＿＿ i as in (eva*d*e/eva*s*ive); then [z] → [s]

Palatalization:

(a) t → č as in (fac*t*/fac*t*ual)

(b) d → ǰ as in (gra*d*e/gra*d*ual)

(c) s → š as in (mi*t*-/mi*ss*ion) (*t* spirantizes to *s*)

(d) s → ž as in (A*s*ia) = A/s/ia; that is, /s/ palatalizes to [š] and then [š] voices to [ž].

Velar Softening:

$$g \rightarrow \text{ǰ} / \underline{\quad\quad} \begin{Bmatrix} i \\ e \end{Bmatrix} \text{as in (le}g\text{al/le}g\text{islate, alle}g\text{ation/alle}g\text{e)}$$

Exercises

1. Technically, the *c* in (*music, musical, musician*) is an anterior, coronal affricate. Students of German will identify it with the romanized (z) segments in (*Zeit:* "time, tide") and *Katze:* "cat"). It is seldom a surface structure form in English save in oddities like (*tsetse fly*). Explain the alternation between [k] and [š] in the forms above. What underlying form does *c* indicate? Observe these alternations and spellings: *face/facial, space/spatial, specie(s)/special/spec-sheet* (i.e., specification sheet). Is the solution below a good one?

$$k \rightarrow c \rightarrow s \rightarrow \check{s} \; / \; \underline{\hspace{1cm}} \begin{Bmatrix} i \\ e \end{Bmatrix}$$

Do the variant spellings (*catsup*) and (*ketchup*) contribute toward a solution?

2. Phonetically transcribe competing pronunciations for these forms.

   (a) miss you
   (b) is your
   (c) hit you
   (d) kid you

Competing Phonetic Transcriptions for English Consonants

In this section we examine four different but compatible systems for phonetically transcribing the consonants of Modern English:

(a) C-H: Chomsky-Halle
     (*The Sound Pattern of English*)
(b) S-T: Smith-Trager
     (*An Outline of English Structure*)
(c) IPA: International Phonetic Alphabet
(d) ITA: Initial Teaching Alphabet[2]

C-H	S-T
IPA	ITA

An easy way to present these four systems is to make use of what is known as a "structural array" which only grossly approximates articulatory positions. The framework is as follows.

	Labial	Dental	Palatal	Velar	Glottal	
Voiceless	x	x	x	x	x	STOPS
Voiced	x	x	x	x	x	
Voiceless	x	x	x	x	x	FRICATIVES
Voiced	x	x	x	x	x	
Resonant	x	x	x	x	x	NASALS

[2]Courtesy of the Initial Teaching Alphabet Publications, Inc., 26 East 43rd Street, New York, N.Y. 10017.

CHOMSKY-HALLE AND SMITH-TRAGER CONSONANT SYSTEMS

	Labial	Dental	Palatal	Velar	Glottal	
Voiceless	p	t	č	k		
Voiced	b	d	ǰ	g		STOPS
Voiceless	f	θ	s	š	h	
Voiced	v	ð	z	ž	γ	FRICATIVES
Resonant	m	n	ɲ	ŋ		NASALS

IPA PHONETIC SYMBOLS

	Labial	Dental	Palatal	Velar	Glottal	
Voiceless	p	t	tʃ	k		
Voiced	b	d	dʒ	g		STOPS
Voiceless	f	θ	s	ʃ	h/hw/ʍ	
Voiced	v	ð	z	ʒ		FRICATIVES
Resonant	m	n	ɲ	ŋ		NASALS

ITA PHONETIC SYMBOLS

	Labial	Dental	Palatal	Velar	Glottal	
Voiceless	p	t	ȼh	(c)k		
Voiced	b	d	j	g		STOPS
Voiceless	f	ŧh	s	ʃh	h/wh	
Voiced	v	ᵵh	z/ꭤ	ʒ		FRICATIVES
Resonant	m	n	n	ꬻ		NASALS

The liquids (+vocalic, +consonantal) are uniformly written [l, r].
Some phoneticians use the symbol [ɫ] as a variant of [l] in non-initial
position as in *lap* ([l æ p] versus *pal* ([p æ ɫ]).

The glide symbols of the four transcription systems are as follows.

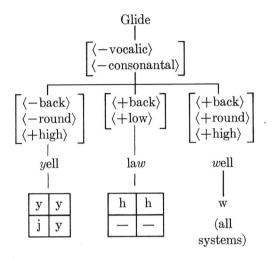

Exercises

1.   The following group of words is arranged in a structural array similar to the chart for the true consonants above. Develop your own array of words and use one of the transcription schemes to represent the consonants phonetically.

*p*ar	*t*ar	*ch*ar	*k*ick
*b*ar	*d*arn	*j*ar	*g*ar
*f*ine	*th*in	*s*ees	*sh*e's *h*e's/*wh*eeze
*v*ine	*th*en	*s*ei*z*e	*s*ie*g*e
ra*m*	ra*n*	ra*ng*e	ra*ng*

2.   Below is a list of homophones, or words which are pronounced alike (*homo* = "same", *phone* = "sound"). How do English speakers know which word is which at the verbal level of speech; that is, in general, how is it that languages tolerate homophones?

   a.   you/yew
   b.   yule/you'll
   c.   discreet/discrete
   d.   cretin/Cretan
   e.   bass/base

3.   What are the main phonetic differences between these words for the common domesticated feline creature which meows?

English French Spanish Portuguese Italian German Greek

cat   chat   gato   gato   gatto   Katze   gata

4. Consult a fairly sophisticated dictionary and investigate these words: *vittles/victuals; critters/creatures.*

Competing Phonetic Transcriptions for English Vowels

As we saw in the section on spirantization, palatalization, and velar softening, often a phonetic form is derived from a phonemic form that one would not suspect was related; that is, we have seen how one form generates another form and how surface phonetic forms are derived from underlying phonemic forms.

Chomsky and Halle, in *The Sound Pattern of English* (1968), have suggested that the underlying vowel system of English consists entirely of simple vowels—there are no so-called "diphthongs" and "triphthongs" but only "monophthongs":

> monophthongs: *a, e, i, o, u* (simple vowels)
> diphthongs: thr*ee*, f*ou*r, t*ow*n (vowel plus glide)
> triphthongs: *you, yew, wow* (glide + vowel + glide)

Before we present the Chomsky-Halle vowel symbology, let us examine the matrix below which delimits the possible types of vowels (+vocalic, −consonantal) that a language may have.

	−back −round	−back +round	+back −round	+back +round
+high −low	X	X	X	X
−high −low	X	X	X	X
−high +low	X	X	X	X

Since vowels may be ⟨+tense⟩ ("long" traditionally) or ⟨−tense⟩ ("short" traditionally), we must double the number of unique segments above so that we have a total of twenty-four possible unique vowel segments. Chomsky and Halle use these underlying vowel segments (a macron marks ⟨+tense⟩ segments):

	−back −round	−back +round	+back −round	+back +round
+high −low	ī/i			ū/u
−high −low	ē/e			ō/o
−high +low	ǣ/æ	ǣ	ā	ɔ/ɔ

Through a series of rules these underlying vowels are converted to surface phonetic vowels. The rules which Chomsky and Halle establish are too complicated and rich for us to present here. However, it is possible for us to furnish the underlying and surface forms of a selected list of English words which fairly well reveals the theoretical soundness of Chomsky-Hallean generative phonology.

	Orthography	Deep Structure	Surface Structure
(1)	beet	/bēt/	[bīyt]
(2)	boot	/bōt/	[būwt]
(3)	bit	/bit/	[bit]
(4)	bull	/bul/	[bul]
(5)	Butte	/bute/	[byūwt]
(6)	bait	/bǣt/	[bēyt]
(7)	boat	/bɔ̄t/	[bōwt]
(8)	but	/but/	[bʌt]
(9)	Berber	/berber/	[bʌrbər]
(10)	bat	/bæt/	[bæt]
(11)	pot	/pɔt/	[pāt]
(12)	law	/lā/	[lɔ̄(h)]
(13)	bet	/bet/	[bet]
(14)	tie	/tī/	[tāy]
(15)	town	/tūn/	[tāwn, tæwn]
(16)	toy	/tɔe/	[tɔ̄y]

We hasten to add that these phonetic forms are valid for Martin and Rulon only; that is, the transcriptions reflect *their* New Mexico and Iowa/Kansas local pronunciations. Below is a list of the same words above in the phonetic notation of S-T, IPA, and ITA.

Orthography	(S-T)	(IPA)	(ITA)
(1) beet	biyt	bit	bɛɛt
(2) boot	buwt	but	bωt
(3) bit	bit	bɪt	bit
(4) bull	bul	bʊl	bωl
(5) Butte	byuwt, byɨwt	bjut	buet
(6) bait	beyt	bet	bæt
(7) boat	bowt	bot	bœt
(8) but	bət	bʌt	but
(9) Berber	bərbər	bɝbɚ	berber
(10) bat	bæt	bæt	bat
(11) pot	pat	pat	pot
(12) law	lɔh	lɔ	l**au**
(13) bet	bet	bɛt	bet
(14) tie	tay	taɪ	t**ie**
(15) town	tawn, tæwn	taUn	toun
(16) toy	tɔy, toy	tɔI	t**oi**

A rule which all dialects of English share is one which "reduces" an unstressed vowel to the so-called "schwa" (ə), which might well be spelled as "uh."

$$\begin{bmatrix} \langle +\text{vocalic}\rangle \\ \langle -\text{consonantal}\rangle \\ \langle -\text{stress}\rangle \end{bmatrix} \rightarrow [\text{ə}]$$

In some dialects of English this reduced vowel schwa is raised to barred-i (ɨ) thus giving rise to a very low level difference between, say, dialect A and dialect B.

Orthography	Dialect A	Dialect B
padded (+Past)	[pǽdəd]	[pǽdɨd]

Notice further that unstressed "uh" will be either schwa or barred-i and that stressed "uh" will be the wedge (ʌ) as in *above* [əbʌv] and *cut* [kʌt] in C-H symbology.

Exercises

1. Phonetically transcribe your pronunciation of the conventional English alphabet.

2.   Phonetically transcribe these English analogues: *long, longer, longest, linger, length, lengthen, elongate, lounge, lunge, Lent, league.*

3.   Transcribe these English analogues: *foot, feet; man, men, woman women; book, beech; goose, geese; foul, filth; full, fill; old, elder; tell, tale,*

Suprasegmental Phonemes

Up to this point we have been concerned only with segmental phonemes, the distinctive units of sound in English. We all know that it is not enough to combine these units without stressing some more than others, without pausing if only for a fraction of a second periodically, or without varying our pitch levels. Otherwise our speech would be appallingly monotonous. Indeed, we can even change the meaning of a sentence merely by changing our intonation pattern. "He drove the car" can become a question, not through the use of the regular question transformation, but by changing the contour of one's intonation: "He drove the car?"

A Thumbnail Sketch of English Stress, Pitch, and Juncture[3]

Stress (accent) refers to the relative acoustic prominence of one syllable over another one. The various kinds of stress which occur in English may be heard in the pronunciation of the paradigm below. Linguists commonly use the terms and symbols sketched below when describing stress assignment. We indicate that a vowel is phonologically TENSE by capitalizing its conventional spelling.

			Numeral Diacritic	Conventional Diacritic
(1)	(a)	primary stress	1 stress	/
	(b)	secondary stress	2 stress	∧
	(c)	tertiary stress	3 stress	\
	(d)	weak stress	4 stress	⌣

(2)   (a)   brief = br$\overset{1}{\text{I}}$Ef = brı́Ef   (adjective)

(b)   briefly = br$\overset{1}{\text{I}}$E$\overset{4}{\text{fly}}$ = brı́Efly̌   (adverb)

---

[3]Based on Chomsky and Halle (1968: 59–162).

$$\overset{2\quad\ 1}{}$$

(c) brief case = brɪɛf cᴀse = brîɛf cǽse   (noun phrase)

$$\overset{1\quad\ 3}{}$$

(d) briefcase = brɪɛfcᴀse = brïɛfcàse   (compound noun)

Just as the phones [s, z, ɪz] of the syntactic category "plural" are predictable by general rule, so is syntactic stress predictable. The phonological features "tense" ⟨+tense⟩ and "non-tense" ⟨−tense⟩ are key items in the prediction of stress. Commonly, polysyllabic (multisyllabic) words are divided into the following units.

(3) (a) ultimate syllable (final syllable)
    (b) penultimate syllable (next to final syllable)
    (c) antepenultimate syllable (third from final syllable)
    (d) antepenultimate   penultimate   ultimate

          syll-   -a-   -ble

The general rules below for the assignment of MAIN STRESS for English (and Latin as well) are a paraphrase of those suggested by Chomsky and Halle (1968:70) in *The Sound Patterns of English:*

(4) (a) Primary stress (1 stress) should be assigned to the penultimate vowel of a word if the last vowel in the word is ⟨−tense⟩ (lax) and if it is followed by no more than a single consonant (C_0^1).
    (b) Primary stress (1 stress) should be assigned to the ultimate vowel in a word if this vowel is ⟨+tense⟩ *or* if it is followed by more than one consonant.

In phonological rules, C = consonant and V = vowel. A superscript numeral specifies the upper bound of sequential segments whereas a subscript numeral specifies the lower bound of sequential segments.

(5) (a) C_0 = zero or more consonants
    (b) C_0^1 = zero or more consonants, but not more than one
    (c) C_1^1 = exactly one consonant
    (d) C_2^2 = exactly two consonants
    (e) C_2^4 = at least two consonants, but not more than four

Informally, one usually lists simply the specified number: C, CC, CCC, etc.

We now return to the matter of stress assignment for individual words. In general, for verbals (verbs and adjectives) ultimate ⟨+tense⟩ vowels receive primary stress; if the ultimate vowel is ⟨−tense⟩ (lax), the stress is placed on the penultimate syllable.

		Ultimate		Ultimate
(6)	(a)	Tense Vowel	(b)	Lax Vowel
		decréAse		ópen
		repéAt		énter
		eráse		stífle
		províde		devélop
		divíne		jéalous
		contríte		lázy
		afráıd		mássive

Consider now the following verbals which are unlike those in (6) in that they terminate in consonant clusters and therefore have underlying lax vowels in the ultimate syllables:

(7)	(a) prevént	(b) contént
	advánce	adépt
	conténd	defúnct
	enthráll	corrúpt

Thus we must refine our generalization concerning stress placement for verbals:

(8) Verbals with ultimate ⟨+tense⟩ vowels receive primary stress on that segment. If the ultimate vowel is ⟨−tense⟩ (lax) and followed by no more than one consonant, then primary stress is placed on the penultimate syllable. If the ultimate vowel is ⟨−tense⟩ (lax) and followed by two or more consonants, then the ultimate vowel receives primary stress.

For some speakers of English, an alternate statement of stress is necessary.

(9) Verbals with ultimate ⟨+tense⟩ vowels receive primary stress on that segment. If the ultimate vowel is lax and followed by at least one consonant, then the penultimate vowel is stressed. This accounts for the following forms:

(10) prévent, ádvance, cóntend, énthrall, cóntent, ádept, défunct, córrupt.

At first glance, the task of accounting for the primary stress assignment of nouns seems insuperable unless one is willing to accept what *seems* to be a bit of linguistic hocus-pocus. To be blunt about it, if one disregards a final lax syllable of nouns, they receive primary stress in the same way as verbals. Consider the following data drawn from that provided by Chomsky and Halle (1968:71):

(11)   (a) cínem-a   (b) arÓm-á   (c) veránd-a
         aspárag-us   hɪʌ́t-us   agénd-a
         metrÓpol-is   horíz-on   amálg-am
         jável-in   corÓn-a   appénd-ix

Additionally, in determining stress for a word, one must make a distinction between derived and non-derived forms. Hence, in *The Sound Pattern of English*, Chomsky and Halle (1968:80–81) distinguish between "primary" (non-derived) and "secondary" (derived) adjectives and nouns for the purposes of stress assignment.

(12)   (a) sOlid, suprɛme, absurd, manifest (non-derived)
        (b) person-al, anecdOt-al, dialect-al, rigor-ous, desɪr-ous, tremend-ous, vigil-ant, defɪ-ant, observ-ant, arrog-ant, adjʌc-ent, indign-ant (derived)
        (c) manage-ment, punish-ment, arrʌnge-ment (derived)

Now we may expand our statement of main stress assignment.

(13)   (a) Disregard the final lax vowel and any consonants that follow it in nouns and derived adjectives.
        (b) Verbals and nouns with ultimate ⟨+tense⟩ vowels receive primary stress on that segment.
        (c) If the ultimate vowel is lax and followed by not more than one consonant, the primary stress should be placed on the penultimate syllable.
        (d) If the ultimate vowel is lax and followed by two or more consonants, the primary stress should be placed on the ultimate vowel.
        (e) In monosyllabic words, the primary stress should be placed on the vowel segment.

Let us consider the derivation of non-primary stresses as in

     1   3   1   3
     vɪolʌte   and   hurricʌne.

The alternating stress rule and the stress adjustment rule account for these forms and others like them.

(14) (a) The ALTERNATING STRESS rule: Add primary stress to the antepenultimate syllable of a noun or verbal which terminates in a ⟨+tense⟩ segment that is already marked with primary stress by the main stress rule.

  (b) The STRESS ADJUSTMENT rule: Reduce all non-primary stresses by a value of one within a word.

The derivations in (15) and (16) illustrate these rules.

(15) (a) *violate*

  1
  (b) VIOLAte = VIOLÁte Main Stress Rule (13b)

  1 2
  (c) VIOLAte = VÍOLÁte Alternating Stress Rule (14a)

  1 3
  (d) VIOLAte = VÍOLÀte Stress Adjustment Rule (14b)

(16) (a) *hurricane*

  1
  (b) hurricAne = hurricÁne Main Stress Rule (13b)

  1 2
  (c) hurricAne = húrricÁne Alternating Stress Rule (14a)

  1 3
  (d) hurricAne = húrricÀne Stress Adjustment Rule (14b)

The rules we have been discussing so far are known as rules of WORD PHONOLOGY. We turn now to the derivation of stress for units other than the word, such as noun phrases (*brief case, black bird*) and compound nouns (*briefcase, blackbird*). To do so, we must take recourse to the notions of "tree diagram" and "labeled brackets."

Let us consider the difference between the forms below.

    2 1
(17) (a) brIEf cAse = brîEf cÁse (Adjective + Noun = Noun Phrase)

    1 3
  (b) brIEfcAse = brÍEfcÀse (Noun + Noun = Compound Noun)

The syntactic structures of (17) are laid out in (18). Tree diagrams are equivalent to labeled brackets. The crosshatch indicates a word boundary.

(18)   (a)

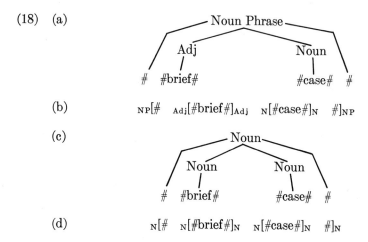

(b) $_{NP}[\# \;\;_{Adj}[\#brief\#]_{Adj} \;\;_{N}[\#case\#]_{N} \;\;\#]_{NP}$

(c)

(d) $_{N}[\# \;\;_{N}[\#brief\#]_{N} \;\;_{N}[\#case\#]_{N} \;\;\#]_{N}$

As the diagrams indicate, *brief* and *case* are simultaneously individual words and part of a larger unit, namely, noun phrase and noun. The rules which supply stress in units larger than a word are said to apply cyclically; that is, they apply first at the lowest and innermost point possible; then, as it were, they apply upward on the tree diagram. The labeled brackets also indicate that #brief# and #case# are individual words as well as parts of the unit noun phrase and the unit noun. Thus as individual words #brief# and #case# receive primary stress by the main stress rule:

rule:

$$\text{(19)   (a)} \qquad\qquad \overset{1}{_{NP}[\# \;\#brief\#} \;\overset{1}{\#case\#} \;\#]_{NP}} = \text{``brief case''}$$

$$\text{(b)} \qquad\qquad \overset{1}{_{N}[\# \;\#brief\#} \;\overset{1}{\#case\#} \;\#]_{N}} = \text{``briefcase''}$$

The COMPOUND STRESS rule and the NUCLEAR STRESS rule complete the derivation of these units.

(20)   (a) Compound stress rule: To an already primary stressed vowel a primary stress should be assigned just in case that vowel is followed by another primary stressed vowel in a noun.

     (b) Corollary: The existing stress in the unit under consideration reduces by a value of one.

$$\text{(21)} \qquad \overset{1}{_{N}[\# \;\#brief\#} \;\overset{1}{\#case\#} \;\#]_{N}} \rightarrow \overset{1}{_{N}[\# \;\#brief\#} \;\overset{2}{\#case\#} \;\#]_{N}}$$

(22)   (a) Nuclear stress rule: To an already primary stressed vowel, primary stress should be assigned just in case that vowel is preceded by another primary stressed vowel in a noun phrase.

(b) Corollary: The existing stress in the unit reduces by a value of one.

$$\text{(23)} \qquad _\text{NP}[\# \overset{1}{\#\text{brief}\#} \overset{1}{\#\text{case}\#} \#]_\text{NP} \rightarrow {}_\text{NP}[\# \overset{2}{\#\text{brief}\#} \overset{1}{\#\text{case}\#} \#]_\text{NP}$$

By applying the STRESS ADJUSTMENT rule, (21) achieves its final form.

(24) Stress Adjustment Rule: Within a *word*, all non-primary stresses are reduced by a value of one.

$$\text{(25)} \qquad _\text{N}[\# \overset{1}{\#\text{brief}\#} \overset{2}{\#\text{case}\#} \#]_\text{N} \rightarrow {}_\text{N}[\# \overset{1}{\#\text{brief}\#} \overset{3}{\#\text{case}\#} \#]_\text{N}$$

The noun phrase *brief case* is unaffected by the stress adjustment rule; however, the compound noun *briefcase* is subject to it, since the two words *brief* and *case* are compounded to form another word.

We repeat, then, that English has the following contrastive pairs:

(26) (a) brief case = briêf cáse (noun phrase)

      (b) briefcase = briéfcàse (compound noun)

As Chomsky and Halle (1968:17) indicate, the compound stress rule applies also to such lexical categories as compound adjectives and compound verbs. The nuclear stress rule applies to adjective phrases, verb phrases, and sentences.

(27) (a) briefcase = bríefcàse (compound noun)

      (b) grief-stricken = gríef-stricken (compound adjective)

      (c) steam-clean = stéam-clèan (compound verb)

      (d) sing the song = sîng the sóng (verb phrase)

      (e) smooth to ride = smoôth to ríde (adjective phrase)

      (f) Dallas won = Dâllas wón (sentence)

Finally, let us simply mention the phenomenon of PITCH. This refers to the relative raising or lowering of one's natural register or voice level. Commonly, four levels of pitch on a 1–2–3–4 increasing scale are recognized, the fourth level being generally limited to states of excitement and the like. Usually one begins a sentence at level 2. Here are two very common patterns.

(28) (a) ²He drove the ³car.¹
      (b) ²She wove a ³rug.¹
      (c) ²Who would ³go?¹
      (d) ²What toy does he ³want?¹
      (e) ²Should he ³worry?³
      (f) ²Would she ³answer?³

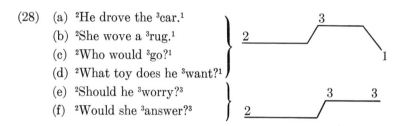

Phonological Boundaries

In *The Sound Patterns of English* (1968:66–67) Chomsky and Halle posit the existence of three phonological boundaries; these boundaries, as it were, are the sounds of silence; that is, they are the absence of sound. These three boundaries are:

Word Boundary	Formative Boundary	Affix Boundary
−segment	−segment	−segment
+WB	−WB	−WB
−FB	+FB	−FB
#	+	=

The following diagram exemplifies these three boundaries.

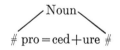

Structural grammarians recognized three kinds of pauses which accompanied the pitch levels mentioned above. These may be symbolized as a falling pause (↓), a rising pause (↑), and a sustained pause (→).

(1) ²He drove the ³car.¹ ↓
(2) ²Should he ³worry.³ ↑
(3) ²The boy on my ³left² → ²came in ³late.¹ ↓

Some structural grammarians used another four symbols to indicate juncture or pause; they are arranged in increasing order of length: +, /, //, #. The so-called "internal juncture" (+) allegedly occurs in the punch line of this anecdote used by Professor John Calvin McGalliard at the University of Iowa.

> It seems that there was a mother skunk and her five little ones walking through the woods. They suddenly encountered a bear. Mother Skunk said: "Let spray!" (Or was it "Let's pray!"?)

In phonetic symbols, these can be transcribed as follows:

(a) Let spray! [let + sprēy]
(b) Let's pray! [lets + prēy]

We conclude now with an informal derivation which shows the intonation contours just discussed as well as phonemic and phonetic transcriptions of an English sentence.

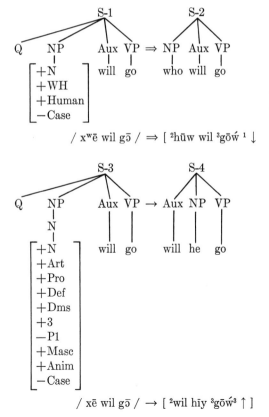

Summary

In this chapter we have examined a number of phonological rules which relate underlying phonemic forms to surface phonetic forms. Indirectly we have hinted that conventional English orthography is primarily a phonemic rather than a phonetic form of writing and that such predictable phenomena as the ⟨+Past⟩ and ⟨+Plural⟩ phonetic alternates [d, t, id] and [s, z, and iz] need not be reflected directly in the writing system.

In the next chapter we suggest that a language such as English is really a collection of dialects that share common underlying forms, which ordered sets of rules convert to alternate surface structures.

References

Chomsky, Noam, and Morris Halle. *The Sound Pattern of English*. New York: Harper and Row, 1968.

Ferguson, Charles A. "Review of *The Sound Pattern of Russian*." *Language*, 38, No. 3 (1962) 284–98.

Halle, Morris. *The Sound Pattern of Russian*. The Hague: Mouton & Co., 1959.

Harms, Robert T. *An Introduction to Phonological Theory*. Englewood Cliffs, New Jersey: Prentice-Hall, 1968.

Harris, James W. *Spanish Phonology*. Cambridge, Massachusetts: MIT Press, 1969.

Hockett, Charles F. *A Manual of Phonology*. Baltimore: Waverly Press, 1955.

Postal, Paul M. *Aspects of Phonological Theory*. New York: Harper and Row, 1968.

Saltarelli, Mario. *A Phonology of Italian in a Generative Grammar*. The Hague: Mouton & Co., 1970.

Schane, Sanford. *French Phonology and Morphology*. Cambridge, Massachusetts: MIT Press, 1968.

Smith, Henry Lee, and George Trager. *An Outline of English Structure*. Washington, D.C.: American Council of Learned Societies, 1957.

Thomas, Charles Kenneth. *An Introduction to the Phonetics of American English*. New York: Ronald Press, 1958.

VI

Dialectal Variations in Today's English

Whenever we move, we invariably take at least one personal possession, our language. When the English colonists appeared at Jamestown in 1607 and at Plymouth in 1620, they brought with them their Early Modern English—the language of Shakespeare, John Donne, John Bunyan, John Milton, and other great writers who seem so far removed from what we today call American English. Depending on the English locale they came from, these early colonists spoke some variety of seventeenth-century British English. Throughout settlement history these various local dialects in America were blended together, usually under the influence of some prestigious cultural and economic center like Boston, New York, Philadelphia, or Charleston. These dialects in turn were subjected to foreign influences (most often related to word borrowing) from at least three different sources: the American Indians already in the country, the Spanish and French-speaking people along the southern and northern borders, and the waves of immigrants whose language was Polish, German, Czech, Norwegian, Swedish, or some other European language, as well as some African languages.

Eventually several major regional dialects appear, and their regional boundaries today can be traced with some accuracy. Furthermore, over a period of three hundred years English in this country undergoes enough change so that it can be clearly distinguished from British English, which in the same period of time has also been undergoing change.

188   The English Language: Yesterday and Today

Since both varieties of language are mutually intelligible to British and American speakers, we cannot say that the British are speaking a different language, even though at one time writers like H. L. Mencken wanted to make a case for two distinct languages. The essential differences are dialectal, and related to pronunciation (*God, lot, got,* for example, have a phonetic [ɔ] which becomes unrounded to [a] in American English) and to vocabulary (*druggist* vs. *chemist; vacation* vs. *holiday*).

A Brief History of Dialect Study

The scientific study of these dialect differences appears rather late in history for at least two reasons. The prescriptivists of the eighteenth century, in their pursuit of a logical, universal, unchanging language, were not interested in dialectal variations, which they considered corruptions of some ideal language. The comparative linguists of the nineteenth century were busy with their descriptions of extant languages, and the structural linguists of the twentieth with a scientific description of English. Until their techniques for description could be refined and systematized, dialect study was not possible.

The first dialect study, the *Deutscher Sprachatlas,* begun in Germany in 1876 under the direction of George Wenker, attempted to describe pronunciation differences throughout Germany. Questionnaires were sent to village schoolteachers asking them to transcribe the local pronunciation of a given set of sentences. Because of the teachers' limited qualifications in transcribing speech, the responses were almost too varied to be useful. However, a wide variety of vocabulary differences became apparent.

The *Atlas linguistique de la France* (1902–1910), by Jules Gilliéron, is considerably more accurate because he enlisted the help of one FIELD-WORKER, who bicycled all over France and interviewed six hundred INFORMANTS. The transcriptions, while more uniform and accurate than the German data, are not quite representative since the fieldworker worked in rural areas, neglecting the larger cities.

A study of the dialects of Italy and southern Switzerland, made by Karl Jaberg and Jakob Jud between 1925 and 1940, is more inclusive, containing both rural and urban responses.

In America the American Dialect Society was founded at Harvard in 1889 for "the investigation of the English dialects in America with regard to pronunciation, grammar, vocabulary, phraseology, and geographical distribution" with the aim of eventually publishing "an authoritative dictionary of American usage." From 1890 to 1939 the Society published *Dialect Notes,* which included both short articles on dialect and full-length monographs. Its successor after World War II was the *Publication of the American Dialect Society*, more commonly called *PADS*.

In 1929 a linguistic atlas of the United States was begun under the editorship of Hans Kurath with the financial support of the American Council of Learned Societies. A staff of fieldworkers was employed, trained in the methodology of Gilliéron, Jaberg, and Jud, and asked to examine the speech habits of 213 New England communities, a task which took over two years to complete—until September of 1933. Since the editing of the findings required several more years, the *Linguistic Atlas of New England*, in three volumes bound in two parts each, was finally published between 1939 and 1943.

In an attempt to obtain a good cross-section of the speakers, Kurath asked for three types of informants:

Type I: little formal education, little reading, and restricted social contacts.

Type II: better formal education (usually high school) and/or wider reading and social contacts.

Type III: superior education (usually college), cultured background, wide reading and/or extensive social contacts.

These types in turn are divided into two subclasses:

A: aged or old-fashioned
B: middle-aged or younger

These informants, of course, were to be people who had lived all their lives in the area and preferably ones whose families also were natives.

The fieldworkers were given work sheets on which they recorded the pronunciation of certain words ([pæθ] vs. [pāθ]), lexical choices (*bucket/pail*), and morphological variants (*dive/dove*). The results were printed in phonetic symbols at the approximate locale on the map represented by the informant. In all, the *Linguistic Atlas* contains some six hundred maps of New England, each one 20 by 24 inches in size.

The remainder of the United States will be described in less sumptuous fashion, when the study of the remaining regions is concluded. To date, very slow progress is being made in the rest of the country chiefly because of a lack of supporting funds. Eventually there will be atlases of the North Central states (Wisconsin, Michigan, Illinois, Indiana, Kentucky, and Ohio), the Upper Midwest (Minnesota, Iowa, North Dakota, South Dakota, Nebraska), the Middle Atlantic and South Atlantic states (New Jersey, Pennsylvania, West Virginia, Virginia, Delaware, Maryland, North Carolina, South Carolina, and eastern Georgia), the Rocky Mountain states (Montana, Wyoming, Utah, Colorado, Arizona, and New Mexico), the Pacific Coast (Washington, Oregon, Idaho, California, and Nevada), and the Inland South (Ala-

MAP 1

PROGRESS OF THE AMERICAN ATLASES*

*Prepared by Mrs. Raven I. McDavid for *The Structure of American English*, by W. Nelson Francis. Copyright ©1958. The Ronald Press Compay, New York.

bama, Arkansas, Florida, Louisiana, Oklahoma, Mississippi, and western Georgia). Of these the atlas of the Upper Midwest, under the direction of Harold B. Allen, is nearly ready for publication as of this writing. The Texas study includes only vocabulary items and has been published in *The Regional Vocabulary of Texas*, by E. Bagby Atwood (1962). (See Map 1.)

New England and the Eastern Seaboard states have made dialect study less formidable because of relatively stable populations. Thus dialect areas were apparent from an early date. Because of the mobility of the American people and the chaotic nature of settlement history, the remainder of the country, especially the west, has been influenced by a variety of cross movenents.

That the various atlases of the United States are so slow in appearing is not indicative of a lack of interest in dialect study. Innumerable articles have appeared in both *PADS* and *American Speech* as well as in other periodicals; numerous doctoral dissertations have explored some facet of dialect; and a few full-length studies have already appeared: Atwood's Texas vocabulary study, Hans Kurath's *A Word*

Geography of the Eastern United States (1949), Atwood's *A Survey of Verb Forms in the Eastern United States* (1953), Hans Kurath and Raven McDavid's *Pronunciation of English in the Atlantic States* (1961), and Virginia G. McDavid's *Verb Forms of the North Central States and the Upper Midwest* (Unpublished doctoral dissertation, University of Minnesota, 1956).

Regional Differences

What is it, then, that tells us that the speech of a person from another part of the country is a different dialect from ours? Why are we amused when we first hear the speech of another region? The obvious differences are pronunciation and vocabulary choice. If the person drops his *r*'s, and we don't, or if he inserts *r*'s where we don't, then we tend to laugh at his strange "dialect." Or if he asks to "carry" us to a movie or to buy us a "tonic," we chuckle at his quaint choice of words. Occasionally a grammatical pattern will betray a different origin—"It's a quarter *to* nine" or "He *dove* off the board."

Dialect study so far has revealed at least three distinct regions in the eastern United States, each with enough differences to be called a separate dialect. The DIALECT GEOGRAPHER's method of study involves interviewing his informants in a given region, noting where one pronunciation ends and another begins. On his dialect map he draws a line called an ISOGLOSS which divides the two areas where, say, *path* is pronounced [pæθ] and [pāθ]. If enough different lines fall within essentially the same area to form a BUNDLE OF ISOGLOSSES, he can be sure of a dialect boundary.

The three main dialect regions in the eastern United States (which to this date has been given the most attention) are Northern, Midland, and Southern, each one having within it several areas with their own particular characteristics. The first of these is VOCABULARY, as these short lists will illustrate. (See Map 2.)

> NORTHERN: *clapboards, pail, spider* (frying pan); *corn husks, co-boss* (call to cow)
>
> > Eastern New England: *bonnyclabber, bonnyclapper* (curdled milk); *sour milk cheese* (cottage cheese)
> >
> > Inland Northern: *Dutch cheese* (cottage cheese); *lobbered milk, loppered milk* (curdled milk)
> >
> > New York City: *pot cheese* (cottage cheese)
>
> MIDLAND: *green beans* (except in Eastern Pennsylvania); *skillet, snake feeder* (dragon fly); *sook* (call to cow)

MAP 2
DIALECT AREAS OF THE UNITED STATES*

Atlantic Seaboard Areas (after Kurath). Tentative Dialect Boundaries. Arrows indicate direction of migrations.

THE NORTH	THE MIDLAND	THE SOUTH
1. Northeastern New England	*North Midland* 7. Delaware Valley (Philadelphia)	14. Delmarva (Eastern Shore)
2. Southeastern New England	8. Susquehanna Valley	15. The Virginia Piedmont
3. Southwestern New England	10. Upper Ohio Valley (Pittsburgh)	16. Northeastern North Carolina (Albemarle Sound & Neuse Valley)
4. Inland North (western Vermont, Upstate New York & derivatives)	11. Northern West Virginia *South Midland*	17. Cape Fear & Peedee Valleys
5. The Hudson Valley	9. Upper Potomac & Shenandoah	18. The South Carolina Low Country (Charleston)
6. Metropolitan New York	12. Southern West Virginia & Eastern Kentucky	
	13. Western Carolina & Eastern Tennessee	

Eastern Pennsylvania: Germanisms like *fatcakes* (doughnuts); *toot* (paper bag)

Western Pennsylvania: *crudded milk* or *cruds* (curdled milk, cottage cheese)

South Midland: *clabber milk* (curdled milk)

SOUTH MIDLAND AND SOUTH: *clabber* (curdled milk); *corn shucks, snack* (food eaten between meals); *snake doctor* (dragon fly).

SOUTH: *carry* (take, escort); *co-wench* (call to cow); *lightwood* (kindling).

Eastern Virginia: *batter bread* (soft cornbread); *croker sack* (burlap bag); *goobers* (peanuts); *hoppergrass* (grasshopper).

South Carolina and Georgia: *groundnuts* (peanuts); *fatwood* (kindling).

A second feature which distinguishes dialect areas is PRONUNCIATION, illustrated by this short list:

Northern: [s] in *greasy*

[ð] in *with*

[ōw] in *mourning* and *hoarse*

[ɔʌ] in *morning* and *horse*

[ɨ] in *careless*

Eastern New England:

[æ] in *barn* and *father*

r deleted except before vowels

[ūw] in *Tuesday* and *new*

epenthetic *r* in (*lawr* and order)

Inland Northern:

[yūw] in *Tuesday* and *new*

r is not deleted

New York City:

r is deleted except before vowels (for many, though not all, speakers)

[ōw] and [ɔʌ] not distinguished in *hoarse* and *horse* (for many, though not all, speakers)

[ā] in *foreign, hog,* and *frog* (for many, though not all, speakers)

[w] rather than [hw] in *wheelbarrow* (for many, though not all, speakers)

Midland:

r is not deleted

[ə] rather than [ɨ] in *careless*

[θ] rather than [ð] in *with*

[z] rather than [s] in *greasy*

Eastern Pennsylvania:

[ūw] in *Tuesday* and *new*

[ōw] and [ɔʌ] not distinguished in *morning* and *mourning*

[ā] in *frog* and *hog*

[w] rather than [hw] in wh*eelbarrow*

South Midland:

Underlying /ī/ is realized as [a•]; thus /ī/ → [āy] as usual, but the glide (y) is replaced by the length feature, in words such as *nice* and *time*

South Midland and Southern:

[yūw] in *Tuesday* and *new*

[a•] in *nice* and *time*

Underlying /ū/ is realized as [æw] rather than [āw] as in *house*

Southern:

r is deleted except before vowels

[ēy] in *Mary* and *dairy*

[i] (or perhaps ɨ) in *haunted*

[z] in *Mrs* and *greasy*

Eastern Virginia:

Underlying /ū/ is realized as [ʌw]; that is, /ū/ → [āw] as usual, but the vowel is raised to wedge.

Underlying /ī/ is realized as [ʌy]; that is, /ī/ → [āy] as usual, but the vowel is raised to wedge.

A third feature which distinguishes one dialect from another (both regionally and socially) is the GRAMMATICAL DIFFERENCE which one finds exhibited in the "principal parts" of English verb segments (+Verbal, +Verb). For example, a speaker of one dialect may have the paradigm *bring/brang/brung*, whereas another speaker may have *bring/brought/brought*. Both paradigms are full-fledged members of the English language. Before we exemplify and discuss this phenomenon further, it is necessary for us to outline briefly what seems to us to be a sane view of the system of English verb segments, first publicly suggested by Professor Silas Griggs (1972).[1] In his analysis he suggests the following classification of English verb segments:

---

[1]A joint lecture presented by Drs. Griggs and Rulon before the East Texas State University Linguistic Circle, Commerce, Texas, April, 1972, entitled "The English Verb Reconsidered in Distinctive Features." (Dittographed.) The main basis of the classification is on the occurrence of the lexical features ⟨+en⟩ or ⟨−en⟩, features which correspond to the perfective affix mentioned in Chapter IV of this text. (See p. 95.) The ⟨+regular⟩ verbs are those which have a predictable dental suffix such as *patt*ed, *padd*ed, *etch*ed, and *edg*ed. Weak verbs (−regular, −en) exhibit an unpredictable dental suffix such as *bring/brought/brought* and *bend, bent, bent*, as well as *can/could* and *may/might*. Strong verbs (−regular, +en) show a fluctuation (ablaut) in the vowel of the stem such as *rise/rose/risen* (+I), *freeze/froze/froze(n)* (+II) and *swim/swam/swum* (+III) for some (though not all) speakers. The mixed verbs (+mixed) exhibit an unusual ⟨+past⟩ or ⟨+perfective⟩ form. For example, the verb *saw* (to cut wood) can be conjugated with a ⟨+regular⟩, ⟨+past⟩ form and a ⟨−regular⟩, ⟨+perfective⟩ form: *saw/sawed/sawn*, whereas *crow* can be conjugated with a strong ⟨+past⟩ form, and a ⟨+regular⟩, ⟨+perfective⟩ form: *crow/crew/crowed*.

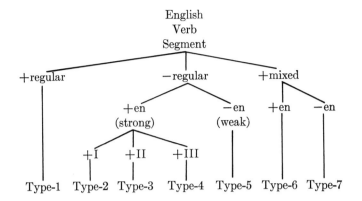

Which particular English verb segment fits into a specific type above depends on the regional and social environments in which one finds himself; also, a given verb may have competing (stylistic?) paradigms such as the weak verb ⟨−regular⟩, ⟨−en⟩ *kneel/knelt/knelt* or the phonologically ⟨+regular⟩ verb *kneel/kneeled/kneeled* within the dialect of one speaker.

Below we exemplify the possible seven types of English verb segments in the essentially northeast Kansas dialect of one of the authors (Rulon), with some actual competing variations in parentheses.

Type-1
(+regular)

1. pat/patted/patted
2. pad/padded/padded
3. etch/etched/etched
4. edge/edged/edged

Types-2-3-4 (strong)
(−regular)
(+en)

(+I)

1. rise/rose/risen
   (rise/riz/riz)
2. blow/blew/blown
   (blow/blowed/blowed)
   (blow/blew/blowed)
3. drive/drove/driven
   (drive/drove/drove)

(+II)

4. climb/clumb/clumb
   (climb/climbed/climbed)
5. dive/dove/dove
   (dive/dived/dived)
   (dive/dove/dived)
6. freeze/froze/froze(n)

(+III)

7. begin/began/begun
   (begin/begun/begun)
8. drink/drank/drunk
   (drink/drunk/drunk)

Type-5 (weak)
(−regular)
(−en)

1. bring/brought/brought
   (bring/brang/brung)
2. buy/bought/bought
3. catch/caught/caught
   (catch/catched/catched)

4. dream/dreamt/dreamt
   (dream/dreampt/dreampt)
   (dream/dreamed/dreamed)
5. fit/fit/fit
   (fit/fitted/fitted)
6. kneel/knelt/knelt
   (kneel/kneeled/kneeled)

Types-6 and 7

(+en)

1. hew/hewed/hewn
   (hew/hewed/hewed)
2. saw/sawed/sawn
   (saw/sawed/sawed)
3. prove/proved/proven
   (prove/proved/proved)

(−en)

4. dive/dove/dived
   (dive/dived/dived)
   (dive/dove/dove)
5. crow/crew/crowed
   (crow/crowed/crowed)
6. thrive/throve/thrived
   (thrived/thrived/thrived)
   (thrive/throve/thriven)

The seven types of verbs listed above may be reduced to essentially five types if such verbs as *hew, dive, saw, crow, prove, thrive* are construed by a speaker to be ⟨+regular⟩.

Our basic point here, however, is that all English speakers (within the entire spectrum of ethnic backgrounds) have the ability (competence) to recognize and understand potentially seven types of English verbs, even though all seven types may not occur in the speech (performance) of an individual speaker. Thus, for example, a given speaker has at least three thoroughly English options for conjugating such a verb stem as *shrink:*

   a.   shrink/shrinked/shrinked (+regular)
   b.   shrink/shrunk/shrunk (−regular, +en, +II)
   c.   shrink/shrank/shrunk (−regular, +en, +III)

In theory, then, there should be no stigma attached to the same or another speaker for his conjugation of such a verb stem as *drink* on the same basis:

   a.   drink/drinked/drinked (+regular)
   b.   drink/drunk/drunk (−regular, +en, +II)
   c.   drink/drank/drunk (−regular, +en, +III)

It is our hope that the above discussion will direct the reader to a humanistic rather than casuistic examination of the regional (Northern, Midland, Southern) and social (Types I and II) variations in the table of verbs below, which were adapted from E. Bagby Atwood (1953) and Virginia G. McDavid (1956); the latter has aptly noted "that such variety is not unfitting in a country of the cultural richness of the United States."

NORTHERN

Verb Stem	−past	+past	+perfect	adjectival
catch	—	catched	catched	—
climb	—	clim	clim	—
dive	—	dove	—	—
have ought	—	hadn't ought	—	—
heat	—	het	—	het
scare	—	—	—	scairt
see	—	see	—	—
will + nt	[wʌnt]	—	—	—

MIDLAND

climb	—	clumb	—	—
see	—	seen	—	—
sweat	—	sweated	—	—

NORTH MIDLAND

get awake	—	got awake	—	—

SOUTH MIDLAND

dog-bite	—	—	—	dog-bit (bitten by a dog)
drink	—	drinked	—	—
give out	—	—	—	give out (tuckered out, tired out)
catch	—	ketched	—	—
rise	—	raised	—	—
see	—	seed	—	—
shrink	—	shrinked	—	—
swim	—	swim	—	—
use to	—	used to didn't/ used to wasn't		

SOUTH MIDLAND AND SOUTHERN

Verb Stem	−past	+past	+perfect	adjectival
boil	—	—	—	boilt (eggs)
buy	—	—	—	bought (bread)
bring	—	brung	—	—
cost	costes	—	—	—
dive	—	div	—	—
drive	—	driv	—	—
draw up (shrink)	—	drawed	—	—
fight	—	fit/fout	—	—
hear	—	heerd	heern	—
be	I is	—	—	—
may-can	—	might-could/ mout-could		
owe to + n't	—	oughtn't to	—	—
ride	—	rid	—	—
rise	—	riz	—	—
take	—	tuck	—	—
be	—	[wʌdnt] (wasn't)		

TYPES I AND II[2]

blow	—	blowed	—	—
bring	—	brung	—	—
drive	—	—	drove	—
drown(d)	—	drownded	—	—
throw	—	throwed	—	—
tear	—	—	tore	—
wear	—	—	wore	—
write	—	—	wrote	—
be + n't	ain't	—	—	—
have + n't	ain't	—	—	—

[2]Note: Additionally, Type I and II speakers mark surface structure progressive forms with the prefix *a-*. This prefix is probably a truncated form of *at*, as in: "The chanteur and chanteuse were *a*-singin' a Wagnerian duet."

It is appropriate here to mention a very significant publication by Juanita V. Williamson (1968), entitled *A Phonological and Morphological Study of the Speech of the Negro of Memphis, Tennessee*, which is a structural (item and arrangement) dialectological analysis of the phonemic inventory and incidence and verb morphology of twenty-three native Memphians and one non-native. Professor Williamson, in comparing her data with that of Atwood's and the *Linguistic Atlas*, finds that in general there is no essential difference between these twenty-four Memphians and the speakers of other regional and social American dialects. Phonologically, the informants in this study exhibit only the surface phonetic differences that one would expect to find in the South. The morphological differences of the verbs parallel that of other well-known and documented American dialects. In the now-familiar terms of this text, she finds no deep structure differences but only the expected surface structure variation that one also encounters in Atlanta, Montgomery, Charleston, Dallas, Houston, and other southern metropolitan cities.

Through the development of television and radio and the increased mobility of the American people, regional dialects are blending together, though they are not likely to become completely uniform in the near future. It would seem that the language of television announcers and newsmen might have a great effect on reducing dialect differences, given the long hours many people spend before their sets; however, little apparent change is taking place, evidently because of the passive nature of television-viewing—the listener doesn't speak back to the set. Given this mobility of Americans and the increased urbanization of the population, it is somewhat misleading to reproduce long tables of words and pronunciations and say that these are representative of the people of a given area. Once a study is made, it becomes a historical relic of the speech habits of a given sampling of people (presumably an adequate cross-section) at a given moment in time. Certainly many words on the lists are relics of a bygone era. *Whiffletree*, like other words pertaining to horses and buggies, is known only to older people of rural upbringing. The *skillet/spider/creeper* distinction is being blurred by *frying pan*, possibly because of the influence of advertising, where this one term might be used nationally. Surely *clapboards* and *weatherboards* are giving way to *siding* since the advent and marketing of aluminum siding. Likewise, *cottage cheese*, the name dairies place on the packaged product, will eventually make antiquated relics out of *lobbered cheese* and its equivalents.

Dialect studies of the western half of the United States reveal a blurring of the many distinctions found in the eastern half, where dialect regions are fairly clear-cut because of the longer period of settlement along the eastern coast and in the South. Generally speaking, the colonists moved westward, so the Great Lakes states and the Pacific Northwest tend to reflect many of the speech patterns of the Northeast. The Southern region extends from southern Delaware south along the Atlantic coast and westward into east Texas. The Midland area extends westward from New Jersey and fans out behind the mountainous ridges of the Alleghenies and the southern Appalachians, reaching through the Midwest and Southwest all the way to the Pacific coast. Needless to say, the unending trek to California from all parts of the country has resulted in a hodgepodge of dialect features there.

Foreign Influence on American Dialects

In their move westward the colonists came in contact with Spanish speakers in the Southwest and with French speakers along the Canadian border; hence American English was subjected to the vocabularies of these languages, resulting in a number of borrowings. *Mosquito* (from *mosca*, "little fly"), *frijoles* (beans), *patio, arroyo* (dry creek), *mesa* (flat land), and *burro* (donkey) are only a few borrowings from Spanish. *Levee* (from French *lever*, "to raise"), *chowder* (from *chaudiere*, "caldron"), *carryall* (*cariole*), and *prairie* are from French.

The colonists who didn't move west were influenced by the language of other settlers of foreign descent. A large number of German words appear in eastern Pennsylvania, where German immigrants settled. *Fatcakes* (doughnuts) has already been mentioned and comes from the German *fettkuche*. *Smearcase* (cottage cheese) is an Anglicization of *schmierkäs*. Dutch words, too, were borrowed back when New York was New Amsterdam: *coleslaw* (*koolsla*, "cabbage salad"), *cooky, cruller, boss, stoop* (porch).

Indian languages make up an obvious source of borrowing (*squash, hominy, succotash, moccasin, tomahawk, wigwam, mackinaw, squaw*), as African languages did later when blacks were brought to the United States as slaves (*banjo, gumbo, voodoo*).

Generative Phonology and Dialectal Variation

We have just seen that a language such as English in both Britain and America is really a conglomerate of mutually intelligible dialects. The adhesive which holds such a language together is the phenomenon of identical (or nearly identical) common deep structures, which undergo different sets of transformations. Conventional orthography (ordinary spelling) works for all dialects of English, then, because it represents common underlying structures which are highly resistant to change. Conventional orthography dates from about 1500 A.D. Thus the underlying structure of English has been stable for about five hundred years.

As we saw in the phonology chapter, such predictable phonological processes as palatalization, spirantization, velar softening, and the like need not be reflected in the spelling system, since they are automatic for the native speaker.

We now see how it is possible for one spelling to serve for six different pronunciations, which are both stylistic and dialectal in nature. English *length*, for example, may be represented phonetically for a variety of speakers as follows:

a. [leŋθ] b. [leŋkθ] c. [liŋθ] d. [liŋkθ] e. [lenθ] f. [linθ]

As native speakers of English, we know that *length* is a nominalized form of the verbal *long* and furthermore that it is also related to *linger*, *lengthen*, *lounge*, and *lunge*. A larger phonological pattern of English is actually involved here, however, in that *long* and *length* are part of a regular alternation between front ($-$back) and back ($+$back) vowels, as the following chart indicates.[3]

	$-$back		$+$back
$+$high $-$low	i	↔	u
$-$high $-$low	e	↔	o
$-$high $+$low	æ	↔	ɔ

s*i*ng	s*u*ng
l*i*nger	l*ou*nge
l*e*ngth	l*o*ng
t*e*ll	t*o*ld
h*e*ld	h*o*ld
*e*lder	*o*ld
br*ea*k	br*o*ke

[3]Chomsky and Halle (1968:209) call these vowel alternations a matter of "backness readjustment" and have formulated a phonological rule (R1, below) which accounts for this phenomenon. One can assume, then, that the underlying form of *length* is /loNg + θ/, which the backness readjustment rule converts to [leNg + θ]. The nasal consonant may be represented as /N/ since, in English, nasals in consonant clusters assimilate to following true consonants. (Cf. Chapter V). The rule of nasal assimilation and backness readjustment can be stated thus:

(R1) Backness Readjustment:

$$\begin{bmatrix} V \end{bmatrix} \rightarrow \begin{bmatrix} -\alpha back \\ -\alpha round \end{bmatrix} / \begin{bmatrix} \underline{\quad} \\ \alpha back \end{bmatrix} \text{ in a certain number of nouns and verbals.}$$

This chart below is a statement of the derivation of the six phonetic reflexes in question.

(a) "length"   (Orthography)

(b) /loNg + θ/   (Underlying form)

(c) leNg + θ   (Backness Readjustment)

(d) leŋg + θ   (Nasal Assimilation)

(e) lenØ + θ   (Voiced Consonant Deletion)

(f) [leŋθ]   Phonetic form in one dialect or style

(g) [liŋθ]   (Lax Vowel Shift); phonetic form in one dialect or style

---

(That is, a vowel which is ⟨+back⟩ is replaced by a corresponding ⟨−back⟩ vowel which is ⟨−round⟩, and a ⟨−back⟩ vowel is replaced by a corresponding vowel which is ⟨+back⟩ and ⟨+round⟩).

(R2) Nasal Assimilation:

$$\begin{bmatrix} +\text{nasal} \\ \text{C} \end{bmatrix} \rightarrow \begin{bmatrix} \alpha\text{ant} \\ \beta\text{cor} \end{bmatrix} / \overset{\prime}{\text{V}} \underline{\qquad} \begin{bmatrix} -\text{nasal} \\ \alpha\text{ant} \\ \beta\text{cor} \\ \text{C} \end{bmatrix}$$

(That is, a ⟨+nasal⟩ consonant following a stressed vowel assimilates to (agrees with) a following ⟨−nasal⟩ consonant for the values of the features ⟨anterior⟩ and ⟨coronal⟩).

The rule of backness readjustment converts the underlying form of *length*, which is /loNg + θ/, to [leNg + θ]. The rule of nasal assimilation converts [leNg + θ] to [leŋg + θ]. Depending on the dialect or style of speech involved, two phonological rules may apply. The *g* of *length* must be either deleted or assimilated for the ⟨voice⟩ feature to the following theta (θ) which is ⟨−voice⟩. The rule of voicing assimilation precedes the rule of voiced consonant deletion.

(R3) Voicing Assimilation:

$$\begin{bmatrix} -\text{nasal} \\ \text{C} \end{bmatrix} \rightarrow \begin{bmatrix} \alpha\text{voice} \end{bmatrix} / \underline{\qquad} \begin{bmatrix} -\text{nasal} \\ \alpha\text{voice} \\ \text{C} \end{bmatrix}$$

(That is, a ⟨−nasal⟩ consonant agrees in the valence for the ⟨voice⟩ feature with a following ⟨−nasal⟩ consonant. The effect here is to convert [leŋgθ] to [leŋkθ]).

(R4) Voiced Consonant Deletion:

$$\begin{bmatrix} -\text{nasal} \\ -\text{cont} \\ +\text{voice} \\ -\text{cor} \\ \text{C} \end{bmatrix} \rightarrow \emptyset / +\text{nasal} \underline{\qquad} [-\text{seg}]$$

(That is, a ⟨−nasal⟩, ⟨−continuant⟩, ⟨+voice⟩, ⟨−coronal⟩ consonant is deleted when it follows a ⟨+nasal⟩ segment and precedes a certain phonological boundary (−segment).

If R3 does not apply, then R4 will. The effect of R4 is to convert [leŋgθ] to [leŋθ]. Clearly, this rule must be restricted, since when comparative −*er* or superlative −*est* are present, the *g* in *longer* and *longest* is not deleted.

A final rule suffices to produce the required phonetic output. This is the rule of "lax vowel shifting" which has the effect of converting an [e] to [i] when [e] precedes a nasal consonant, rendering *pin* and *pen* as homophones in some dialects.

(a) "length"   (Orthography)
(b) /loNg + θ/   (Underlying form)
(c) leNg + θ   (Backness Readjustment)
(d) leŋg + θ   (Nasal Assimilation)
(e) leŋk + θ   (Voicing Assimilation)
(f) [leŋkθ]   Phonetic form in one dialect or style
(g) [liŋkθ]   (Lax Vowel Shift); phonetic form in one dialect or style

(a) "length"   (Orthography)
(b) /loNg + θ/   (Underlying form)
(c) leNg + θ   (Backness Readjustment)
(d) leNØ + θ   (Voiced Consonant Deletion)
(e) [lenθ]   (Nasal Assimilation); phonetic form in one dialect or style
(f) [linθ]   (Lax Vowel Shift); phonetic form in one dialect or style

We see now how difficult it becomes to assert that there is one "right" way to pronounce *length*, or any other word in the language for that matter. Indeed, one speaker may use more than one different pronunciation of a given word, depending on the writing or speaking style he has chosen at the moment. If those pronunciations are not the same as ours, we cannot automatically conclude that he is a sloppy speaker with a lazy tongue, as many people are prone to conclude.

As we noted in the first chapter, one regional dialect very often occupies a prestigious position and becomes the language which speakers of less prestigious dialects begin to imitate. Several dialects of Old English at one time or another assumed such a position as the political and economic power of those regions came into prominence. East

---

(R5) Lax Vowel Shifting:

$$\begin{bmatrix} -\text{back} \\ -\text{tense} \\ -\text{low} \\ V \end{bmatrix} \rightarrow [+\text{high}] \, / \, \underline{\quad} \, [+\text{nasal}]$$

(That is, a ⟨−back⟩, ⟨−tense⟩, ⟨−low⟩ vowel becomes ⟨+high⟩. The effect of this rule is, for example, to convert [lenθ] to [linθ]).

The rules above as formulated and ordered will account for these phonetic forms: [lenθ], [leŋkθ], [linθ], [liŋkθ]. To account for [lenθ] and [linθ] it is necessary to assume that for some dialects and for some styles, R4 must precede R2. Thus, underlying /loNg + θ/, which has been converted to [leNg + θ], will then convert to [leN + θ]; that is, the *g* is deleted before nasal assimilation. Now, the nasal consonant assimilates to −*th* ([θ]) giving [lenθ], which R5 may optionally convert to [linθ].

Midland, the dialect of Chaucer, eventually superseded other Middle English dialects in status because of the favorable geographical location of London. Likewise, Central French came to have more prestige than Norman French because of the cultural importance of Paris.

In the United States the English of educated speakers of each region has the same status as that of the next region. Our last six presidents—Roosevelt, Truman, Eisenhower, Kennedy, Johnson, and Nixon—represent a wide geographical spread with only one distinct region not represented, the South. And all represent educated English with, of course, regional variations. Those who favor the speech of John Kennedy over that of Lyndon Johnson either are from New England or place more status on the life style Kennedy represented. Likewise, the Texan might feel that New England speech sounds affected. What usually happens is that we are influenced more by the person or what he represents than by his language.

Each dialect region in the United States has subdialects within it which lack the social status of academic English within the same community. Variant pronunciation is one item which stigmatizes the speakers of those dialects, pronouncing *thing* as [tiŋ], *mouth* as [māwf] or reducing consonant clusters in words like *wasp* [was] and *first* [fʌrs].[4] More often, however, it is grammatical features which prove to be the the most stigmatizing:[5] multiple negatives, lack of agreement between subject and verb, omission of inflectional endings, and omission of the copula (*be*):

[4]A phonologist can theorize that these phonetic variations might be linguistically (but perhaps not socially or politically) resolved in the usual generative manner; that is, he can speculate that such variant pronunciations of *mouth* and *thing* have a common underlying phonemic form something like /mūθ/ and /θiNg/ which pandialectal rules convert to [māwθ] and [θiŋ] respectively. It may well be that, like many British Cockney speakers, many American speakers have a rather low level (late) conversion rule which relates [θ] to [f] in final position before word boundaries: /mūθ/ → [māwθ] (→ [māwf]). However, this formulation does not explain the initial [t] in some dialects in such words as (th*ing*/t*ing*) and (th*ree*/t*ree*), or the initial [f] in (th*ing*/f*ing*) and (th*ree*/f*ree*). But if we were to assume an underlying /t/ in both *mouth* and *thing*, we might be well on our way toward capturing the actual process which relates these phonetic forms. These derivations would then be in order:

(1) (a) "mouth" (Orthography)
    (b) /mūt/ (Underlying form)
    (c) [māwt] (Vowel Shift and Rounding Adjustment) Dialect-A
    (d) [māwθ] (Spirantization) Dialect-B
    (e) [māwf] (Labialization) Dialect-C

(2) (a) "thing" (Orthography)
    (b) /tiNg/ (Underlying form)
    (c) [tiŋφ] (Nasal Assimilation; Consonant Deletion) Dialect-A
    (d) [θiŋ] (Spirantization) Dialect-B
    (e) [fiŋ] (Labialization) Dialect-C

The alternation between orthographic *t* and *th-* (reflecting the phonetic alternation between a ⟨−continuant⟩ segment and a ⟨+continuant⟩ segment) is something one

I ain't gonna do nothin' about it.

He have a new car.

This my brother hat.

Traditionally the attitude of teachers and laymen is that speakers of such divergent dialects are slovenly speakers who don't hear all the sounds in a word, who don't think clearly in complete thoughts, who come from "nonverbal" backgrounds where language is little used in communicating, or who merely delight in being perverse. Recently a number of studies have been made by sociolinguists of the speech of several minority groups from Appalachian whites to inner-city blacks in cities like Detroit, New York, and Washington, D.C.[6] These studies have revealed that the speakers of these dialects have internalized a complex grammatical system with sophisticated rules of a high order. In fact, some shades of meaning are possible in these dialects which are not possible in the English of the educated majority. "He workin' " and "He be workin' " are not the same as "He's working," as we shall see presently.

In the preceding phonological analysis of *length*, we saw how it is possible to derive several phonetically different but semantically equivalent surface structures from one underlying form. This same type of analysis holds for whole sentences as well. Jean Malmstrom (1969:49) reports certain types of syntactic dialectal variation, which we might illustrate with the following sentences:

---

must recognize between Southern British English (and therefore American English) and Anglo-Scottish, where in many dialects one finds (the*gither*) vis-à-vis (to*gether*) and (the *night*) vis-à-vis (*tonight*). The point is that if English speakers can tolerate the parallel *gh* syndrome in (*tough*), [tʌf], (*rough*), [rʌf] (Cf. *ruffian*), (*trough*), [trɔf], [troθ], (*drought*), [drãwt], [drãwθ] (from *dry* + *th*), (*height/heighth*), (*through*), [θrūw], (*though*) [ðōw], (*draught*), [dræft], (*laugh(ter*), [læftər] and so on, why can they not accept the [t, θ, f] syndrome for what it is, namely, an inconsequential, low-level, surface structure phonetic choice open to speakers of the language? After all, is the consonant cluster reduction of *wasp* and *first* to *was'* and *firs'* really any different from such pandialectal reduction in words like (*Christ/Christmas*, soft/ *soften, chaste/chasten*) as well as (*thistle, whistle*,) and (*mustn't*)? Finally, if numerous Southerners can learn to read *Baptist* and *rinse* as (bæbdist] and [rinč] (rather than [bæptist] and [rins]), then surely there is no reason why all English speakers can't operate on the basis of a conventional orthography such as the one that is being read now.

[5]Stigmatizing from the viewpoint of the educated speaker. The speaker of a divergent dialect, of course, sees nothing wrong with what he says, and, of course, he shouldn't.

[6]William Labov, *The Social Stratification of English in New York City* (Washington, D.C.: Center for Applied Linguistics, 1966); Walter A. Wolfram, *A Sociolinguistic Description of Detroit Negro Speech*, (Washington, D.C.: Center for Applied Linguistics, 1969); Juanita Williamson, "A Phonological and Morphological Study of the Speech of the Negro of Memphis, Tennessee " *Publications of the American Dialect Society*, No. 50 (November 1968).

(1)   (a)   The man workin' (here) in Denton.
      (b)   The man be workin' (there) in Dallas.   Dialect-1
      (c)   The man's workin' (here) in Denton.
      (d)   The man's a-workin' (there) in Dallas.   Dialect-2
      (e)   The man's working (here) in Denton.
      (f)   The man's working (there) in Dallas.   Dialect-3

Allegedly, Dialect-1 and Dialect-2 make a surface structure distinction
which Dialect-3 does not; that is, ignoring *here* and *there*, "the man
workin' " contrasts supposedly with "the man be workin' " in the same
way that "the man's workin' " contrasts with "the man's a-workin'."
Thus, it is alleged that (1a) and (1c) refer to proximal (nearby) situa-
tions, and that (1b) and (1d) refer to either chronic or continual situa-
tions or to non-proximal (remote) ones. There is no denying that the
surface structure differences in (1) exist. However, we propose to
demonstrate somewhat simplistically how and why natural languages
can tolerate such variation.

Jacobs and Rosenbaum (1971:75–76) indicate that under one analysis
it is possible to construe all auxiliary verbs as main verbs in the deep
structure. In such an analysis, the *be* of progressive aspect will be a
main verb. Additionally, one must posit *at* as an underlying constituent
which may or may not be deleted. The informal underlying structure
of the sentences in (1) is indicated in (2) below.

(2)

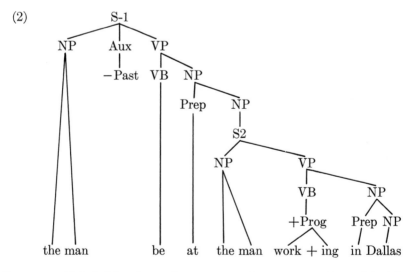

In sentence-labeled brackets, the structure above is approximated in (3).

(3) $_{S1}$[the man ⟨ −Past ⟩ be at $_{S2}$[the man work + ing in Dallas]$_{S2}$]$_{S1}$

In all dialects the repeated noun phrase (*the man*) is deleted as in (4) below.

(4)   the man ⟨−Past⟩ be at work + ing in Dallas

Depending on the dialect and the style, in theory, the structure in (4) may be transformed into one of the structures below.

(5)   (a) The man's at working in Dallas. (Aux agreement, Aux incorporation)
      (b) The man at working in Dallas. (Person deletion)
      (c) The man's aØ working in Dallas. (Consonant deletion)
      (d) The man's a-working in Dallas. (Affixation)
      (e) The man's Ø working in Dallas. (Preposition deletion)
      (f) The man's workin' in Dallas. (Voiced consonant deletion)

Had the structure in (2) been marked negatively for progressive aspect (−progressive), the sentences in (6) would have been generated.

(6)   (a) The man at work in Dallas. (Dialect-1)
      (b) The man's at work in Dallas. (Dialect-2 and Dialect-3)

The uniformity and regularity of the partial and complete deletion of *at* can be seen by examining the sentences below in (7).

(7)   (a) The man sleepin'. (Dialect-1)
      (b) The man's a-sleepin'. (Dialect-2)
      (c) The man is sleeping. (Dialect-3)
      (d) The man('s) *at sleep* ⇒ The man('s) *asleep*. (Pandialectal)

The forms *asleep, awake, away,* and others like them are pandialectal (occurring in all dialects) whereas *a-sleepin'* and *a-workin'* are not. What the full data suggest is that all speakers of English have a rule which reduces *at* to *a-* and some speakers have a rule which deletes *a-* in progressive forms (*sleeping*) but not in derived adjectives (*asleep*).

Conclusion

According to our deep structure–surface structure analysis of English, we saw in Chapter III that Modern English pronunciation can be derived from an earlier stage in the language (represented rather well by our spelling system) through a series of phonological processes. From a

diachronic point of view we can see why Chaucer's [hūswīf] becomes
Modern English [hāwswāyf] through a process affecting the tense vowels.
From a synchronic vantage point (Chapter V) we can understand why
there are still variations of the modern pronunciation so that Tidewater
Virginians say [hʌws], South Midlanders say [hæws] with [æ] rather than
[a] and [wa•f] with a monophthong rather than a diphthong. We see why
some speakers say [pen] and others [pin]. These differences are surface
differences which do not affect the communication process.

Furthermore, we see how different speakers use different grammatical
rules to arrive at different surface constructions which are the same
underneath; i.e., "He my friend" and "He is my friend" come from
the same deep structure. A speaker of the latter may contract the verb
to 's without attracting any attention. If he deletes the verb entirely,
he is guilty of stigmatized speech, at least in the opinion of some of his
associates. Thus one construction, considered "standard," has more
social status than the other.

Up to this point we have been hesitant to define standard English,
mainly because of the elusiveness of the term. Presumably it is the
English spoken by the educated classes in our society, by the dominant
social and cultural groups. Yet several questions immediately present
themselves. What about the pronunciation of *pen, house, time, length,
path*? Certainly it varies from region to region. What is the standard
pronunciation [hæws] or [hāws]? Does the majority rule in cases of
divided speech? Older editions of *Webster's New International Dictionary*
(Second Edition) listed [paθ] as the preferred pronunciation of *path*,
even though this pronunciation is typical only of New England. What
about levels of style? Our language choices vary from one occasion to
the next, and are intimately related to our audience and our purpose.
Are contractions, so common in speech, to be considered standard in
writing? What about older forms? Do they have a greater sanction
because of age? If so, should we reassess the verb *help*, once a strong
verb with a preterit form *holp*, which is still used by many speakers
today? Will grammaticality serve as a test for what is standard? That is,
if native speakers say it, is it all right? Many sentences with intransitive
verbs and prepositional phrases can be made passive.

> They slept in that bed ⇒ That bed was slept in.
> They stood in the rain ⇒ The rain was stood in.

Certainly the last sentence sounds a bit peculiar to most speakers. Could
we get everyone to agree on what is standard anyway?

What we can say with some certainty is that differences in grammar
and pronunciation exist and that they represent surface variations of
identical deep structures. Each of us must determine for himself what

his "tolerance quotient" is and how much linguistic diversity he can stand before lashing out at those whose speech is not like his.

In this text we have defined such natural language as English as a set of sentences, and we have suggested that the language is made up of a set of autonomous dialects, each of which is sufficient to its own purposes. In turn, the English language is a member of the set of dialects that make up the Germanic family of languages, which includes the North branch (Danish, Icelandic, Norwegian, Swedish), the West branch (Frisian, German, English), and the now extinct East branch, Gothic.

An eminent American theoretical linguist, Emmon Bach, in *Universals in Linguistic Theory* (1968:121), has made the claim that there is a universal base rule component of grammar; thus, the suggestion, in his own words, is "that it is possible to convey any conceptual content in any language, even though the particular lexical items will vary widely from one language to another." If this is so, it should follow that dialects of the same language should share identical or nearly identical deep structures that transformations convert to surface structures, which, of course, may vary systematically across dialects in the same way that the English sentence "It is me/I" may surface in Paris as *C'est moi*, in Berlin as *Ich bin es*, in Stockholm as *Det är jag*, or in Copenhagen as *Det er mig*, etc.

Finally, if the type of grammar we have been discussing can, in fact, easily relate English "Ask him is he coming" to German *Frage ihn, ob er kommt* (And we believe it can!), then it surely is a minor task to relate both of these to English "Ask him if/whether he is coming (or not)." Similarly, it is simple to relate the English deep structure s[Neg I know]s to the full surface structure "I don't know" or the alternate surface structure [āy ō nō] or [āy dəno], and so on *ad infinitum*.

It is clearly time to abandon linguistic isolationism and the mythical concept of *a* standard English, or *a* standard German, Spanish, or French for that matter, for cultural plurality in the United States at least demands linguistic heterogeneity. Let us not spoil the milk of human diversity by a puritanical insistence upon linguistic pasteurization and homogenization. After all, variety *is* the spice of life!

Public attitudes toward language, however, are the result of many years of public schooling and are highly resistant to change. Perhaps we should glance at the history of those attitudes as they are reflected in grammars and dictionaries.

Exercises

Nota bene: The year 1971 witnessed the publication of two excellent texts of interest to the student of English linguistics and American dialectology: (1) *A Various Language*, edited by Juanita Williamson and Virginia Burke; (2) *Readings in American Dialectology*, edited by Harold Allen and Gary Underwood. Many classic articles not readily available to general audiences are included in these texts. In the exercises below, we make reference, for the convenience of the reader, to the articles appearing in these volumes by the initials WB (Williamson and Burke) and AU (Allen and Underwood) plus the sequential number in either text. Thus WB5 refers to the fifth article in the text by Williamson and Burke, and so on.

1. Obtain a copy of the recording entitled *Our Changing Language* and/or *Americans Speaking* and construct a unit on dialectology based on one or both of these recordings and the information supplied therewith.

Americans Speaking, accompanied by a very useful pamphlet, is currently available from the office of the National Council of Teachers of English, 1111 Kenyon Road, Urbana, Illinois 61801. The geographical areas represented on the record include Topsfield, Massachusetts; London, Kentucky; Brooklyn, New York; Prattville, Alabama; and Madison, Wisconsin.

Our Changing Language, with an informative record jacket, is currently available from McGraw-Hill, Webster Division, Hightstown, New Jersey 05820. The geographical areas represented on the record include Alabama, California, New Hampshire, Illinois, Texas, Newfoundland, South Carolina, Metropolitan New York City, Salt Lake City, West Virginia, and Alberta.

2. Form a panel discussion around the publications listed below. These give (sometimes polemical) attention to the topic of bidialectalism in the United States.

   (a) "Bidialectalism: The Linguistics of White Supremacy," by James Sledd, *English Journal*, (December 1969).

   (b) "Doublespeak: Dialectology in the service of Big Brother," by James Sledd, *College English* (January 1972).

   (c) "The Politics of Bidialectalism," by Wayne O'Neil, *College English* (January 1972).

   (d) *Linguistic-Cultural Differences and American Education*, Special issue of the *Florida Foreign Language Reporter*, 7, No. 1 (Spring/Summer 1969).

3. Consult the publications listed below; then compile a list of verb forms which have competing principal parts (*sing, sang, sung* vs. *sing,*

sung, sung) in your area of the United States. Make a limited survey and tabulate the results.

   (a) "Some Dialectal Verb Forms in England," by W. Nelson Francis. (WB10) or (AU22)

   (b) *A Survey of Verb Forms in the Eastern United States*, by E. Bagby Atwood, University of Michigan Press, 1953.

   (c) *Verb Forms of the North Central States and the Upper Midwest*, by Virginia G. McDavid, unpublished doctoral dissertation, University of Minnesota, 1956. Available from University Microfilms, P. O. Box 1346, Ann Arbor, Michigan, 48106.

   (d) "Grammatical Differences in the North-Central States," by Virginia G. and Raven I. McDavid, Jr. (WB28)

   (e) *A Phonological and Morphological Study of the Speech of the Negro of Memphis, Tennessee,"* by Juanita V. Williamson, *Publications of the American Dialect Society*, No. 50 (November 1968).

4. Compare and contrast the differences between a structural approach to dialectology and a transformational approach by examining the publications listed below.

   (a) *Handbook of the Linguistic Geography of New England*, by Hans Kurath, American Council of Learned Societies, 1219 Sixteenth Street, N. W., Washington, D. C., 1939.

   (b) *The Pronunciation of English in the Atlantic States*, by Hans Kurath and Raven I. McDavid, Jr., University of Michigan Press, 1961.

   (c) "Review of the *Pronunciation of English in the Atlantic States*," by Samuel Keyser, *Language*, 39, No. 2 Part 1, (April-June 1963).

   (d) "Is a Structural Dialectology Possible?" by Uriel Weinreich. (AU26)

   (e) "Structural Dialectology: A Proposal," by Robert Stockwell. (AU27)

   (f) "Overall Pattern and Generative Phonology," by Rudolph Troike. (AU28)

   (g) "The Methods of American Dialectology," by E. Bagby Atwood. (AU1)

   (h) "Linguistic Geography: Achievements, Methods, and Orientations," by Gino Bottiglioni. (AU25)

(i) "Phonemic and Prosodic Analysis in Linguistic Geography," by Trevor Hill. (AU29)

5. Investigate the topic of vocabulary differences among dialects by consulting the publications listed below.

(a) *A Word Geography of the Eastern United States*, by Hans Kurath, University of Michigan Press, 1966.

(b) *The Regional Vocabulary of Texas*, by E. Bagby Atwood, University of Texas Press, 1962.

(c) *A Compilation of the Work Sheets of the Linguistic Atlas of the United States and Canada and Associated Projects*, edited by Alva L. Davis, Raven I. McDavid, Jr., and Virginia G. McDavid, University of Chicago Press, 1969.

(d) "What Do You Call It?", by Hans Kurath. (WB19)

(e) "Early American Speech: Adoptions from Foreign Tongues," by Thomas Pyles. (WB7)

(f) "Some Aspects of Atlantic Seaboard English Considered in Their Connection with British English," by Hans Kurath. (WB9)

(g) *Survey of English Dialects*, by Harold Orton and Eugen Dieth, E. J. Arnold & Son Limited, Leeds, England, 1962.

(h) *Survey of Scottish Dialects*, by Angus McIntosh, Thomas Nelson and Sons Limited, Edinburgh, Scotland, 1961.

(i) *Down in the Holler: A Gallery of Ozark Folk Speech*, by Vance Randolph and George P. Wilson, University of Oklahoma Press, Norman, Oklahoma, 1953.

6. Obtain a copy of the journal called *Publications of the American Dialect Society* (*PADS*) such as Juanita Williamson's "A Phonological and Morphological Study of the Speech of the Negro of Memphis, Tennessee (PADS, No. 50, November 1968) (WB45) or PADS (No. 51, April 1969) and replicate the dialect studies contained therein for your geographical area. A list of *PADS* can be obtained by writing to University of Alabama Press, University, Alabama.

7. Consult the publications listed below; then write an essay in which you discuss such a topic as this: "What the Teacher of English Needs to Know about Dialectology."

(a) "Sense and Nonsense about American Dialects," by Raven I. McDavid, Jr. (AU2) or (WB6)

(b) *Linguistics and the Teaching of Standard English to Speakers of Other Languages or Dialects,* edited by James E. Alatis, 20th Annual Round Table, Monograph Series on Languages and Linguistics, No. 22, 1969, Georgetown University Press, Washington, D. C. 20007.

(c) *Bilingualism and Language Contact: Anthropological, Linguistic, Psychological, and Sociological Aspects,* edited by James E. Alatis, No. 23, 1970. See item 7b above.

(d) "The Standard of American Speech," by Fred Newton Scott. (WB1)

(e) "Cultural Levels and Functional Varieties," by John S. Kenyon. (WB3)

(f) "A Projection of Sociolinguistics: The Relationship of Speech to Social Status," by Haver C. Currie. (WB5)

(g) "Towards a New Perspective in Negro English Dialectology," by Beryl Loftman Bailey. (AU35)

(h) "On the Structure of the Verb in a Dialect of American Negro English," by Marvin D. Loflin. *Caveat Emptor!* (AU36)

(i) "Sociolinguistic Factors in the History of American Negro Dialects," by William A. Stewart. (AU37)

(j) "Continuity and Change in American Negro Dialects," by William A. Stewart. (AU38)

(k) A Checklist of Significant Features for Discriminating Social Dialects," by Raven I. McDavid, Jr. (AU39)

(l) "Stages in the Acquisition of Standard English," by William Labov. (AU40)

(m) *The Study of Nonstandard English,* by William Labov, National Council of Teachers of English, 1111 Kenyon Road, Urbana, Illinois 61801, 1970.

(n) *Teaching Standard English in the Inner City,* edited by Ralph W. Fasold and Roger W. Shuy, Center for Applied Linguistics, 1611 North Kent St., Arlington, Virginia 22209, 1970.

(o) *A Sociolinguistic Description of Detroit Negro Speech,* by Walter A. Wolfram, Center for Applied Linguistics, 1969. See item 7n above.

(p) *Teaching Black Children to Read,* edited by Joan C. Baratz and Roger W. Shuy, Center for Applied Linguistics, 1969. See item 7n above.

(q) *Conversations in a Negro American Dialect,* transcribed and edited by Bengt Loman, Center for Applied Linguistics, 1967. Available with accompanying tape. See item 7n above.

(r) "The Language of the City," by Raven I. McDavid, Jr. (WB41)

8. Investigate the phenomenon of literary dialect by examining some of the publications listed below.

   (a) "The Psychology of Dialect Writing," by George Philip Krapp. (WB3)
   (b) "A Theory of Literary Dialect," by Sumner Ives. (WB13)
   (c) "Eye Dialect as a Literary Device," by W. Edward Farrison. (WB14)
   (e) "Geographical Delimitation of the Dialect Areas in *The Adventures of Huckleberry Finn*," by Curt M. Rulon. (WB16)
   (d) "Poe's Use of Negro Dialect in *The Gold-Bug*," by Eric Stockton. (WB15)
   (g) "Dialect Differentiation in the Stories of Joel Chandler Harris," by Sumner Ives. (WB17)
   (h) "Dialects in Eugene O'Neill's Plays," by Ruth M. Blackburn. (WB18)
   (i) "The Phonology of the Uncle Remus Stories, by Sumner Ives, *PADS*, No. 22 (November 1954).
   (j) *Features of New England Rustic Pronunciation in James Russell Lowell's Biglow Papers*, by James Walker Downer, unpublished doctoral dissertation, University of Michigan, 1958. Available from University Microfilms, P.O. Box 1346, Ann Arbor, Michigan, 48106.
   (k) *The Representation of Negro Dialect in Charles W. Chesnutt's The Conjure Woman*, by Charles William Foster, unpublished doctoral dissertation, University of Alabama, 1968. For availability, see 8j above.
   (l) *The Dialects in Huckleberry Finn*, by Curt M. Rulon, unpublished doctoral dissertation, University of Iowa, 1967. For availability, see 8j above.

9. The following narratives, spoken by a ten-year old Denton, Texas, girl, were transcribed by Barbara McDaniel, a graduate student at North Texas State University. Examine one or both of them and determine what, if any, grammatical features characterize this speaker's dialect. Which features, if any, are stigmatizing from your point of view? What features might be considered "hyper-corrections"?

A. "Goldilock and the Three Bears"
   One day it was three bears there was in the house, eating some por-

ridge. And the mother bear, she was cooking some porridge; and it was too hot. And so they went for a walk, and Goldilock came there. Goldilock was walking through the woods and she saw this little house; so she went and knock on the door. And she didn't think that anyone lived—that any lived there and so she just walked in. And she saw this table with three bowls of porridge for a mother, father, and little baby. So she tasted the mother's and it was too warm. She tasted the father's—and it was too hot. Then she ate the little baby porridge up.

So she went to a chair, and she broke the little baby chair. And the mother chair was too soft. And the father chair was too hard. So she went to the beds, and she slept in the father's bear bed and it was too hard, slept in the mother bed and it was too soft, and she got in the little baby bear bed and she sayed, "This one's just right."

So the bears came back home, and they found out that Goldilock had been eating their porridge, and have sit in their chair. And then they went up to stairs they saw her in bed. They frightened her and she ranned away.

B.   "Cinderella"

She have three step-sisters and one step-mother, and they make her do all the work. She don't have—hardly never get a bite. So one night the prince was giving a ball, and the three sisters fussed at her and everything—made her clean up the house, and she had to fetch everything they tell her to do; and when it was time to go, well she sayed "Are we going to the ball?" And the old step-sisters sayed, "You! They wouldn't take you! They wouldn't take you in no clothes like that!"

So her fairy godmother came and gave her a beautiful dress, and had a pumpkin, and made it out of a stagecourt. And she went to the ball.

And before twelve midnight struck, well she left one of her shoes and the princess [prince] went to house to house to see if the one that could wear it. So he got to Cinderella's house and her sisters couldn't wear it, so he was gonna go; and so Cinderella ranned out—ran out— befront— behind the house and he tried the shoe on her. And they got married.

References

Atwood, E. Bagby. *A Survey of Verb Forms in the Eastern United States.* Ann Arbor: University of Michigan Press, 1953.

———. *The Regional Vocabulary of Texas.* Austin, Texas: University of Texas Press, 1962.

Bach, Emmon, and Robert T. Harms, eds. *Universals in Linguistic Theory.* New York: Holt, Rinehart, and Winston, 1968.

Chomsky, Noam, and Morris Halle. *The Sound Pattern of English.* New York: Harper and Row, 1968.

Jacobs, Roderick A., and Peter S. Rosenbaum. *Transformations, Style, and Meaning.* Waltham, Massachusetts: Xerox College Publishing, 1971.

Kurath, Hans. *A Word Geography of the Eastern United States.* Ann Arbor: University of Michigan Press, 1966.

———, and Raven I. McDavid, Jr., *The Pronunciation of English in the Atlantic States.* Ann Arbor: University of Michigan Press, 1961.

Labov, William. *The Social Stratification of English in New York City.* Washington, D.C.: Center for Applied Linguistics, 1966.

Malmstrom, Jean. "Dialects—Updated." *The Florida Foreign Language Reporter,* Special Anthology Issue, 7, No. 1 (Spring/Summer 1969), 47–49, 168.

Williamson, Juanita V. "A Phonological and Morphological Study of the Speech of the Negro of Memphis, Tennessee." *Publications of the American Dialect Society,* No. 50. (November 1968).

Wolfram, Walter A. *A Sociolinguistic Description of Detroit Negro Speech.* Washington, D.C.: Center for Applied Linguistics, 1969.

VII

Usage and Lexicography: Yesterday and Today

In the previous chapter we saw that dialectal variations are surface variations, each dialect having its own set of rules to convert underlying forms to surface forms. We suggested that some surface variations have more prestige than others, depending, of course, on the viewpoint of the person judging the dialect in question. Still, to most people today "nonstandard" dialects are considered "bad English," something which teachers should strive diligently to stamp out.

Part of the problem stems from a misunderstanding of terms or a failure to define terms clearly so that linguist and layman are using them synonymously. As we saw in Chapter III, GRAMMAR to the linguist means the system of the language or the description of that system. To the layman it means acceptable speech. That is, a person uses "good grammar" or "bad grammar"; hence his USAGE is good or bad. Thus the term "usage," as it is used by writers of handbooks, is equated with linguistic etiquette, and such writers admonish their readers to exemplify "good usage" by listing countless expressions which are considered "correct" or "incorrect." One is told to say *reason is that* . . . rather than *reason is because* . . . because, if one follows the "rule" (stated in a "grammar" book), he must use a noun clause rather than an adverb clause after a copula. The fact of the matter is that many educated speakers say *reason is because* . . . ; thus this expression has become a part of standard usage in English. Hence the problem lies in the apparent disparity between what people say and what the usage books tell them to say.

The linguist, whose interest is in scientific data, records language which people use, and to him such debatable items of usage as *reason is because* . . . would be considered acceptable standard usage. The rhetorician, on the other hand, is concerned with stylistic matters—what sounds more euphonious, more formal, or more appropriate to a given audience. And the lexicographer is caught in the middle. As a scientist his job is to record the language which people use, but the layman looks to him for his opinion on what should be used. Thus when he fails to use enough status labels, he is branded as overly permissive and as one who is hastening the decay of the language.

Where and when did the highly conservative attitudes toward usage begin?

The Renaissance

Until printing was firmly established in England and until literacy was fairly widespread, there could be little concern on the part of the public in matters of usage. Presumably people of high social position set the style in matters of language; even Caxton himself, the first English printer, handed his work over to the Duchess of Burgundy who, probably less literate than he, "oversawe and corrected" it.

Renaissance writers are noted for their exuberant spirit in borrowing words freely from Latin and Greek (and less frequently, from French, Italian, and Spanish), coining new words based on Latin and Greek originals, or giving older words new meanings, fantastic though they often were. New coinages and adaptations were not always the result of an attempt on the part of a writer to be clever, however. Many new words were necessitated by a sixteenth-century knowledge explosion in which new words were needed in certain technical fields and others were borrowed rather freely by translators of Latin and Greek works. In fact, the first dictionaries were mere lists of "hard" words which the average reader, whose knowledge of Greek and Latin was very slight, might not have known.

Sir Thomas Elyot's *The Governour* (1531) is sprinkled with Latinisms in a conscious attempt to enrich the language. Sir John Cheke, on the other hand, objected to classical borrowings, and wrote in a latter to Sir Thomas Hoby: "I am of this opinion that our own tung should be written cleane and pure, unmixt and unmangeled with borowing of other tunges . . . "

Certainly many of the borrowed words bordered on pedantry and were justly ridiculed as "inkhorn" terms, sprinkled liberally in a passage of English prose from the author's inkwell. Though they may have sounded strange to the men of that time, words like *compendious, figurative, inveigle, penetrable, indignitie, audacious,* and *compatible,* though they sound learned, do not sound particularly un-English to the modern speaker. And surely no one today would lament the demise of *anacephalize, deruncinate, adminiculation,* or *illecebrous.*

That contemporary speakers were often baffled by the flood of strange new words can be seen in the sudden need for dictionaries. Robert Cawdrey's *The Table Alphabeticall of Hard Words* (1604) explains some three thousand difficult or unusual words borrowed into English. John Bullokar's *English Expositor* (1616), besides difficult words, lists famous people in real life and in classical mythology. Henry Cockeram's *English Dictionarie* (1623), the first with "dictionary" in the title, has as its subtitle *An Interpreter of Hard English Words.*

Not only dictionaries but grammars as well began to appear with increasing frequency. William Bullokar's *Pamphlet for Grammar* (1586), considered the first, is a slim volume of sixty-eight pages but one in which the author (in a verse preface) hopes to regularize English. As C. C. Fries says, "Most of the grammars published from 1586, the date of the first English grammar, to the end of the seventeenth century were of two kinds. They were either directed to foreigners who wished to learn English and for this purpose were often written in Latin or in French; or they were quite frankly introductions to the study of Latin, and aimed simply to take advantage of the use of the pupil's native language in grammar." (Fries, 1949:10).

The Eighteenth Century

From the latter half of the seventeenth century through the eighteenth century, both grammars and dictionaries continue to appear, most of them predicated on certain basic assumptions which automatically make them highly prescriptive in matters of usage.

Several factors contributed to the advent of prescriptivism. Perhaps the leading assumptions were that the universe is characterized by order and that man's greatest asset is his reason. To aid his rational faculty, man might look back to classical examples or precepts to see what ordered laws exist in the universe. By extension those same fixed, unchanging laws might be seen in operation in languages; hence the popular notion that languages could be standardized and fixed so that they would not be subject to decay. Furthermore, some universal language was thought to exist, and Latin was elevated to that position and held in great respect.

Just as one looked back to the Greeks and Romans for literary styles worthy of emulation, one looked back to earlier stages in the history of English when the language was in a "purer" form. Dryden praised Chaucer as the father of English poetry, the poet from whom "the purity of the English tongue began," stating that he "refined his mother tongue," presumably from a barbarous late Old English. Swift hearkened back to the Elizabethan age: "The period wherein the English tongue received most improvement, I take to commence with the beginning of Queen Elizabeth's reign, and to conclude with the great rebellion in forty-two." Nathaniel Bailey in 1772 also glanced wistfully back to the Golden Age of Elizabeth, noting that "nothing can exceed the beauty of periods in our old writers Ascham and Hooker."

A Language Academy

So certain were some writers that the language could be regulated that they tried to establish a language academy which would pass judgment on all linguistic matters. Such academies had been founded in Italy in 1582, France in 1635, and Spain in 1713 to keep those languages "pure and eloquent," though to this day they have not really achieved their original goals. Languages continually change, and academies (and grammars, for that matter) can do little to stop the change. A good example of a recent attempt to stop change was the action of the French Academy in preparing a dictionary of Anglicisms with French equivalents so that Frenchmen might stop using American English words like *call-girl*, *cliff-dweller*, *fairway*, *melting-pot*, *snack-bar*, *teen-ager*, and use appropriate French synonyms instead. The dictionary was facetiously named *Parlez-vous Franglais?* (*Time*:80.)

English men of letters who favored the establishment of an academy were Edmund Bolton, 1617; John Dryden, 1664, 1679; John Evelyn, 1665; Stephen Skinner, 1671; Daniel Defoe, 1697; Joseph Addison, 1711, and Jonathan Swift, 1712.

In *An Essay upon Projects* (1697), Defoe lamented the lack of esteem which English has when compared to French and wished that a society might be established "to polish and refine the English tongue, and advance the so much neglected Faculty of Correct Language, to establish Purity and Propriety of Stile, and to purge it from all the Irregular Additions that Ignorance and affectation have introduced." Such a society must not be comprised of learned men "whose English has been far from Polite, full of Stiffness and affectation, hard Words, and long unusual coupling of *syllables* and Sentences, which sound harsh and untuneable to the Ear, and shock the Reader both in Expression and Understanding." Then, he facetiously adds, "There should be no room in this Society for neither *Clergyman, Physician,* or *Lawyer.*" The remainder of the essay "Of Academies" is devoted to the first task of such an academy, to oppose swearing.

Swift's "Proposal for Correcting, Improving and Ascertaining the English Tongue" (1712) was perhaps the most eloquent and impassioned argument for the establishment of an academy. He praised the high stage of perfection which Latin had reached in the heyday of the Roman empire, and hoped that English might be "fixed forever" and not "perpetually changing." Swift censured "illiterate Court-Fops, half-witted-Poets, and University-Boys" for their cant phrases, their flowery styles, their bawdy humor, and for clipping syllables from words for the sake of meter in a line of poetry, thus shortening *drudged, disturbed, rebuked,* and *pledged* to *drudg'd, disturb'd, rebuk't,* and *pleg'd,* which incidentally are mere graphic changes rather than changes in pronunciation anyway.

Swift's reference to shortening words by deleting vowels is based on his earlier conversations with Joseph Addison, who also felt that English had too many monosyllables and that writers helped propagate more by "closing in one Syllable the Termination of our Praeterperfect Tense, as in the Words *drown'd, walk'd, arriv'd,* for *drowned, walked, arrived . . .* " Thus, he says, they have "very much disfigured the Tongue, and turn'd a tenth part of our smoothest Words into so many clusters of consonants." (*Spectator* 135). He failed to note that not since Middle English times have the vowels in those final syllables been pronounced, and, like Swift, he was confusing the nature of writing and speech.

Addison further lamented the substitution of the verb ending -*s* for -*eth,* which has "added to that *hissing* in our Language, which is taken so much notice of by Foreigners." Only an academy, he felt, could decide what forms should be used.

The Rise of Grammar Books

Needless to say, the plan for a language academy withered on the vine, to be revived periodically in both England and America. In the meantime the grammarian and the lexicographer had taken over the duties of an academy and were willing to establish certain linguistic norms which they felt would represent the "best" English. The first half of the eighteenth century has fewer than fifty books on grammar, rhetoric, criticism, and linguistic theory, according to a study by Sterling Leonard. Between 1750 and 1800 more than two hundred titles appeared. (Leonard:12.)

These books were not written for foreigners learning English but for Englishmen who wanted or needed to "improve" their speech. The study of English grammar replaced the study of Latin grammar, the method of study being almost identical—the memorization and application of rules. Such rules, according to Charles C. Fries, "were generally either carried over from Latin syntax or the new creation of a so-called 'rational grammar' and thus based upon 'reason' or the laws of thought.' " (Fries, 1949:17.)

A respect for "rules" and for the "authority" in language is thus directly related to the eighteenth-century attitudes toward order and stability in the universe. One of the most influential grammars was written by Bishop Robert Lowth and called *A Short Introduction to English Grammar* (1762). His Preface states:

> The principal design of a Grammar in any language is to teach us to express ourselves with propriety in that Language, and to enable us to judge of every phrase and form of construction whether it be right or not. The plain way of doing this, is to lay down rules, and to illustrate them by examples. But, besides shewing what is right, the matter may be further explained by pointing out what is wrong. (p. x.)

It is from Lowth that we get our rules banning the double negative and the superlative to indicate one of two ("the smallest of the two"). His book was quite popular in the United States and was used at Harvard as late as 1841. (Pooley, 1933:23.)

Robert Pooley suggests three influences in America which "greatly enhanced the value and appreciation of fixed rules in English": a great deal of public speaking which called for a polished style (based on certain rules of acceptable speech), the necessity for an authoritative standard of acceptable usage for immigrants who often blended their own grammatical patterns with English or transliterated their own idioms into English, and certain feelings on the part of pioneer people of social and educational insecurity. (Pooley, 1933:24.)

Such feelings of insecurity have always been a necessitating factor behind the publication of dictionaries, grammars, and rhetorics as middle-class people become more prosperous and want to imitate the dress, manners, and speech of the upper classes. *The Art of Speaking* (1708) suggests that "The best Expressions grow low and degenerate, when profan'd by the populace, and applied to mean things." *The Royal English Grammar* (1737) notes that *yes* "is more usual and modish than *yea*" and that *ay* is "rude and ungenteel." In fact, one of the early dictionaries, Henry Cockeram's *The English Dictionarie* (1623), was written not only to "interpret hard words" but also to assist in "the more speedy attaining of an Elegant Perfection of the English Tongue."

Lindley Murray, who borrowed his rules from Lowth, published his *English Grammar, Adapted to the Different Classes of Learners* in 1795. He wrote an *Abridgement* in 1797, *English Exercises* in 1802, and a two-volume *English Grammar* in 1814. These books ran to "over 120 editions of 10,000 copies each, so that more than 1,000,000 copies of his books were sold in America before 1850." (Pooley, 1933:24) Noah Webster's *Plain and Comprehensive Grammar* appeared in America in 1784 to enjoy popularity both here and in England.

Not all eighteenth-century grammars and rhetorics were prescriptive, however. Joseph Priestley, the scientist who dabbled in linguistics, asserted in *The Rudiments of English Grammar* (1761) that usage rests on custom. George Campbell, in *Philosophy of Rhetoric* (1776), also declared that the "Supreme authority" in language is use. On matters of divided usage he would resort to what is "univocal," analogous to other terms or expressions in the language, euphonious, simple, and "conformable to ancient usage."

The Rise of Lexicography

If the majority of the eighteenth-century grammarians were eager to settle points of grammar and syntax, the lexicographers were willing to tackle the word stock of the language. As noted earlier, the Renaissance writers borrowed and coined words freely, and the writers of the Restoration and eighteenth century added their special brand of coffee-house jargon; hence, writers like Swift felt the necessity for an academy to purge the language of "quaint Fopperies" and "gross Improprieties."

Johnson's plan for his dictionary, which he sent to Philip Dormer Stanhope, the Earl of Chesterfield, stated his chief intent: "to preserve the purity, and ascertain the meaning of our English idiom." He recognized the general audience to which it was directed, and in the spirit of the neoclassical ideal of *dulce et utile*, added: "It is not enough that a dictionary delights the critic, unless, at the same time, it instructs the learner; as it is to little purpose that an engine amuses the philosopher by the subtlety of its mechanism, if it requires so much knowledge in its application as to be of no advantage to the common workman," an ideal worthy of any modern dictionary.

Though he later affirms his desire to correct and fix the language, one can read between the lines and see that Johnson himself must have realized that there were several inconsistencies to which he would "interpose" his own judgment and support what appears "consonant to grammar and reason." Nevertheless he still thought of himself as a purist during his seven years as a "harmless drudge" when he wrote in the *Rambler* (No. 208), "I have laboured to refine our language to grammatical purity, and to clear it from colloquial barbarisms, licentious idioms, and irregular combinations."

Before the dictionary appeared, Lord Chesterfield wrote a letter to *The World* (November 28, 1754) praising Johnson's labors and lamenting the fact that there had been nothing in English except "what our neighbors the Dutch and the Germans call theirs, WORD-BOOKS. . . ." He then added that "all words, good and bad, are there jumbled indiscriminately together, insomuch that the injudicious reader may speak and write as inelegantly, improperly and vulgarly as he pleases, by and with the authority of one or other of our WORD-BOOKS." Interestingly enough *word book* is as accurate a name as *dictionary*, which is also a book of words of a given language. What Lord Chesterfield was apparently objecting to was the fact that the earliest dictionaries had included only "hard" words, with the exception of works like Stephen Skinner's *Etymologicon Linguae Anglicanae* (1671), which was the basis for many of Johnson's etymologies, and Nathaniel Bailey's *Universal Etymological Dictionary* (1721), which is probably the first complete dictionary in the sense in which we use the term today.

Lord Chesterfield, like others before him, admitted "that our language is at present in a state of anarchy" and stated that the time of borrowing from other languages had come to an end:

> The time for discrimination seems to be now come. Toleration, adoption and naturalization have run their length. Good order and authority are now necessary. But where shall we find them? We must have recourse to the old Roman expedient in times of confusion, and chuse a dictator. Upon this principle I give my vote for Mr. Johnson to fill the great and arduous post. And I hereby declare that I make a total surrender of all my rights and privileges in the English language, as a freeborn British subject, to the said Mr. Johnson, during the term of his dictatorship. Nay more; I will not only obey him, like an old Roman, as my dictator, but, like a modern Roman, I will implicitly believe in him as my pope, and hold him to be infallible while in the chair; but no longer. More than this he cannot well require; for I presume that obedience can never be expected when there is neither terror to enforce, nor interest to invite it.

That Johnson would have made a good dictator is apparent to anyone who reads Boswell's *Life of Johnson* or knows of the character of Johnson. On countless occasions Johnson refuses to be bullied and proves both his physical and mental prowess. As Boswell says of him, "There is no arguing with Johnson; for when his pistol misses fire, he knocks you down with butt end of it."

Whether others would have been so eager and willing to submit to the authority of Johnson remains for speculation. When the *Dictionary* appeared the next year, Johnson fortunately rejected the notion that he could have settled all matters of orthography, etymology, and usage "to put a stop to those alterations which time and change have hitherto suffered to make" in the language. Words and phrases cannot, he adds, be preserved from mutability, and no lexicographer "can embalm his language, and secure it from corruption and decay."

Though the dictionary would be considered inadequate by today's standards, it did set a pattern for modern lexicographers to follow. Its basic flaws are its personal bias and its incorrect etymologies. Johnson includes words whose place in the language might be questioned— *opiniatry, ariolation, clancular, conclusible, discubitory,* etc. (Baugh:327). Many of his etymologies are incorrect (numerous words are erroneously listed as having Celtic origins), because he lived before the great historical and comparative studies of the Indo-European family of languages in the nineteenth century.

His personal bias is reflected in a few definitions, which the modern reader finds amusing:

> *excise.* A hateful tax levied upon commodities, and adjudged not by the common judges of property, but wretches hired by those to whom excise is paid.

> *oats.* A grain, which in England is generally given to horses, but in Scotland supports the people.

> *patron.* (1) One who countenances, supports or protects. Commonly a wretch who supports with insolence, and is paid with flattery.

> *pension.* An allowance made to any one without an equivalent. In England it is generally understood to mean pay given to a state hireling for treason to his country.

Finally, Johnson was the first lexicographer to illustrate meanings with quotations. Since many words were pronounced differently by different people, he made no attempt to indicate pronunciation. William Kenrich's *New Dictionary* (1773) is the first to do so, followed by *A Complete Dictionary of the English Language* (1780), by Thomas Sheridan (father of the playwright Richard Sheridan), a teacher of elocution who wanted to teach the "true pronunciation" of words. "Many pronunciations," Sheridan says in his Preface, "which thirty or forty years ago were confined to the vulgar, are now gaining ground; and if something be not done to stop this growing evil, and fix a general standard at present, the English is likely to become a mere jargon, which everyone may pronounce as he pleases."

John Walker, another elocutionist, achieved greater fame as an authority on pronunciation, however, and his dictionary of 1791 was "for a hundred years regarded both in England and America as the chief authority on pronunciation." (Mathews:31.) From this time on, pronunciation becames a standard feature of dictionaries.

Noah Webster was the first American lexicographer and in 1806, published his *Compendious Dictionary of the English Language*, a book which was revised in 1828 and on several other occasions throughout the nineteenth century. His chief competitor was Joseph E. Worcester, whose dictionaries also appeared in revised form throughout the century. Eventually other great dictionaries appeared: *The Century Dictionary*, based on various revisions and abridgements of John Ogilvie's *Imperial Dictionary*, and Funk and Wagnalls's *Standard Dictionary* (1893–94).

Nineteenth-Century Grammars

The impact of early nineteenth-century comparative philology, as seen in the work of linguists like Grimm, Verner, Rask, and Bopp, was not felt by the grammarians or lexicographers of the nineteenth century, who continued the prescriptive tradition of the eighteenth. Lindley Murray's *English Grammar*, published in 1795, along with his other works, continued its influence far into the next century. Murray had no qualms about "correcting" the grammar of writers of the sixteenth and seventeenth centuries, nor for that matter, of the King James version of the Bible. Goold Brown's *Grammatical Institutes* (1825) had countless "rules to memorize, exercises to parse, and quotations from standard authors to 'correct.' " (Pooley:25.) In his Preface he states: "The only successful method of teaching grammar is to cause the principal definitions and rules to be committed thoroughly to memory, that they may ever afterwards be readily applied." Even today most people remember their grammar study as a long list of "rules."

A few other grammarians were paying some lip service to custom, or usage. Samuel Kirkham's *English Grammar in Familiar Lectures* (1825) begrudgingly admitted that he often had "to bow to custom." Peter Bullion, in his *Principles of English Grammar* (1834), also agreed that the grammarian "must take the language as it *is*, not as he would wish it *to be*." Samuel Greene's *First Lessons in Grammar* (1848), like the "functional" grammars of a later day, stressed the sentence as a grammatical unit. Later in the century William Dwight Whitney, in a series of lectures entitled *Language, and the Study of Language* (1867) concluded that "Men's usage makes language." T. R. Lounsbury, in his *History of the English Language* (1879), affirmed that "the test of any tongue is not the grammatical or linguistic resources which it may be supposed to possess; it is the use which it makes of the resources it does possess. . . . "

The Twentieth Century

The advent of the twentieth century brought no new attitudes toward language behavior to the typical grammarian or to the public at large. The grammarian was still prescribing "correct" English, and the public wanted to know the "rules." Typical of such attitudes was an editorial in *The Detroit Free Press* (December 9, 1928) which stated that "a vast amount of wretched English is heard in this country. The remedy does not lie in the repeal of the rules of grammar; but rather in a stricter and more intelligent enforcement of those rules in our schools. . . . " (Fries 1940:2.) One grammar book (W. W. Charters, *Teaching the Common Branches,* rev. ed., 1924) defined grammar as a "series of rules and definitions," and added that since "ninety-five per cent of all children and teachers come from homes or communities where incorrect English is used, nearly everyone has before him the long, hard task of overcoming habits set up early in life before he studied language and grammar in school." (Fries, 1940:2.) If any credence could be given to such statistics, it might behoove the American public to speak another language entirely; surely two years of high school French or Spanish could produce a better batting average.

Robert C. Pooley's study, *Grammar and Usage in Textbooks on English,* published in 1933, traces the history of prescriptivism with its concomitant theories of "correctness" and concludes that times have not changed: "Eighteenth-century theories of language resulted in attitudes and specific rules concerning usage which became fixed and arbitrary in nineteenth-century schoolbooks, and which still persist in the textbooks of today in total disregard for the objective facts of English usage." (p. 12.) His study analyzes sixteen widely used textbooks in grammar and composition written between 1900 and 1930 for three instructional levels—elementary, secondary, and college. The books, he says, are all predicated on two basic fallacies: good usage is equivalent to literary English, and the existence of a fixed standard of language which one must not depart from. "In practice as well as theory," he adds, "the books are hopelessly outmoded." (p. 51.)

Two more recent studies don't offer much optimism. Jean Malmstrom examined 312 language arts textbooks published between 1940 and 1955 and discovered a great discrepancy between textbook pronouncements about "correct usage" and linguistic atlas findings concerning what people really say. The textbooks often fail to recognize regional variants, fail to make distinctions between written and spoken English, and are seldom in agreement with each other. "Since the textbook writers as a group approach current American usage normatively," she adds, "their statements are based on a premise that some arbitrary standard of 'correctness' exists, that it can be discovered, and that it should be taught." (Malmstrom:196.)

Teachers are equally conservative, according to a study made by Thurston Womack, who sent one thousand questionnaires containing fifty items of debatable usage to members of the National Council of Teachers of English (NCTE), asking them to label each item according to its acceptability in formal or informal speech and formal or informal writing.

Though most items have been labeled acceptable in numerous current books on usage, at least in informal speech, most of the 339 teachers who returned the questionnaries rejected most of the debatable items. Besides revealing the conservatism of many typical teachers, assuming that NCTE members are typical, the study also showed that "the teacher, then, most likely to reject items of debatable usage is the high school teacher with more than ten years of teaching experience living in a small town, who holds either an A.B. or an M.A. degree. On the other hand, the teacher most likely to accept items of debatable usage is the college teacher in a city of more than 50,000 people with less than ten years of teaching experience and a doctor's degree." (Womach:189.)

If the teacher is as conservative as these studies indicate, the general public is even more reluctant to accept items of debatable usage and still places great faith in the little books on grammar and usage. They look to the lexicographer, who, like Emily Post or Amy Vanderbilt, should, they think, tell them what to say.

Twentieth-Century Dictionaries

Perhaps the lexicographer is partly guilty for providing the notion that his book is "authoritative," though such claims might be blamed on the advertising department instead. Indeed Noah Webster's books are not only "authoritative" but chauvinistic as well, as he extols the distinct features of American English and cites quotations from Americans to illustrate his definitions.

The Century Dictionary, which first appeared in 1891, and Funk and Wagnalls's *Standard Dictionary of the English Language,* first published in 1893, both took modern views toward the nature of language and the lexicographer's function to record that language. The great *Oxford English Dictionary,* originally entitled *A New English Dictionary on Historical Principles,* published from 1884 to 1928, states its descriptive function, "to present in alphabetical series the words which have formed the English vocabulary from the time of the earliest records down to the present day, with all the relevant facts concerning their form, sense-history, pronunciation, and etymology." (p.v.)

The Controversy Over Webster's *Third*

Before the third edition of *Webster's New International Dictionary* appeared in 1961 (the previous edition, the *Second*, appeared in 1934), the editor, Philip B. Gove, announced in a prepublication essay in *Word Study* (October 1961) his endorsement of the principles set down by the NCTE:

1. Language changes constantly.
2. Change is normal.
3. Spoken language is the language.
4. Correctness rests upon usage.
5. All usage is relative.

Since the speakers of the language have added new words (*astronaut, beatnik, countdown, den mother, sit-in,* etc.) and have given new meanings to old words, the permanent staff of a hundred specialists at the Merriam-Webster Company headquarters in Springfield, Massachusetts, where the dictionary was published, had to amass a gigantic file of recorded evidence, or citations (over ten million), before publishing the new edition with its 50,000 new words (not in the Second) and 50,000 new meanings.

Unfortunately, the first reviewers of the dictionary assumed that Mr. Gove's announcement was a complete about-face from former editorial policy and that he was abdicating his throne as linguistic ruler. The inclusion of *ain't* (as well as other borderline cases), plus the lack of status symbols so common in the Second (symbols which told the reader immediately whether a word was colloquial, illiterate, etc.), caused an immediate outcry from the critics, as the titles of those reviews so clearly indicate: "Dig Those Words," "Good English Ain't What We Thought," "Say It Ain't So!", "The Death of Meaning," "Sabotage in Springfield," "Keep Your Old Webster's" and "Anarchy in Language," to name only a few. These reviews plus others have been printed in *Dictionaries and THAT Dictionary*, edited by James Sledd and Wilma R. Ebbitt (Glenview, Illinois: Scott, Foresman, and Co., 1962).

The inclusion of *ain't*, which schoolteachers had attacked for so many years, was unforgivable to many critics, who saw the imminent decay of the language through the permissiveness of the lexicographer. The dictionary entry said, "though disapproved by many and more common in less educated speech, used orally in most parts of the U.S. by many cultivated speakers esp. in the phrase *ain't I*," a fairly accurate appraisal of current use. But critics were unwilling to accept the word despite the findings of dialect geographers, preferring instead such stilted expressions as *am I not?* or even the somewhat awkward *aren't I?*

Nevertheless the critics were undaunted in their condemnation. "What Webster's has done," said the Toronto *Globe and Mail*, "is to cast the mantle of its approval over another example of corrupted English," and concluded by saying, "A dictionary's embrace of the word 'ain't' will comfort the ignorant, confer approval upon the mediocre, and subtly imply that proper English is the tool only of the snob; but it will not assist men to speak truly to other men. It may, however, prepare us for that future which it could help to hasten. In the caves, no doubt, a grunt will do." (September 8, 1961.)

The *Third* also tried to be objective toward other informal constructions like "Who was that lady I saw you with?"—once condemned because of the final preposition—by labeling the sentence as "used by speakers on all educational levels and by reputable writers." Dryden had decided that, since *preposition* means *"pre-*position," the preposition must logically precede the noun.

Too many critics who attacked the book felt that the lexicographer is a sentry whose duty it is to guard the language. A review in the Detroit *News* ("New Dictionary Cheap, Corrupt") stated, "If a great dictionary forsakes its post as the guardian of our language, how can one avoid disappointment?" (February 10, 1962.) The *American Bar Association Journal* also censured the *Third* because "it has utterly abdicated any role as a judge of what is good English usage" (January 1962) by failing to make fine distinctions between *like* and *as, imply* and *infer*, and *enormity* and *enormousness*. Furthermore it includes "that most monstrous of all non-words 'irregardless.' " The *Second*, the reviewer added, "referred to this as erroneous or humorous. As far as the new Webster's is concerned this meaningless verbal bastard is just as legitimate as any other word in the dictionary." The reviewer concluded that the shade of Noah Webster "must now have become a restless and tormented spirit."

The permissive attitude of the new edition was allied with a "general decay in values" ("Good English Ain't What We Thought," Chicago *Daily News*, October 20, 1961). The Detroit *News* review, mentioned above, concluded by citing Dean Inge, the "gloomy dean" of St. Paul's, London, who favored "the traditions, disciplines, and standards of the past" and who allied any departures from those standards with the "bolshevik spirit," which, he said, "is to be found everywhere, not just in Russia."

Some critics, in panning the *Third*, heaped praise on the Second, which, ironically enough, was almost equally descriptive in tone. The Washington *Post* (January 17, 1962), in a review entitled "Keep Your

Old Webster's," admonished the reader to "hang on to it" and "don't throw it away," expressions labeled colloquial or not found at all in the second edition. The *Nation* solemnly announced that it "will continue to cite the Second Edition of *Webster's International* as its authority." (March 10, 1962.)

The first review of the *Third* to appear in the New York *Times* was quite flippant in tone and suggested that the dictionary editors had not lived up to their public responsibility when they included words like *confab, yak, finalize,* and *swell* with "no suggestion that they are anything but standard" (October 12, 1961). In a letter to the editor of the *Times* (November 5, 1961), Mr. Gove reminded the journalist that the *Times* is cited at more than seven hundred entries. "We plan to continue reading and marking the *Times*," he added, "as the number one exhibit of good standard contemporary cultivated English."

Perhaps one of the longest book reviews in any modern magazine was that of Dwight Macdonald, entitled "The String Untuned," in the *New Yorker* (March 10, 1962). The title of the review is taken from Ulysses' speech in Shakespeare's *Troilus and Cressida* in which Ulysses comments on the order *(degree)* in the universe:

> Take but degree away, untune that string,
> And, hark, what discord follows!

Macdonald lamented the "trend toward permissiveness, in the name of democracy, that is debasing our language by rendering it less precise and thus less effective as literature and less efficient as communication."

As Neil Postman and Charles Weingartner said in *Linguistics: A Revolution in Teaching*, "*Webster's Third* was viewed as a kind of linguistic Kinsey Report, condemned because its authors felt obliged to describe human behavior rather than dictate its course." (p. 155.)

Eventually the controversy over the *Third* subsided, and those who were so adamant in condemning the book had time to see its merits. As Albert Marckwardt said, two years after the publication of the dictionary when the shouting had stopped:

> It is the English-teaching profession which should be seriously disturbed by the dictionary controversy. If the Webster war has proved little or nothing about dictionaries, it has demonstrated our ineptitude, if not absolute failure, in teaching our students what a dictionary is for, how it is made, and the proper way to use it. Much of the misunderstanding of principle, of the confusion of principle and practice, of the failure to read and interpret accurately can, with considerable justice, be laid at our door. After all, the embattled critics were once our students; had our teaching of the dictionary been soundly based, this comedy of errors should have been at least somewhat less comic. (Marckwardt: 344–45.)

More Recent Dictionaries

When *The Random House Dictionary of the English Language* appeared in 1966, it did not provoke the bitter wrath of the critics, largely because of its attempt to take a middle position on the thornier problems of usage. The Preface announced the middle stance:

> Should the dictionary be an authoritarian guide to "correct" English or should it be so antiseptically free of comment that it may defeat the user by providing him with no guidance at all? There is, we believe, a linguistically sound middle course. Language, most people agree, is never static—except when dead. It has a capacity for constant change and growth that enables it to serve effectively the requirements of the society in which it exists. It is, therefore, the function of a dictionary to provide the user with an exact record of the language he sees and hears. That record must be fully descriptive. Since language is a social institution, the lexicographer must give the user an adequate indication of the attitudes of society toward particular words or expressions, whether he regards those attitudes as linguistically sound or not. The lexicographer who does not recognize the existence of long-established structures in usage has not discharged his full responsibility. He has not been objective and factual; he has reported selectively, omitting references to a social attitude relevant to many words and expressions. He does not need to express approval or disapproval of a disputed usage, but he does need to report the milieu of words as well as their meanings. In this dictionary, on the basis of extensive research and thoughtful consideration, we have used usage labels to guide the reader to effective and appropriate use of words.[2]

Besides an excellent introductory essay on "Usage, Dialects, and Functional Varieties," by Raven I. McDavid, Jr., there are *Usage* entries following certain debatable words like *ain't* and *already* which attempt to clarify the current status of the particular item in question. Possibly for a commercial reasons, a conservative stance is taken toward *ain't*, which is labeled "Nonstandard in U.S. except in some dialects; informal in Brit. *am not.*" The *Usage* entry gives more information:

> AIN'T is so traditionally and widely regarded as a nonstandard form that it should be shunned by all who prefer to avoid being considered illiterate. AIN'T occurs occasionally in the informal speech of some educated users, especially in self-consciously or folksy or humorous contexts (*Ain't it the truth! She ain't what she used to be!*), but it is completely unacceptable in formal writing and speech. Although the expression *ain't I?* is perhaps defensible—and it is considered more logical than *aren't I?* and more euphonious than *ain't I?*—the well-advised person will avoid any use of AIN'T.[3]

[2]From the Preface of *The Random House Dictionary of the English Language*, copyright 1970, 1969, 1967, 1966 by Random House, Inc. Reprinted by permission.
[3]From *The Random House Dictionary of the English Language*, copyright 1970, 1969, 1967, 1966 by Random House, Inc. Reprinted by permission.

Like *Webster's Third*, the *Random House Dictionary* includes all of the four-letter obscenities except one, and this one is included in the newest dictionary which appeared in the fall of 1969, *The American Heritage Dictionary of the English Language*. The inclusion of this one obscenity so far has not caused a public furor. The outcry was greater over *Webster's* inclusion of *ain't* than over the four-letter obscenities. The second edition of *Webster's New World Dictionary* has omitted all of them on the grounds that everyone knows them anyway. If lexicography is a science, then perhaps these words that have been just outside the realm of respectability—like so many cant terms and slang expressions that have become respectable—should be admitted to the published lexicon. Surely they appear in print often enough in modern fiction. Interestingly enough, these Anglo-Saxon obscenities have had quite stable meanings unaffected by time, unlike other words which have undergone pejoration, amelioration, specialization, generalization, or other types of semantic change.

The *American Heritage Dictionary* is the first to include an appendix of reconstructed Indo-European roots so that one can find further information concerning entries whose etymology can be traced to Indo-European. Dictionaries in the past traced words back to Latin, Greek, Primitive Germanic, etc., but seldom any farther.

Like *Webster's Third* and *The Random House Dictionary*, *The American Heritage Dictionary* editors assert that usage is the authority for correctness. They add that statements about usage are actually value judgments and should be labeled as such. Furthermore, the persons best qualified to make those value judgments "are those professional speakers and writers who have demonstrated their sensitiveness to the language and their power to wield it effectively and beautifully." (p. xxiii.)

To get a broad view of preference in usage, the makers of the dictionary "commissioned a Usage Panel of about a hundred members—novelists, essayists, poets, journalists, writers on science and sports, public officials, professors. . . . The panelists have in common only a recognized ability to speak and write good English." (p. xxiii.) To this panel was submitted a list of approximately eight hundred items of debatable usage, and the results were summarized in brief *Usage* entries following each word.

Needless to say, opinion was not uniform in most cases. Ninety-nine percent of the panelists disapproved of *ain't I?* and *between you and I* in writing; ninety-seven percent objected to the adverb *thusly* and to the use of *debut* as a verb. Ninety-six percent approved of *slow* as an adverb, and ninety-four percent approved of *anxious* to mean *eager*. On countless other items, however, opinion was much more diversified.

The usage editor, Morris Bishop, concluded that "the counselors found . . . no absolute standard of rightness. Though naturally believing in their own superiority, they do not presume to dictate. They seem to conclude, without explicit statement, that usage is its own affair,

with due regard to the usage of other good writers and speakers."
(p. xxiv.) Surely this is as safe and sensible a course as one might take
in such a publishing venture.

Conclusion

Where does the teacher stand in all of this? Most probably he is
trained in the traditional manner and may have attended an in-service
workshop course, at the request of his principal or superintendent,
"to learn something about linguistics." Unfortunately, too many teachers
have not been back to school or have not kept up with new trends as they
are described in the professional journals. Thus they carry on in the
tradition of the prescriptive schoolmarm of the last century. And in the
meantime the man on the street keeps asking for answers—"correct"
answers—about what is right.

A middle road might possibly be taken, what Robert Pooley calls
"an enlightened prescriptivism." He suggests that teachers ignore distinctions between *shall* and *will*, split infinitives, *like* as a conjunction,
the possessive case before a gerund, and other minute matters and con-
centrate instead on the standard use of pronouns, verb tenses and
agreement with subject, the elimination of double negatives, etc. (Pooley,
1963:176–81.)

In the previous chapter on dialects we suggested that we would not
attempt to "eliminate" anyone's speech. We certainly oppose the
teaching of standard English through repetition and substitution drills
as if it were a foreign language, because nonstandard dialects are *not*
like foreign languages. We even have some reservations about the
current attempts, with undue emphasis, to make students bidialectal,
because in saying to a child, "You need to learn this other dialect
because it will help you to get ahead in the world," we are implying
that his own dialect is not good enough. We agree with Bergen Evans
that "custom is illogical and unreasonable, but it is also tyrannical.
The latest deviation from its dictates is usually punished with severity.
And because that is so, children should be taught what the current
and local customs in English are." (Evans:82.)

Charles C. Fries summed up the problem several years ago in his
American English Grammar:

> The schools, therefore, have assumed the burden of training every boy
> and girl, no matter what his original social background and native speech,
> to use this "standard" English, this particular social or class dialect. To
> some pupils it is almost a foreign language; to others it is their accustomed

speech. Many believe that the schools have thus assumed an impossible task. Certainly the widespread and almost unanimous condemnation of the results of their efforts convinces us that either the schools have not conceived their task adequately or they have chosen the wrong materials and methods to accomplish it. We shall find, I think, that seldom have school authorities understood the precise nature of the language task they have assumed and very frequently have directed their energies to teaching not "standard" English realistically described, but a "make-believe" correctness which contained some true forms of real "standard" English and many forms that had and have practically no currency outside the classroom. (p. 14).

Once teachers see the "precise nature of the language task they have assumed" and the complexity of the questions of usage and of dialect differences, then perhaps they can interest students in several of the highly interesting facets of language study, whether it be in controversial matters of usage, the history of words, the reasons behind language change, or (fantastic as it may seem) even the study of grammar.

Exercises

1.   Examine the prefatory material in several different dictionaries to see what they say about matters of usage. Then look up some items of debatable usage (items from this chapter or from any of the many usage manuals currently available) to see if the dictionary editors follow the principles they set forth in their prefaces.

2.   What do the same editors say about stylistic levels? What labels do they use to indicate such levels? How accurate are these labels, especially when applied to isolated words and phrases? How much do they overlap?

3.   It was noted in the chapter that *The American Heritage Dictionary* editor chose a "Usage Panel" to give its opinion on several hundred items of debatable usage. How much "authority" does such a panel have and how much faith does the average person place in the opinions of its members?

4.   What is the main reason recent slang terms are not included in most desk dictionaries? Should obscenities which have been in existence for hundreds of years also be omitted? What makes a word obscene?

5.   Most dictionaries use the term *Dial.* to indicate that a particular word or expression is restricted to one region. How valuable is this label anyway? Should more information be included following the label? Look up some regionalisms like *tonic, fat stock show, blintz, bagel, dragon*

fly, snake doctor, mosquito hawk, firefly, lightning bug, firebug, glowworm to see how precisely your dictionary identifies the region in which they are used.

6.   Check several current dictionaries and grammars to see how they define "standard English." What weaknesses or inadequacies do you find in their definitions?

7.   Check the following words to see if they vary in pronunciation in the United States: *either, gaseous, roof, status, almond, pecan, avocado, falcon, peninsula, sumac*

8.   AMELIORATION and PEJORATION are terms used to indicate, respectively, that a word has taken on more pleasant connotations or less pleasant ones. Check the etymology of the following words to find out which process they have undergone: *knave, marshall, hussy, knight, chivalry, lord, lady, lewd, lust, steward, sheriff, churl, villain, angel, nice, crafty*

9.   GENERALIZATION is the process whereby a word broadens in meaning. The opposite process is called SPECIALIZATION. Which process have the following words undergone? *deer, meat, starve, hound, dog, loaf, fowl, undertaker*

References

Baugh, Albert C. *A History of the English Language*, Second Edition. New York: Appleton-Century-Crofts, Inc., 1957.

Evans, Bergen. "Grammar for Today." *The Atlantic Monthly*, 205, (March 1960), 79–82.

Fries, Charles C. *American English Grammar*. New York: Appelton-Century-Crofts, Inc., 1940.

———. *The Teaching of English*. Ann Arbor, Michigan: The George Wahr Publishing Co., 1949.

Leonard, Sterling. *The Doctrine of Correctness in English Usage, 1700–1800*. Madison, Wisconsin: University of Wisconsin Studies in Language and Literature, 1929.

Malmstrom, Jean. "Linguistic Atlas Findings versus Textbook Pronouncements on Current American Usage." *The English Journal*, 48 (April 1959), 191–98.

Marckwardt, Albert H. "Dictionaries and the English Language." *The English Journal*, 52 (May 1963), 336–45.

Mathews, M. M. *A Survey of English Dictionaries*. London: Oxford University Press, 1933.

"Parlez-vous Franglais?" *Time*, November 29, 1963, p. 80.

Pooley, Robert C. "Dare Schools Set a Standard in English Usage?" *The English Journal*, 49 (March 1960), 176–81.

———. *Grammar and Usage in Textbooks on English.* Madison, Wisconsin: University of Wisconsin Bureau of Educational Research, Bulletin No. 14, 1933.

Postman, Neil, and Charles Weingartner. *Linguistics, A Revolution in Teaching.* New York: Dell Publishing Company, 1967.

Sledd, James, and Wilma R. Ebbitt, eds. *Dictionaries and THAT Dictionary.* Glenview, Illinois: Scott, Foresman and Co., 1962.

Womack, Thurston. "Teachers' Attitudes Toward Current Usage." *The English Journal,* 48 (April 1959), 186–90.

VIII

Implications for Teachers

In this book we have attempted to give our readers a quick overview of language study, particularly as it relates to the phonological and grammatical structure of English, the historical development of the language, the attitudes of people toward the spoken and written word, and the nature of language in general. We have attempted to incorporate the latest in linguistic scholarship, some of which will seem difficult because it is new. However, we feel that many new textbooks are using those new approaches and that teachers will need to become familiar with them.

Our general purpose has been twofold: to present the more difficult material in as concise a manner as possible, and to survey the other aspects of language study in an introductory course for those with little background in linguistics. We have tried to raise pertinent questions about language, many of which as yet have no pat answers. Because we assume that a great part of our audience are teachers or teachers-to-be, we have purposely directed our material to what teachers need to know, and we trust that those readers will emerge with a more knowledgeable and sophisticated attitude toward language study.

In Chapter I we defined language as a highly intricate system, one which preschool children master effortlessly through mere exposure to whatever system is used in their environments. Indeed, if two systems are used, they will master both, thus becoming bilingual. Hence teachers cannot respect enough the highly complex verbal system which students bring with them to the classroom, and certainly they must not belittle that system if it differs in the least from theirs. It is the children's primary tool of communication which up to this point has served them well. The fact that competing English surface structures such as *bringed*, *brang*, and *brought* (parallelling deep structure *bring + past tense*) occur in the speech of young children does not point up indecision and stupidity but rather demonstrates the fact that, in general, prepubescent children have an ability to hypothesize about language, not limiting themselves to the one form which most adolescents and adults cling to.

The spoken aspect of language was also emphasized in Chapter I. Everyone will agree that the average volume of speech produced in a day's time far outweighs the volume of language written or read. Since the two types of language vary considerably, they must not be treated as if they are alike. Even stylistic levels within each type will differ according to time and circumstance. One junior high teacher in a metropolitan city in Texas announced to her students on the first day of class, "We are going to use only good English in this classroom," presumably her brand of classroom English. She made no distinctions between written and spoken English or formal and informal speech and writing, as if one spoke and wrote the same way at all times. Quite often a writing assignment will of necessity dictate its own style. A theme assignment on "What I Did Last Summer" should not be marked down if it fails to follow the more conservative stylistic practices of formal academic English. Likewise, "Dark-Light Symbolism in *The Scarlet Letter*" would probably not be appropriate if written in the language of the street.

The study of grammar was the subject of Chapters III and IV. It is important, first of all, that teachers are aware of the different meanings of the term as used by laymen and linguists. The survey of grammar study in Chapter III was designed to show how grammarians in the past viewed language study and what they were hoping to achieve in writing grammars. It was also noted how Latin grammarians of the Middle Ages influenced grammarians for centuries to come, how English grammarians attempted to model English on Latin, and how English grammarians sought to prescribe what the English language ought to be in terms of Latin grammar. This overview was designed to help explain why traditional school grammars approach the language as they do and to give the reader some insight into some of the antiquated teaching practices we have all suffered through these many years. It is hoped that the teacher can see both the strengths and weaknesses of these several approaches to the study of grammar and feel free to adapt the best from any one of them.

We have chosen the transformational-generative grammatical model over the traditional and structural ones for reasons already noted in Chapter III. However, its very great explanatory and descriptive powers, coupled with its mathematical formalism, explicitness, and precision, are very clearly appealing attributes. A key theoretical Chomskyan concept that we have touched upon many times is the distinction between LINGUISTIC COMPETENCE (what we know) and LINGUISTIC PERFORMANCE (what we say). A parallel key concept is the distinction between DEEP STRUCTURE and SURFACE STRUCTURE and the corollary that a sentence is a device for relating or pairing a deep structure (meaning) with a surface structure (pronunciation). Also, we have indicated that the three (apparently) universal transformational processes of INSERTION, DELETION, and SUBSTITUTION relate deep structures to surface structures.

The particular grammatical model which we elaborated on consists of three major components: a SYNTACTIC component which generates basic (kernel) sentences and which assigns to each sentence a structural description; a SEMANTIC component which assigns to each sentence a meaning or interpretation; a PHONOLOGICAL component which assigns a pronunciation or phonetic interpretation to each sentence.

The phonological component ought to be of special interest to reading and spelling teachers, who should be happy to learn that, of the three basic types of writing systems (the other two are *syllabic* and *ideographic*) English is conventionally written with the most economic and versatile system, namely, *alphabetic* characters. As we have seen, the guiding principle of an alphabetic system of writing is that, in general, words which have the same meaning are spelled the same way. For example, it is appropriate to have *t* both in *demonstrate* and in *demonstration* and *e* and *o* in *telephone/telephonic/telephony* even though there is phonetic surface structure variation. It is evident, then, that conventional English orthography represents deep rather than surface structure. This fact leads one to suspect that phonic alphabets are probably unnecessary tools in the initial teaching of reading and spelling skills; that is, conventional English orthography is sufficient to its task of representing the language for young and old, for rich and poor, for black and white and yellow, brown, and red alike.

Because it is true in general that the more you know the better off you are, we feel that we can recommend grammar study (like a dose of castor oil) merely because it is good for a person. We make no claim on the transfer of linguistic knowledge of a language to more or less logical thinking, better or worse written compositions, more or less persuasive speaking. In short, because language is one of the major vehicles for human communication and because education is a humanizing process, what could be more important than a study of the one main characteristic that sets man apart from other forms of life? Beyond this, grammar study allows us to describe and explain the sometimes puzzling varieties of language forms that we encounter in different usage environments and dialect areas.

In the first chapter we noted that languages change and that change is normal. Chapter II, a short history of English from its Germanic beginnings to the present, illustrates some of the major changes which have taken place. The alert teacher, who knows something of this history, can explain why some verbs have a dental stop in the preterit while others have an ablaut series, why some plurals end in -*s* while others have an internal vowel change, why so many Modern English words are of foreign origin, why English is more like German than French, and countless other matters which arise daily when one studies English.

The ongoing process of language change is evident today in the United States in the number of regional dialects we have (Chapter VI). These variations are interesting in themselves and should prove a stimulating topic for discussion in the classroom. If the difference between the teacher's speech and that of the children is only a matter of regional variation, then certainly the teacher should realize the basis for the difference and not send a child off to speech correction class because his dialect is different. Raven McDavid tells the story of an anthropologist friend, a Cherokee Indian from Oklahoma, who was placed in a "corrective speech" class when he moved from Oklahoma to Detroit. He was surprised to find that the class contained no stammerers, cleft palates, lispers, or foreign accents. Rather the boys and girls in the group were from Arkansas, Missouri, Kentucky, Tennessee, and other states not representative of Inland Northern speech. "We all realized immediately that they were planning to brainwash us out of our natural way of speaking; and it became a point of honor among us to sabotage the program," the Oklahoman confided. (McDavid: 2, 5-7.)

If the child is from the South or South Midland area, he will not make a distinction between the vowels in *pen* and *pin*, and it is useless for the teacher to try to teach this distinction. One Texas teacher, in an exercise on syllable stress, corrected the child from California who marked the second syllable of *cement* as the stressed syllable. The teacher's rejoinder after she was made aware of regional differences was that her pronunciation (*cément*) was right and that "two things can't be right or it will confuse the children." (Horn: 124.) The children, in this case, were probably less confused than the teacher. Still another teacher was attempting to correct the peculiar pronunciation of a child from New England so that he could talk correctly—like other Texas students. A final example is the teacher who spent a good deal of time denouncing the "improper" expression *hadn't ought*, an expression not used in that particular region. The children were so taken with the novel expression that they started to use it. If the teachers know the differences in regional speech, then they will not be guilty of such absurdities.

Regional differences may pose a few problems related to reading and spelling. Like *pen* and *pin* other pairs of words are homophonous in certain regions of the country: *horse, hoarse; morning, mourning; whale, wail; caught, cot; Mary, merry, marry; guard, god; fort, fought,* etc. The phoneme-grapheme correspondence, we have already noted, is not as close as teachers would like to think. One teacher attributed her students' inability to spell words ending in [əns], like *appearance, experience, valence,* to their incorrect pronunciation of these words. Evidently in her mind the written symbol on the page made her think she was pronouncing the words differently. How many people will argue that they *do* pronounce the *b* in *dumb, thumb,* and *comb?*

Besides accepting the regional dialect of the child the teacher might also add a unit or two on dialect, first, to make students aware of dialectal differences and, second, to teach a mutually respectful and cooperative attitude toward those differences. Surely enough inexpensive books and recordings are available: paperback books like Jean Malmstrom and Annabel Ashley's *Dialects — U.S.A.* (NCTE,1963); Carroll E. Reed's *Dialects of American English* (World, 1967); and Roger Shuy's *Discovering American Dialects* (NCTE, 1967); as well as the two recordings *Our Changing Language* (Webster Division of McGraw-Hill) and *Americans Speaking* (NCTE). Two recent collections of readings on dialect are Harold B. Allen and Gary N. Underwood's *Readings in American Dialectology* (Appleton-Century-Crofts, 1971); and Juanita V. Williamson and Virginia M. Burke's *A Various Language: Perspectives on American Dialects* (Holt, Rinehart and Winston, 1971).

If there are students in the classroom from other regions, their speech might be compared to the speech of other members of the class and prominent differences noted. Certainly vocabulary lists of regional expressions are easy enough to compile. The tape recorder is an excellent tool for recording for future use a few paragraphs (perhaps the same passage) by a speaker not native to the area. Students can also record the speech of a friend or neighbor which would illustrate dialectal differences; or, if a tape recorder is not available, they might use one of the dialect questionnaires in the above-mentioned books and make their own survey. Such a discovery approach to language would serve several purposes — sparking some interest in what is too often a tedious course, teaching the students something about language, and familiarizing them with the scientific approach to language study.

Finally, the study of dialect in literature can be equally interesting. Surely enough samples are available, from the poetry of Robert Burns to the ghetto speech in the writings of a number of modern black authors.

If the dialect which the child brings to the classroom is one of the less prestigious ones, we must certainly not make him feel inferior because of it. We do not reject children because they are poorly clothed or poorly housed; why should we reject them for linguistic reasons? Too often, especially in many inner-city schools, the dialect of the child is so completely different from that of the teacher that communication between them is difficult, and will be practically impossible if the teacher is not well-informed, open-minded, and resourceful about language differences. As noted in the chapter on the nature of language, anybody's language is adequate if it communicates. The child who has no problem communicating at home or in his neighborhood too often fails to communicate in the classroom. That teachers fail to understand the divergent language and culture of students can be verified by their naïve remarks about language and culture. Many will argue that the child's language is inadequate because he comes to school totally without linguistic or cultural experiences. If ghetto life is half as bad as reported—what with all the rats, crime, and dope pushing—one finds it difficult to believe that the deprived child comes to school totally without experiences. His experiences are the exact opposite of those of the middle-class teacher. Too often the teacher has no concept whatsoever of the realities of life in the inner city—the poverty, the squalor, the rigors of daily survival.

In *Teaching Disadvantaged Children in the Pre-School*, Carl Bereiter and Siegfred Engelmann report "a considerable number of children who at four years of age hardly speak at all" (p. 31), a statement predicated on the assumption that such children come from nonverbal backgrounds, often ones with an absent father and a working mother. Yet there are often numerous siblings to talk to and certainly enough people around who are anything but nonverbal. These writers state further that the speech of severely deprived children does not consist of distinct words "but rather of whole phrases or sentences that function like giant words." Thus "He's a big dog" becomes "He bih daw," and "That is a red truck" becomes "Da-re-truh" (p. 34). When we account for the deletion of the copula and the reduction of consonant clusters found in some dialects, (and perhaps some blurred perceptions on the part of speaker and transcriber), we see that the sentences are meaningful and follow a different set of highly ordered rules.

If the student's dialect is so completely different that he has problems in reading, he may even need materials written in a nonprestigious dialect to help him learn to read. Then gradually he can shift to materials in classroom English. So far the proponents of nonstandard materials have met with a good deal of resistance both from teachers, who fear that such materials will perpetuate or reinforce nonstandard English, and from parents, who do not want undue attention called to their own speech habits. If the advocates of nonstandard materials lose their battle, perhaps some materials might be introduced in the schools which would stress basic deep structure similarities in our language, or reading texts which would at least be more relevant to students than the ordinary fare of the "Dick and Jane" readers. At least teachers might be more sympathetic toward the multiplicity of problems faced by the disadvantaged child. A remedial teacher in north Texas tells of her attempts to help a poor reader and the victory she achieved when he was finally able to complete an entire book. He wrote a report on the book and gave it to his English teacher, only to have it returned with thirty-five red marks and circles. Needless to say, he didn't want to read another book.

The situation above, we hope, is not typical, but it does point out a situation which often arises—the teacher and the school system manage to kill any interest the child may have in learning, largely through attitudes held, techniques used, or misunderstandings of the way language functions. How successful have classroom attempts to stamp out "bad English" been, anyway?

Once teachers see some of the dialect barriers to communication and to reading, they may lose some of their faith in the many placement and achievement tests which are directed toward the white middle-class student and in many of the reading materials written for the same audience. Is the deprived child familiar with the language of the tests, or does it serve only to confuse him? If there are pictures to identify or objects to be described, are they ones with which he would be familiar? One professor of education asked a black educator why lower-class children do so poorly on the Metropolitan Reading Readiness Test. The black, holding up the test, replied, "Here is a picture of a wagon with three wheels. What is wrong with it? The child sees nothing wrong with it. He often plays with a wagon with no wheels at all. Here is a table with three legs. This is not uncommon in his home. Why should he see anything wrong with it?" (Dale: 780.)

If tests are slanted toward one audience, what about the basic readers? Do they reflect the interests and the culture of the inner city, or are they oriented exclusively toward rural and small-town America? Fortunately, some educators are seeing a need for relevant books at the lower levels, and such books are slowly beginning to appear. Publishers have been slow to print books with a limited market or books about the life of certain minority groups which might prove offensive in white communities.

What about the child who comes to school without even English at his disposal, one whose native tongue is something else? In 1960 there were about five million children of school age whose native tongue was not English. About 1.75 million of these were Spanish-speaking, mainly Cubans in Miami, Puerto Ricans in New York, and Mexican-Americans in the Southwest. Studies of the educational success of these minority groups show that the dropout rate of Mexican-American students is higher than that of the black. In Texas, which has the highest Mexican-American dropout rate in the Southwest, almost fifty percent of the Mexican-Americans who begin school do not finish. (See the reference list.) Only the American Indian fares worse in the public schools.

The obvious reason for the poor performance of the Mexican-American is the language barrier that he encounters from the very first grade. Add to this the school regulations which forbid him to speak his native language, the textbooks which make no mention of his culture or his contributions to American society, the attitudes of society which subtly or openly reject his culture; it is indeed a wonder that he ever finishes school. Fortunately, since the passage of the Bilingual Education Act in 1968, a number of bilingual programs have been put into operation that will teach the children in their native tongue until they have mastered enough skills to begin the study of English.

It is our hope that language study (and dialect study in particular), once it becomes widespread enough, will help to enlighten the populace on matters of language diversity and will make people more tolerant of speech patterns unlike their own. Perhaps it is not too optimistic to expect that mutual tolerance for linguistic and cultural differences will someday become a reality, and that diversity will be a virtue which makes Americans more interesting because of their multi-ethnic and multilingual backgrounds.

Chapter VII traced the history of attitudes toward language use and toward language change. Mention was made of several attempts to found an academy to purify English and stop it from changing. Today the notion still persists that English existed in an erstwhile state of perfection. Actually there was never a "Golden Age" of English, though people like to think of Renaissance English as the "height" because of Shakespeare and the King James version of the Bible.

The meanings of words change, too, and teachers must stop clinging to antiquated forms because presumably they are older, better, more beautiful, or more logical. *Dilapidated* once referred to stone buildings, but now may refer to any building that is run down, and no one would question this current meaning. *Disinterested* has ceased to mean only *impartial*, and to most people means *uninterested*. In other words there is nothing sacred about the older meaning, which presumably is the "real meaning" of the word. Hence, the teacher needs to realize that words mean what people make them mean and that dictionaries should record the current meaning. Too often, naïve teachers ask students to look up a word in *the* dictionary (as if there were only one) to find its real meaning, as if it had only one.

Furthermore, teachers should stop clinging to older grammatical forms merely because they are listed in a textbook on usage. A teacher at an English workshop in Oklahoma was asked by the director why she still taught the distinctions between the use of *shall* and *will*. She replied, "I somehow feel that we as teachers owe it to the children to teach them the finer things in life." If this is one of them, can we blame the students when they cry out for relevance?

Since language change is normal, there can be no ideal language which is eternally "correct" and free from mutability. Consequently, teachers need to divest themselves of the notions of right and wrong, good and bad. It is highly important that the teacher have a clear notion of the meaning of the terms *good* and *bad* if and when they are used. Is *good* synonymous with *effective*, as it is to many English teachers? If so, would Huck Finn's speech, labeled "bad English" by many teachers and laymen, be ineffective, while journalese and educationese and the garbled prose of government reports would be considered effective?

Can *good*, then, be equated with "standard" and *bad* with "nonstandard"? Hopefully, teachers are taking a more tolerant view of divergent dialects, realizing that speakers of those dialects are not slovenly speakers expressing fragmented thoughts in broken sentences. These dialects are fully developed and quite adequate for communication. Could we say, then, that good English is that which communicates? If so, then "I ain't done nothin' about it," which is certainly clear, would have to be considered good, thus adding further confusion to the term.

It might behoove us all to avoid the terms *good, bad, correct,* and *incorrect* and to replace them with terms less charged with emotional or personal bias. For example, we can talk about what is grammatical (i. e., is used by native speakers) and what is not grammatical (i. e., not used by native speakers) with some certainty. Thus *I have already done it* and *I done it* are grammatical, while *It makes three days that I am here* is not grammatical in the scientific meaning of the term as used in Chapter I. We can also talk about the social value people place on various pronunciations and grammatical constructions. Certainly enough sociolinguistic studies are now available which list the stigmatizing features of certain nonprestigious dialects.

Problems related to syntax, choice of idiom, word choice, and punctuation are actually problems of style that come under the heading of rhetoric. Thus it is not a matter of writing a correct composition but rather an effective one, well organized and written in a style suitable for a given audience. At the high school and college level, these matters of rhetoric will consume most of the teacher's time. At the elementary level, however, especially where the classroom contains a large number of children who do not speak classroom English, the problems are quite different, as we have already seen.

We have dealt with the English language as *language*. When we consider the study of composition and literature, there is no limit to the general area of "English" or "Language Arts." If we include the whole field of communication, these areas become even broader. But no matter how wide they become, they still are based on that most important substructure—language. Throughout the English-speaking world the surface differences will be many, yet we remain English speakers whose dialects and idiolects are mutually intelligible because they all come from a common deep structure — English. To extend the analogy we might say that, like human beings, these many differences are all alike under the skin. However, it is the surface differences which are the most interesting, once we learn to accept them, even if they vary considerably from ours.

The study of one's language and literature could—and should—be the most exciting part of the school curriculum. Or, if not the most exciting, at least the most relevant.

References

Baratz, Joan C., and Roger W. Shuy, eds. *Teaching Black Children to Read.* Washington, D.C.: Center for Applied Linguistics, 1969.

Carter, Thomas P. *Mexican Americans in School: A History of Educational Neglect.* New York: College Entrance Examination Board, 1970.

Dale, Edgar. "Vocabulary Development of the Underprivileged Child." *Elementary English*, 42 (November 1965), 778–86. Reprinted in *Dimensions of Dialect*, edited by Eldonna L. Evertts (NCTE, 1967), pp. 30–38.

Fasold, Ralph W., and Roger W. Shuy, eds. *Teaching Standard English in the Inner City.* Washington, D.C.: Center for Applied Linguistics, 1970.

Gaarder, A. Bruce. "Statement before the Special Subcommittee on Bilingual Education of the Committee on Labor and Public Welfare, U.S. Senate, May 18, 1967." Reprinted in *The Florida Foreign Language Reporter*, 7 (Spring/Summer 1969), 33–34, 171.

Horn, Thomas D., ed., *Reading for the Disadvantaged.* New York: Harcourt, Brace, and World, 1970.

Johnson, Henry S. and William J. Hernández, eds. *Educating the Mexican American.* Valley Forge, Pa.: Judson Press, 1970.

Manuel Herschel T. *Spanish-Speaking Children of the Southwest: Their Education and Public Welfare.* Austin, Texas: University of Texas Press, 1965.

McDavid, Raven, Jr. "Sense and Nonsense About Regional Speech." *Humanities in the South*, Newsletter No. 24, (Spring 1966), 2, 5–7.

Appendix

Table of Symbols and Abbreviations Used in this Book

1. / /
parallel slant lines (virgules, solidi) enclose systematic phonemic forms, e.g., orthographic "sign" = /sign/.

2. [ ]
small square brackets enclose systematic phonetic forms, e.g., orthographic "sign" = [sāyn].

3. þ
Old English orthographic symbol (thorn) for phonetic [θ] (theta) as in "e*ther*" and [ð] (eth) as in "either."

4. ȝ
Old English orthographic symbol (yogh) for phonetic [γ] (gamma) as in German "sa*g*en" and Spanish "ami*g*o".

5. V
Capital V is an informal orthographic symbol for any vowel.

6. V̄
Macron capital V is an informal orthographic symbol for a phonologically ⟨+tense⟩ (long) vowel.

7. C
Capital C is an informal orthographic symbol for a consonant.

8. →
A single-shafted arrow symbolizes the concept "rewrites as, consists of, comprises, becomes," as in A → B; that is, A rewrites as B.

8a. >
A directional marker indicates historical development, as in: hit > it

9. ⇒
A double-shafted arrow symbolizes the concept "is transformed into," as in A ⇒ B; that is, A is transformed into B.

10. ( )　Parentheses in formulas enclose rule options, as in A → B (C); that is, A rewrites as B, or, A rewrites as B + C.

11. { }　Braces enclose choices, as in A → $\begin{Bmatrix} B \\ C \end{Bmatrix}$; that is, A → B, *or*, A → C.

12. *　An asterisk marks hypothetical or reconstructed forms in the historical chapter, as in *pətḗr (father); it also marks ungrammatical forms in the grammar chapter, as in *Maon Yksmohc setirw srammarg.

13. ⟨F₁⟩　Angle brackets enclose phonological, lexical, or syntactic features such as ⟨+nasal⟩, ⟨+animate⟩, or ⟨+en⟩.

14. $\begin{bmatrix} \langle F_1 \rangle \\ \langle F_2 \rangle \end{bmatrix}$　Large square brackets enclose simultaneously-occuring features which comprise a segment.

15. +/−　Plus and minus are used to mark the valence of phonological, lexical, or syntactic features on an antonymous adjective basis; thus ⟨+animate⟩ = animate and ⟨−animate⟩ = non-animate, and so on.

16. #　The double-cross (crosshatch) bounds words and sentences: # #this# #marks# #a# #sentence# #

17. +　A single plus bounds formatives (morphemes) as in the word #proced + ure#; a single plus is also used to symbolize concatenation as in this formula: S → NP + Aux + VP; that is, a sentence consists of a noun phrase plus (+) an auxiliary plus (+) a verb phrase.

18. ′　An acute mark symbolizes primary stress (1 stress) as in brĭef and cáse in isolation.

19. ∧　A caret (circumflex mark) symbolizes secondary stress (2 stress) as in briêf cáse and bluê bĭrd.

20. ˋ　A grave mark symbolizes tertiary stress (3 stress) as in brĭefcàse and bluébìrd

21. ˘　A breve symbolizes weak stress (4 stress) as in brĭefly.

22. ∅　Slash-zero indicates deletion or the null element.

23. XAY → XBY is equivalent to A → B / X_____Y: algebraic rule form which is to be read as: A rewrites as B in the context (/) of the left-hand boundary X and the right-hand boundary Y. A simple example is where "not" contracts to "n't," which can be stated:
A → ∅ / X_____Y
o → ∅ / n_____t

24. Inventory of Chomsky-Hallean Systematic Phonetic Symbols

A. Vowels

Orthography	*Phonetic*
b<i>ee</i>t	[īy]
b<i>i</i>t	[i]
b<i>ai</i>t	[ēy]
b<i>e</i>t	[e]
b<i>a</i>t	[æ] (called *ash/digraph*)
b<i>oo</i>t	[ūw]
l<i>oo</i>k	[u]
b<i>oa</i>t	[ōw] (called *close-o*)
b<i>ough</i>t	[ɔʌ] or [ɔh]
p<i>o</i>t	[ā] or [ɔ] (called *open-o*)
b<i>ou</i>t	[āw] or [æw]
b<i>oy</i>	[ɔy] or [ōy]
b<i>u</i>t	[ʌ] (called *wedge*)
B<i>ér</i>ber	[ʌ́r, ɚr]
b<i>uy</i>, b<i>i</i>te	[āy]
B<i>u</i>tte	[yūw]
Cub<i>a</i>	[ə] (called *schwa*)

B. True Consonants

<i>p</i>ar	[p]
<i>b</i>ar	[b]
<i>t</i>ar	[t]
<i>d</i>arn	[d]
<i>ch</i>ar	[č]
<i>j</i>ar	[ǰ]
<i>k</i>ick	[k]
<i>g</i>ar	[g]
<i>f</i>ine	[f]
<i>v</i>ine	[v]
<i>th</i>in	[θ] (called *theta*)
<i>th</i>ine	[ð] (called *eth*)
<i>s</i>ue	[s]
<i>z</i>oo	[z]
Aleu<i>t</i>ian	[š]
allu<i>s</i>ion	[ž]
<i>h</i>e's	[h]

Orthography	*Phonetic*
wheeze	[h(w)]
Ba*ch* (German pronunciation)	[x] (called *chi*)
ra*m*	[m]
ra*n*	[n]
ra*n*ge	[ɲ]
ra*ng*	[ŋ]

C. Liquids

| *l*ip, pi*ll* | [l, ł] called "light-l" *vs.* "dark-ł" or barred ł" |
| *r*ip | [r] |

D. Glides

*y*ell	[y]
*w*ell	[w]
la*w*	[h/ʌ] ([lɔh, lɔʌ])

Common Abbreviations

1. Adj = Adjective
2. Adv = Adverb
3. Anim = Animate
4. Ant = Anterior
5. Art = Article
6. Aux = Auxiliary
7. C = Conjunction
8. Com = Common
9. Con = Concrete
10. Cons = Consonant
11. Cont = Continuant
12. Cor = Coronal
13. Def = Definite
14. Dem(on) = Demonstrative
15. Fem = Feminine
16. Imp = Imperative
17. IOI = Indirect Object Inversion
18. Mod = Modal
19. N = Noun
20. Nas = Nasal
21. Neg = Negative
22. NP = Noun Phrase

23. Pass = Passive
24. Perf = Perfect
25. Pl = Plural
26. Poss = Possessive
27. PP = Prepositional Phrase
28. P(rep) = Preposition
29. Pro = Pronoun
30. Prog = Progressive
31. Prox = Proximal
32. PSR = Phrase Structure Rule
33. Q = Question
34. S = Sentence
35. Seg = Segment
36. Son(or) = Sonorant
37. Spec = Specific
38. SSR = Segment Structure Rule
39. Stat = Stative
40. Strid = Strident
41. Subj = Subject
42. V = Verb
43. Voc = Vocalic
44. VP = Verb Phrase
45. WH = Interrogative or Relative

Index

(Proper names among References not listed here. All transformations listed under one entry.)

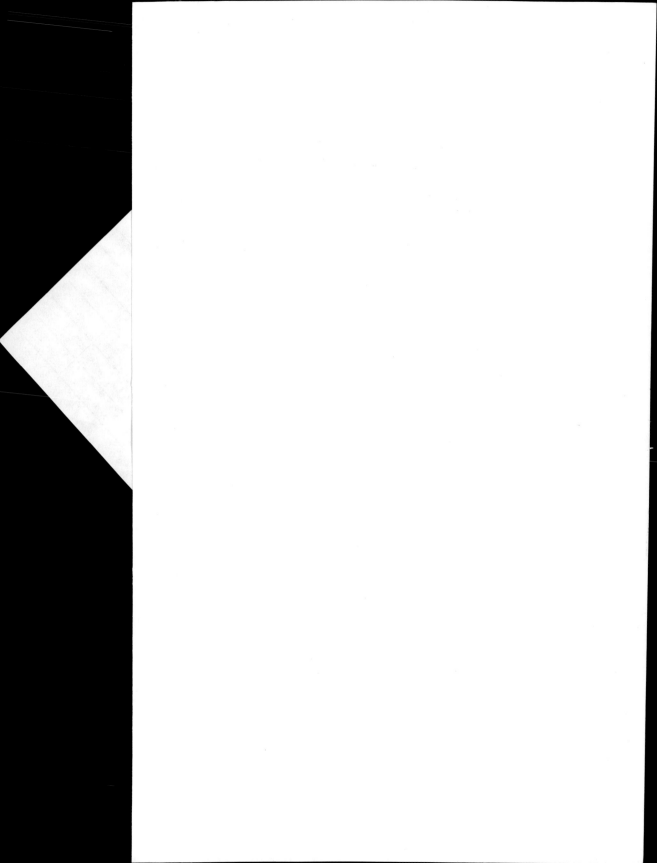

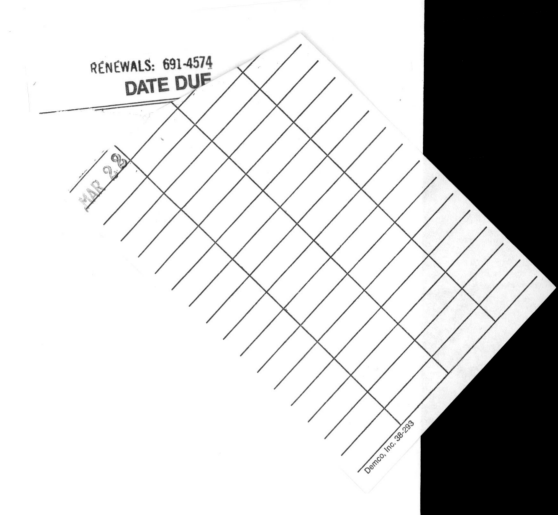

RENEWALS: 691-4574

DATE DUE

MAR 22

Demco, Inc. 38-293